JEWS ON

Jews on Broadway

An Historical Survey of Performers, Playwrights, Composers, Lyricists and Producers

Second edition

Stewart F. Lane

McFarland & Company, Inc., Publishers

Jefferson, North Carolina

LIBRARY OF CONGRESS CATALOGUING-IN-PUBLICATION DATA

Names: Lane, Stewart F., author.
Title: Jews on Broadway : an historical survey of performers, playwrights, composers, lyricists and producers / Stewart F. Lane.
Description: Second edition. | Jefferson, North Carolina : McFarland & Company, Inc., Publishers, 2017. | Includes bibliographical references and index.
Identifiers: LCCN 2017004762 | ISBN 9781476667058 (softcover : acid free paper) ∞
Subjects: LCSH: Jews in the performing arts—New York (State)—New York—History—20th century. | Jewish entertainers—New York (State)—New York—History—20th century. | Jews in popular culture—United States. | Theater—New York (State)—New York—History—20th century. | Musicals—New York (State)—New York—20th century—History and criticism. | Broadway (New York, N.Y.)
Classification: LCC PN1590.J48 L35 2017 | DDC 791.089/924—dc23
LC record available at https://lccn.loc.gov/2017004762

BRITISH LIBRARY CATALOGUING DATA ARE AVAILABLE

ISBN (print) 978-1-4766-6705-8
ISBN (ebook) 978-1-4766-2877-6

Front cover images © 2017 iStock

Printed in the United States of America

McFarland & Company, Inc., Publishers
Box 611, Jefferson, North Carolina 28640
www.mcfarlandpub.com

To my wife, Bonnie,
who has always encouraged me
to push the envelope

Acknowledgments

Putting together a book of this nature is not an easy task.
With that in mind, I'd like to acknowledge
several people for their work and contributions.

Thank you to Rich Mintzer for assistance;
Janis Gibson for research; Ellen Adler, Nahma Sandow,
Charles Strouse and Tovah Feldshuh for input;
Tom Oppenheim, Karen Schauben and of course
the many Jewish talents who have contributed
for the past 100-plus years to Broadway.

Table of Contents

Preface

When I first came up with the idea of writing a book on the history of the American theater in the 20th century, I was daunted. What an unimaginable undertaking. Huge, epic in its proportions and so complex with its multi-faceted, interconnected families, names and shows, I knew it would be a significant challenge. However, because I love the theater and have spent my entire life learning about it, working in it and being a part of it, I began to break it down.

Each century is, of course, unique. The 20th century, however, was extra special for the American theater because it finally came into its own. The theater of a country reflects that country's culture and politics. The early attempts at playwriting and musicals in the United States could actually be called British theater or, at best, Colonial theater. General Burgoyne, the English military strategist during the Revolutionary War, was also a playwright and had his work performed in New York, even as he tried to level the city.

As the nation began to mature, it slowly developed its own identity, and this was reflected in the works of the writers and poets of the time. American theater in the 19th century tended to center on melodramas and local issues: largely newcomers (greenhorns) arriving as immigrants in a new land, or city mouse versus country mouse themes. President Lincoln was watching the melodrama *Our American Cousin* at the Ford Theater in Washington, D.C., when he was assassinated. Although emigrants were constantly streaming into America during this century, like the Irish escaping the potato famine or the German Jews escaping persecution, it wasn't until the next century that theater matured and started to find a voice from a generation either born overseas or emigrating as children.

It was from this point of view that I was inspired to write this book. America is a wonderful country that embraces people from all nations. It is this mix of cultures that makes Americans truly citizens of the world. So, starting with the Jewish contribution to American theater, I embarked on what I hoped would be an extensive study of this rich and productive period. The result of this effort was the first edition of *Jews on Broadway*, which was tremendously received. It did, in fact, inspire me to write about another significant cultural impact on Broadway, which resulted in *Black Broadway: African Americans on the Great White Way*. This book was chock full of interesting theater stories along with a number of amazing photographs.

This new edition has more than two dozen photos, featuring some major Broadway luminaries and even yours truly. The new version also delves deeper and brings to the forefront a number of acclaimed Jewish actors who made their mark in film or television. Some impacted Broadway while others were impacted by Broadway. In addition, I've included more of Jewish theatrical instructors, whose methodology influenced numerous performers, plus the latest generation of Jewish talent who are shaping Broadway in the second decade of the twenty-first century.

A lot has changed in the short time since the first edition of *Jews on Broadway*. Attendance has continued to grow, with shows about Mormons, Disney's favorite Genie, musical giants such as Carole King and Gloria Estefan and a huge hit about, of all people, Alexander Hamilton—who would have guessed?

As for me, I continue to be involved in some of the latest Broadway musicals while, at the same time, launching a new endeavor. I have brought together Broadway and technology as never before, through the founding of an internet company called BroadwayHD (Broadwayhd.com). Now anyone can bring live captured Broadway shows right into their living rooms via Apple, Roku, or internet services. It's Broadway at your doorstep.

Of course, along with exciting news, there is often sobering news and for me—and the theater industry—that came in the passing of my friend and partner, Broadway legend James M. Nederlander. Nederlander, who passed away during the summer of 2016 at the age of 94, spent most of his adult life owning theaters, producing countless shows and shaping Broadway as we know it today. He was certainly a trailblazer in the industry, from which many, myself included, learned how this business operated. I miss him and will never forget him.

Introduction: Setting the Stage

Before we take a look at over a century of Jewish contributions to Broadway, let's take a moment to reflect upon the roots of such theatrical participation. How did the Jewish people come to have such a passion and a strong connection to the theater? From where did this theatrical enthusiasm evolve?

There are some who link the Jewish involvement in theater to the plays created and performed for the holiday Purim, called Purim Shpiels. The holiday custom dates back centuries and recounts the events outlined in the book of Esther. Joyous in nature, the Shpiels were originally designed to be family entertainment, and today are often presented for young children to learn the story of the holiday. However, in the 16th century, Purim Shpiels turned into professional performances with groups of touring actors playing the roles, complete with costumes and makeup. By offering a mocking commentary, the Purim Shpiel presented a Jewish version of political justice in the world, not unlike the political satire that would become a large part of the Jewish playwright's repertoire.

Performing, for the Jewish people, was also a manner of self-expression in societies in which they dealt with persecution. It was a means of storytelling outside of the synagogue, which was especially important when the Jewish people were unable to practice their religion publicly. Theater also served as a means of growth and learning when formal education was hard to come by.

Part of the impetus for Yiddish theater, which precluded the Jewish involvement in American theater, came from the Jewish Enlightenment throughout Europe in the late eighteenth and nineteenth centuries, called Haskalah. This was a philosophical and social movement that encouraged the Jewish people to explore secular subjects and to enter fields such as agriculture, science and the arts. Haskalah influenced education by stressing not only Jewish teaching, but also the need to put emphasis on a secular education, which meant learning both Hebrew and the European languages. The idea was to reach out beyond the Jewish community to also integrate with the larger community.

3

For the American Jews, the concept of Haskalah was evident in the assim-ilation of the Jewish immigrants into mainstream society. This was apparent first in Yiddish theater, particularly as it grew to include the works of Gordin and adaptations of classic literature not based on Jewish history. It was even more evident in the second generation of American Jews, who gravitated from Yiddish, which during the enlightenment was no longer spoken throughout most of Europe, to English-speaking theater.

Also evident from this period of enlightenment was the writing of books that presented Jewish characters in current settings rather than focusing on historic events or religious themes. This too spilled over to the American Jewish writers, including the many playwrights who focused on the current Jewish experience as it pertained to being part of American customs and culture. While Haskalah ended in Europe, it had lasting effects on Jewish theater and the arts.

In the Pages That Follow

Through the next eight chapters, we take a look at the Jewish experience as it pertains not just to theater, but to Broadway, which came to be accepted in the early part of the century as the apex of American theater.

The Jewish theatrical story in America begins with immigration to the land of hope and freedom and with the evolution of Yiddish theater in America which, during its heyday, was every bit as noteworthy and successful as Broad-way.

In the coming chapters we will travel with the Jewish performers, play-wrights, composers and lyricists from Yiddish theater to the next generation of vaudeville performers and then on to the years leading up to the Second World War. We will take a chapter to pay tribute to the immense contributions of a handful of composers and lyricists that re-defined the American musical forever. Then we will explore The Group Theater and the dramas that depicted life during the Great Depression amid the growing anti–Semitism that existed prior to World War II.

Following the patriotism of the war years and the many plays and musicals that depicted life during and after wartime, we will take a look at the Commu-nist trials of the 1950s, which affected many Jews in theater. Finally, in the 1960s and '70s Jewish themed shows made their way to Broadway, and assim-ilation was complete. By the 1990s, gay Jewish playwrights were stepping up in an attempt to gain their own acceptance and promote their own social con-cerns including HIV/AIDS.

We conclude the book by bringing the reader into the new century, which was not even two years old when we, as a nation, endured the tragedy of 9/11. Broadway's response was quick and the footlights were shining within days, sending a clear message that America would not be silenced by terrorism. From that point forward, despite the all too familiar budget challenges, Broadway has seen greater diversity on the stages, increased behind the scenes production activity from women and some wildly innovative productions.

Featured in the upcoming pages are many great talents, their stories, their accomplishments and in some cases how they held onto and even brought their Jewishness into their craft. Jacob Adler, Boris Thomashefsky, Oscar Hammerstein, Fannie Brice, Al Jolson, Irving Berlin, the Gershwins, Rodgers and Hammerstein, Clifford Odets, Stella Adler, Comden and Green, Arthur Miller, Zero Mostel, Neil Simon, David Merrick, Tony Kushner, Wendy Wasserstein, Alan Menken and Mel Brooks are all included in the Jewish contribution to Broadway ... along with many others.

Also, throughout the chapters, I have tried to include the changes in Jewish life, culture and acceptance as it paralleled that which took place onstage. After all, the productions and the people behind them typically reflected the Jewish experience in America and abroad. From those who changed their names because they were fearful of being "too Jewish" to those who clamored to play Tevye in *Fiddler on the Roof*, the acceptance of the Jewish people in theater and in society has certainly changed, and such changes were also reflected on Broadway.

Hopefully the melting pot that has been, and still is, Broadway Theater can serve as an example to society at large.

1

Immigration, Yiddish Theater and Building Broadway

If there is any definitive starting point for the Jewish impact on theater in America, it is the Yiddish theater of the late nineteenth and early twentieth centuries. Between 1880 and 1914, the Jewish population in America grew from 250,000 to 2.5 million, as the Jews fled persecution, primarily from Eastern Europe. They landed at Ellis Island in New York Harbor and settled nearby in what would become the overcrowded ghettos of the Lower East Side of Manhattan. Many brought with them little more than the clothes on their backs, or perhaps their few worldly possessions. However, they also brought with them an indelible spirit, a strong sense of community and the desire to build a better life for themselves and for their children. Particularly important to these immigrants were both tradition and culture, which included a relatively new form of entertainment known as Yiddish theater. This new form of theater had emerged in the 1870s in Eastern Europe and then in London.

As a means of retaining Jewish cultural roots and sense of community and embracing their newfound freedom of expression, Yiddish theater in America was born. From its emergence in the 1880s, Yiddish theater grew as a phenomenon for the immigrants, producing star performers and generating a "buzz" that spread beyond the Lower East Side of Manhattan into other cities, and even outside of the Jewish community. But for those on the Lower East Side, most of whom were working in sweat shops by day, or as laborers, the theater was a significant bond that held the community together. Harold Clurman, well-known drama critic and founder of the Group Theater of the 1930s, was first inspired by Yiddish theater as a child. He noted in 1968 that "even more than the synagogue or the lodge, [it] became the meeting place and the forum of the Jewish Community in America between 1888 and the early 1920s."[1]

Yiddish theater was more than what we know of today as "community theater." It was much more, including featured performers who made their way to the United States for the purpose of acting without the restraints imposed by foreign governments. Boris Thomashefsky and Jacob P. Adler, whose daughter Stella would become one of the legendary acting teachers of the 20th century, were two of the most celebrated national figures of this magical era. A wide range of material from melodramas to comedies was presented, often inspired by the culture and the life of the European Jews, especially those emigrating from Russia.

The appeal of the many shows presented in large theaters, some housing over 2,000 people, crossed socio-economic boundaries and made theater a rich part of the lifestyle of the Jewish people in America. However, to better appreciate the impact of Yiddish theater as the foundation for Jewish involvement in American theater, it is important to look back briefly at the emergence of Yiddish theater in the 1870s in Europe.

The Father of Yiddish Theater

Abraham Goldfadn, born in Starokonstantinov, Russia, in 1840, was heralded as the father of Yiddish theater. It was Goldfadn, a Russian intellectual, who wrote and produced the first Yiddish theater productions in Jassy, Romania, in 1876. Nahma Sandrow, author of the book *Vagabond Stars: A World History of Yiddish Theater,* describes Goldfadn as a "folk singer and folk poet, product of the popular Yiddish cultural tradition of the townlets of Eastern European countryside."[2] She goes on to expand upon his reputation as a jack of many trades, adding that Goldfadn was "a trouper, an artist, a dreamer, an intellectual, a hustler, a scrapper, a con man, a romantic, a dandy, an optimist and a one man band."[3] This was exemplified by his various careers, which included shop owner and editor of several newspapers, all of which eventually failed. He was also a songwriter for some of the Broder singers of the era, who were flashy, somewhat flamboyant life-of-the-party entertainers.

In fact, it was one such Broder singer, a Lithuanian Jew named Israel Grodner, who inspired Goldfadn to start writing and producing plays that would incorporate a story along with the music of the era. According to Sandrow, there are many versions of how the first Yiddish theater production came to be. Whether Goldfadn came to see Grodner perform, or Grodner summoned Goldfadn and suggested that he use the music in play form, remains debatable, but what is known for sure is that Goldfadn first took the stage to perform sophisticated poems and essentially bombed. Grodner, however, saved the show with his comedy and lighthearted songs. Upon seeing the response of the audience to Grodner's performance, Goldfadn was hooked. He would write musical numbers into his plays and then produce them.

Yiddish Theater Was Born

The songs, the humor and the storylines were all provided by Goldfadn, who made sure his actors, usually two in a performance (which was all he could afford to pay), understood exactly what was expected of them. He did not write out most of the dialogue but had the actors improvise based on the storyline. While the shows lacked the precision of a Shakespearian play, they brought together important elements in Jewish culture, including song and humor. They were neither complicated nor scholarly, but met the demands of an audience that simply sought out good entertainment. While he did receive his share of criticism from those who thought he could provide more substance and sophistication in his works, Goldfadn learned quickly the importance of "giving the people what they wanted." And with that in mind, he kept the songs light and humorous, simple and relevant to the performances, at least until the audiences became more familiar with the idea of theater.

Sandrow also points out in her book that Goldfadn began what would become a tradition in Yiddish theater, known as the curtain speech. This occurred at the end of the show when Goldfadn would come out and talk to the audience. "He was a combination teacher, elocutionist and barker," she explains.[4]

Early comedies, including *Shmendrik* and the *Two Kumi-Lemls*, were based on simple premises, such as arranged marriages, and were immediately hits. Another popular show, *The Witch*, was about superstition. Soon other shows emerged about a wide range of familiar topics, each a hit. As Goldfadn's legacy grew, so did Yiddish theater and his own company. His performers included Broder singers, cantors, cabaret performers, local workers, drifters, gamblers and yes, even actors ... some of the best of the time, including Jacob P. Adler.

Goldfadn maintained tight control over everything from the venues to the costumes and the scenery to the props. He was steadfast in his ways and wanted everything to meet his wishes. Despite his control and his rising stardom, he was still unable to make very much money. Goldfadn was constantly promoting the shows to anyone who would listen, sometimes with great success and other times resulting in small turnouts.

Long engagements were uncommon, and the company remained on the road for months at a stretch. As the overall popularity of Yiddish theater grew, other companies appeared. Some, like Goldfadn's, were a diverse mix of talent, while others were family troupes. Some worked long hours to put on a first-rate production while others loosely organized a show and hoped for the best. There was little regard for copyright law, which was rarely enforced, so troupes that enjoyed the work of Goldfadn simply performed the same plays in another town or city. Often performers who had worked with Goldfadn would leave his company and start their own. There was no great loyalty among most of the performers who often just wanted to keep working. Acting was then, as it is today, a difficult career choice.

In a short time, Yiddish theater, in one form or another, was emerging as a cultural phenomenon throughout Eastern Europe. For the Jewish people, theater was becoming a way of life, providing entertainment and, as plays became more sophisticated, providing food for thought. It would all come to an abrupt end, however, with the assassination of Czar Alexander II, who had allowed great freedom for the Jewish people. Under his successor, Czar Alexander III, organized religious persecution against the Jewish people swelled throughout all of Eastern Europe. The Jewish people were forced into ghetto life, few were allowed to study or own land, and theater was all but eliminated. As Sandrow writes in her book, "The entire communities of Moscow, St. Petersburg and Kharkov were marched in manacles to the railway stations and expelled."[5]

Many of the Jewish actors fled to London, which would soon emerge as the new home of Yiddish theater. Israel Grodner, Jacob P. Adler and Anna Held were among the performers who settled in London's Jewish section to take part in any of several Yiddish theater productions. The Jewish immigrants who had fled the persecution of Eastern Europe were thrilled to once again have the cultural connection that came from Yiddish theater. Shows were plentiful, even in rooms adjacent to taverns, which were established as theater clubs. Jacob P. Adler once wrote of the Yiddish theater experience in London, "If Yiddish theater was destined to go through its infancy in Russia, and in America grew to manhood and success, then London was its school."[6] Adler was correct in acknowledging that the Jewish thespians were able to hone their craft without fear of religious persecution. Of course, in observance of the Sabbath, plays were not performed on Friday nights or until sundown on Saturdays.

In a few years, however, there were more performers than shows in which to appear. Additionally, London had its own English-speaking theaters already established, thus creating more competition as the immigrants also began exploring the established theater. London's East End was a poor neighborhood to begin with, so the influx of Jewish immigrants, including the many actors, was taking its toll on the inhabitants. Adding to the overcrowded living conditions were strict fire laws that were also imposed on the theaters. This made it more difficult for performers to find work on the stages of London. While Yiddish theater would continue successfully in London for several decades, it was destined to find a new home on the other side of the pond, so to speak, in America.

Coming to America

Along with many immigrants heading to the United States directly from Eastern Europe, many of London's Jewish immigrants, including some of the top performers on the Yiddish stages, boarded ships for America. Ellis Island was the final stop for millions of immigrants, including the Irish, the Italians, and the Jews, among others, seeking a better life in this new land of hope. Starting in 1881, some 1.3 million Jews would immigrate to America over a span of 22 years. While it was hard to find jobs and the living conditions on the Lower East Side were difficult and overcrowded, the freedom afforded to the Jewish people was better than life in Russia, Romania or Poland, along with slightly more living space and more job opportunities than in London.

In 1882, Yiddish theater would first appear in America. It would blossom very quickly and become the cultural explosion of the era. "The Yiddish theater stars quickly became matinee idols, generating fanfare wherever they went. These were among the most influential actors of their time and they would go on to influence Jewish, and non–Jewish, performers and playwrights for decades," explains Nahma Sandrow.[7]

Despite the eminent popularity of Yiddish theater, it got off to an inauspicious start in New York City. Two Russian performers, Leon and Miron Golubok, along with four members of their acting troupe, crossed the Atlantic Ocean to join Abe Golubok, who was already in New York City, working at a cigar factory with a young 12-year-old co-worker named Boris Thomashefsky. Together they formed the company that planned to stage what would be the first production of Yiddish theater in the United States, Goldfadn's hit musical, *The Witch*. As the story goes, Thomashefsky and Abe Golubok persuaded a saloon owner, Frank Wolf, to finance the performance, as well as bring the company from Russia.

Opening night, August 12, 1882, at Turn Hall on East Fourth Street, did not go as planned. As the story goes, something mysterious happened to the diva, who at the last minute had a headache and didn't show up for the performance. Some claim that she was bribed by German Jews living uptown, who were embarrassed by what they considered the vulgar Lower East Side Yiddish-speaking crowd. As a result, the show never took place.

While various versions of the same night differ regarding the influence of the uptown Jews, it is widely agreed that a large crowd showed up for the big event. Some say the diva was eventually bribed by Thomashefsky and finally showed up late, while other accounts say she did not. Either way, the show was never staged and the crowd left disappointed. Nonetheless, Yiddish theater would commence shortly thereafter and the crowds returned. Soon it would become a distinct part of the Jewish lifestyle. Sweatshop workers would set aside whatever money they could spare and buy tickets for the latest production. In time, the uptown Jews and those from all over the city, as well as non–Jews, were also taking in the shows. The old Bowery Garden, a beer hall known mostly for vaudeville, was home to Yiddish shows on Friday afternoons, and despite the Sabbath, on Saturday afternoons. Even orthodox Jews attended the shows; however no actual business was transacted, and the lights were turned on the day before. Goldfadn's productions were frequently presented at the Bowery Garden.

Within a year, the Goluboks would form their own troupe, and Thomashefsky, along with his sisters and his father, would form another. Other troupes were also soon emerging as more actors were emigrating from London to the American stage, including Jacob P. Adler. Every theater on the Lower East Side, and even some makeshift theaters, were clamoring for Yiddish theater productions. In fact, at one point there were as many as 14 shows being staged at once, rivaling Broadway.

BORIS THOMASHEFSKY AND JACOB P. ADLER: LEGENDS OF YIDDISH THEATER

Boris Thomashefsky came to America in 1881 from the area around Kiev, in the Ukraine. He was 12 at the time and made the long trip with his family. Within a year, while working at the cigar factory, he began singing in a local synagogue. He possessed an outstanding voice, which was not surprising, since he came from a long line of cantors. At work, he learned from his elders some of the songs from the old country, where Yiddish theater had once flourished. Determined to bring those songs, along with the shows from which they originated, to his newfound home in New York, the young Thomashefsky would put together that first Yiddish theater production, *The Witch*.

Despite the opening night disaster mentioned above, immigrants remained eager to see Yiddish theater productions, and Thomashefsky launched his career with his own companies. Just as Goldfadn was widely considered the father of Yiddish theater, Thomashefsky would soon be heralded as the founder of American Yiddish theater. Still a teenager, he would also take shows on the road and introduce Yiddish theater to Jewish communities in other cities. For a while he was even based in Chicago, building up the theater base in the Windy City.

It was while touring, however, that he would land in Baltimore, where at the age of 18 he would meet a 14-year-old actress named Bessie Baumfeld-Kaufman. She was enamored with the theater and especially Thomashefsky, whom she first saw dressed as a girl. She went backstage to meet the actress only to find out that under the wig was a handsome young teenage boy. Within days, Bessie would run away from home to join the company, and in a few years she and Thomashefsky would get married.

Thomashefsky had a penchant for light operettas, musicals and comedy, much as Goldfadn had had in Eastern Europe. His voice, his good looks and his stage persona all rolled up into his becoming one of the major celebrities of the era. As Goldfadn had learned many years before, in Eastern Europe, Thomashefsky discovered early on that it was important to give the people what they wanted, and light musical entertainment fit the bill perfectly. When a new wave of half a million Jewish immigrants came into the country in the years between 1905 and 1908, he was ready with the light musical fare that they anticipated from the old country.

Thomashefsky was a force in Yiddish theater and an icon whom young Jewish performers aspired to emulate. "A rock star of his time, women would swoon at his mere appearance on stage and he built a huge fan base not only on the Lower East side, but in other cities, from the tours of his company," notes Sandrow.[8] Among the many notable shows he produced and adapted for Yiddish theater, including those in which he performed, were *Uncle Tom's Cabin, East Lynn, Faust* and *The Green Millionaire.*

While many of the immigrants who flocked to Yiddish theater were still toiling away in sweatshops or as manual laborers, Thomashefsky became the wealthiest of the performers. Together with his wife Bessie, they became theater owners and magazine publishers while living in a 12-room home on Bedford Avenue in Brooklyn. They also raised funds for the needy and spent their own money to bring young actors from Eastern Europe to the United States.

While a few of the stars of Yiddish theater made the crossover to American theater, Thomashefsky did not, as he was less comfortable performing in English. Years later, in 1931, he did co-write and perform in the Broadway musical *The Singing Rabbi*. The show only lasted three performances, but the legend of Thomashefsky lasted much longer. In fact, George Gershwin mentioned him in a couple of his songs and in the hit musical *The Producers*, Max Bialystock attributes his success as a Broadway producer to the tutelage of the great Boris Thomashefsky. A famous theater joke also surrounds Thomashefsky; whether it is accurate or not is anyone's guess. It seems that Thomashefsky reputedly spent the night with a local prostitute. At the end of their time together he handed her a pair of tickets to a performance that evening of his latest play. The prostitute responded, "I really don't need tickets, I need bread." To this Thomashefsky replied, "If you wanted bread you should have slept with a baker."

Jokes notwithstanding, Thomashefsky remains a legendary figure from Yiddish theater, and his contributions had a lasting effect on American theater.

Jacob P. Adler, meanwhile, was among those who came from London to take to the American stages of the Lower East Side. "He was a showoff, and he was gorgeous," says Ellen Adler, granddaughter of Jacob and daughter of Stella Adler. "He was the most famous of them all," adds Ellen, regarding her grandfather's much-heralded days on stage.[9]

They called him the Great Eagle, since Adler is the German word for eagle, and because Adler soared as a performer. He was respected by his peers and revered by his fans. Adler first made his mark as a young actor in his hometown of Odessa in the Russian Empire. He had a brief boxing career as a teenager, then took the footwork he'd learned and parleyed it into a brief dancing career, all the while gaining local notoriety. He was inspired by watching Israel Grodner perform and soon joined a Yiddish theater group in the 1870s. He would work hard and hone his acting skills in performances throughout Russia and Poland.

After being forced out of Russia by religious persecution and strict laws that severely limited the activities of Jewish people, Adler moved his acting career to London. Adler starred in *The Odessa Beggar*, which became one of the roles he would return to several times during his long career.

The poverty and the overcrowded conditions of London's East End would prompt him to pick up and move to the United States, where Yiddish theater had already taken off. After establishing himself as a leading player in several productions, Adler started his own company, which would perform the works of novelist-turned-playwright Jacob Gordin. While musicals and comedies were enjoyed by the mainstream, Gordin wrote dramatic works based on classic literature, including a Yiddish version of *King Lear*, based loosely on the Shakespearian play. The play drew the usual Yiddish theater crowd plus a more sophisticated audience, not typically found in these theaters. The production starred both Jacob P. Adler and his third wife, Sara. "She was a great actress in her own right, very beautiful and well disciplined on stage," says her granddaughter Ellen, a prolific painter. "There was so much talent in the Adler family," she adds, recounting more than a dozen theatrical performers.[10]

In the ensuing years, Adler would bring a significant number of more serious, noteworthy dramatic works to Yiddish theater, broadening the genre and introducing the immigrant audiences to great works including those of Shaw and Ibsen. Plays written in English were now performed on the Yiddish stages along with the original Yiddish works. In Shakespeare's *The Merchant of Venice*, Adler played the role of Shylock to adoring audiences at the People's Theater. Then, in 1903, the play would go to Broadway, in English, and Adler was asked to play the role again, which he did, speaking in Yiddish. The result was triumphant.

When the play closed, however, Adler headed back to Eastern Europe in an attempt to bring his family to America. His sister and her seven children would eventually come to the United States a few years later. Adler meanwhile returned to play Shylock on Broadway in a revival of the hit show. Having created a new character, a Yiddish Shylock on Broadway, Adler gained far more notoriety than ever before.

Despite his Broadway success, the tradition that came from Yiddish theater was still closer to his heart. He would take on greater challenges, such as taking Tolstoy's *Power of Darkness*, written in Russian, and bringing it to the stage in Yiddish. The play was a hit, as was Tolstoy's *Resurrection*. Both starred Adler, who in 1904 built the Grand Theater at the corner of Bowery and Canal Street.

Until a stroke nearly ended his career and his life in 1920, Adler continued as a leading force in Yiddish theater, going on tour with Thomashefsky at one point, but more significantly legitimizing the genre through the serious, thought-provoking works of Gordin, whom his daughter Stella has credited with making Jacob P. Adler's career. While there was more money to be made through the lighter upbeat shows of Thomashefsky, Adler knew that given time, serious dramatic works would also become a staple in Yiddish theater, and he was right. He made an indelible mark in theater as a performer and as the patriarch of one of the most significant families in American theater.

Adler and Thomashefsky were adored by the Yiddish community, especially by the women. While Thomashefsky was married to Bessie for many years, Adler was known as a carouser. Along with reviews of the plays, the local newspapers featured gossip columns, typically filled with tidbits on the two leading men as well as other stars of the Yiddish stages. Devoted fans sent gifts to their favorites and picked up the tab when they were seen at a café or tavern. There was also the practice of staging benefits for specific performers, which was popular in American and British theater. A benefit performance was one in which the actor chose the show, of course starred in it, and was afforded the box office profits. Yet, neither Adler nor Thomashefsky needed the benefit performances to survive.

Alder and Thomashefsky were friends, sometimes business partners and at other times rivals. While Thomashefsky was the song and dance man, a star of musical comedies, Adler was a serious "actor." Yet they maintained a usually friendly competitive spirit. For example, in response to Adler playing *King Lear*, Thomashefsky took on a serious role, performing in the first Yiddish-language production of Shakespeare's *Hamlet* ... and the reviews were positive.

Of course there were other stars, such as David Kessler, whose dramatic acting gained respect and great attention. There were the comic stars, Sigmund Mogulesko and Ludwig Satz. While not a star, actor Edward G. Robinson also made his debut in Yiddish theater. Born Emanuel Goldenberg to a Romanian family, Robinson immigrated to the United States with his parents in 1903. Shortly thereafter, he had his Bar Mitzvah at the first Romanian-American temple and set his sights on acting. Robinson started out taking roles in Yiddish theater productions before moving to Broadway starting with the 1915 Roi Cooper Megrue original play *Under Fire*. He would later go on to great success in film, appearing in more than 100 motion pictures.

Larger-than-life performers of their time, the stars of Yiddish theater performed in a very bold, deliberate manner with a strong stage presence. It was a style that was not subtle, yet it was still considered realistic by its audience.

Unlike the American theaters, the atmosphere within the Yiddish theaters was far more casual, with a carnival-like ambiance. Vendors sold their goods, people congregated during long intermissions, changed seats to sit with friends and laughed, jeered and applauded loudly, while eating and drinking during the show. Some of this behavior spilled over into vaudeville, where the audiences were sometimes as busy as the performers. The theater was a meeting place of sorts, in which to visit with friends, mingle, talk, gossip and enjoy the camaraderie. It was an escape from the difficult working and living conditions, and it provided the community with a much-needed sense of Jewish unity. The audiences laughed, cried and sang along with the stars on stage. Most of the Yiddish theater productions were shows designed for the mass audience. They were not highly sophisticated, nor were they vaudeville. They had story lines that were either easy to follow, familiar to the culture or taken from classic literature but adapted for the audience. Most of the immigrants were denied much education in their homelands, so, while some shows were enlightening, many were simply entertaining. The audiences could enjoy and discuss their theater experience with their neighbors ... and did they ever. The shows and the stars were the talk of the Lower East Side, and in time, throughout Jewish neighborhoods in Brooklyn and other parts of New York City. Quite devoted to their favorite stars, some fans even got into fights, literally, when debating which celebrity was the better performer.

THE ACTRESSES

As Nahma Sandrow describes in her book, the actresses in Yiddish theater fell into several categories. They were "vivacious spubrette or hoyden, stately prima donna, emotional heroine, character comedienne or villainess. They all had to have good voices, and usually they had to be able to dance. In looks, the public favored flavored flashing eyes, adorable smiles, and zaftik (juicy) figures."[11]

Bessie Thomashefsky, Boris' wife, was a leading star of the era. Bessie and Boris were the preeminent couple in show business of their time. Michael Tilson Thomas, conductor and grandson of the Thomashefskys, recreated the legendary couple on stage at Carnegie Hall's Zankel Hall in New York City. Tilson Thomas would comment that they were "the Richard Burton and Elizabeth Taylor of their time," based on their notoriety, their wealth and their adoring public.[12] Together they would perform in numerous shows in New York, Boston, Philadelphia and Chicago. Bessie's versatility on stage allowed her to take on a great range of roles. She could play the diva, take on comical roles with a Fanny Brice flair for wisecracks, or perform a dramatic role as well as any actress of her generation. When the couple eventually separated, her career continued with what was often considered her greatest, most highly acclaimed role as the seductive lead in Oscar Wilde's *Salomé*. She would also go on to manage her own Lower East Side theater troupe and revive some of her favorite roles. An independent woman, Bessie would even take on the leading role in a play called *Chantzhe* [Hannah] *in Amerika,* about a woman who wanted nothing more than to be a chauffeur, something that was unheard of at the time, in what still remains a heavily male-dominated field.

Among the Yiddish actresses of the era was Bertha Kalish, an immigrant from the Austro-Hungarian Empire. She had moved to Romania and become a star of Yiddish theater before making her way to America where she grew to prominence in a Yiddish version of Henrik Ibsen's classic *A Doll's House,* as well as in *Fedora* and *The Kreutzer Sonata.* In fact, she was so highly acclaimed in *The Kreutzer Sonata* that she would play the role on Broadway in 1906. Kalish would go on to play various other significant roles in both Yiddish and English and was always described as being a beautiful woman with a magnificent voice.

There were other women of the Yiddish theater, such as Jenny Goldstein, known as the reigning queen of melodrama, musical tearjerkers and full-blown musical spectaculars. Sara Adler, Jacob's wife, who began her American stage career as Sara Heine, the wife of Maurice Heine, another Yiddish actor, was featured in nearly 300 roles. Sara, who spoke Russian, supposedly learned Yiddish while performing in Yiddish theater. Although many of her performances were with her husband Jacob, she also performed across the river from the

Several women appear on the bill as the New Delancey Theatre features a gala midnight show during the heyday of Yiddish theater (Museum of the City of New York).

Lower East Side, in Brooklyn, presenting the works of Ibsen and Shaw to Yiddish-speaking audiences.

The legendary Molly Picon, discussed in greater length in Chapter Two (during her days in vaudeville), also honed her skills in Yiddish theater. Fanny Thomashefsky taught her piano, Michael Thomashefsky put her on stage at 15 (in his Yiddish repertory troupe at the Arch Street Theater) and she performed in Boris Thomashefsky's *Uncle Tom's Cabin.* Clearly, she was trained by one of the preeminent theatrical families. While she was to go on to great notoriety in English theater, Picon never forgot her roots.

THE PLAYHOUSES AND THE PLAYWRIGHTS

Like popular television shows and mainstream mass-appeal movies, the shows of Yiddish theater were the premiere entertainment for the Jewish audience, rivaling Broadway at the box office.

Six theaters were the most prominent of the many venues for Yiddish theater. In the Bowery, The Windsor, which opened in 1893, was the largest, with a seating capacity of 3,500, dwarfing even the largest Broadway theaters of the time. The Windsor housed the most mainstream popular shows. The People's Theater was a spacious 2,500-seater leased at the start of the 20th century by Thomashefsky. Adler managed the Grand Theater, a 2,000-seat venue featuring what Adler called "better theater," meaning the more sophisticated plays adapted by Gordin. Another large theater was the Thalia, built in the 1880s holding 3,000 theatergoers and featuring shows starring David Kessler. Each theater had its own repertory system presenting new shows on a regular basis, plus "benefits" for the stars and occasionally for charities. Prices were typically in the $.25 to $1.00 range for tickets, and the collective 11,000 seats in these four prominent theaters were filled nearly every night.

Two more prominent theaters would open in 1911 and 1912, north of the Bowery on Second Avenue. The nearly 2,000 seat Second Avenue Theater was built for David Kessler and the National, also at roughly 2,000 seats, was built for Boris Thomashefsky. At the time, these were the "state-of-the-art," elegant theaters that highlighted an area that would become known as the "Yiddish Broadway." In fact, the opening of these theaters brought numerous dignitaries including the mayor of New York City, William Jay Gaynor, who might not have understood Yiddish, but nonetheless was on hand for the festive occasions.

The sheer size of the theaters meant that a new show could be seen by many people in a short time. As a result, it also meant there was an ongoing demand for new material. The early light musicals of Goldfadn, Grodner and those emulating their style were one of several genres that marked the era.

There were the "crowd pleasers" from the early years of Yiddish theater, which continued to draw large audiences as new waves of immigrants descended on the Lower East Side. The stories were simple and the songs brought back the spirit of their homeland.

By contrast, there were Gordin's "high-brow" dramatic plays, which would not only fuel the career of Jacob P. Adler, but also legitimize Yiddish theater for those who looked down upon it, calling the populist plays shund, a Yiddish word roughly meaning "trashy." However, the term eventually came to describe the "commonplace" shows that appealed to the masses. Similarly, popular reality television shows today might be referred to by critics as a "shund" despite being money-making ventures with great mass appeal. It took time for the Jewish "intellectual elite" to accept Yiddish theater, which they considered to have more of a circus-like atmosphere than actual theater.

While Gordin was more concerned with quality, there was a definite need for quantity. Playwrights Moyshe Hurwitz and Joseph Lateiner were two of the most prolific of the era, each writing hundreds of plays. Their works included melodramas, comedies, tragedies and lavish spectacles, sometimes all in the same play. They turned out plays like bakers turn out bread, and their craft became known as baking plays because it was similar to the process of shaping the dough, cooking it and repeating the same process again and again. The plays followed a few similar story lines and were baked hastily, sometimes missing an act, but always fresh out of the oven for opening night ... even if they didn't always totally make sense. Plots, storylines and even lines of dialogue were often lifted from one play and dropped into another to finish a scene or make a smoother transition.

One of the most successful plays of the time, *The Jewish Heart,* in 1908, mixed comedy and drama into a relatable storyline to capture the hearts of the audience, making them cry and making them laugh. *The Jewish Heart* was not only a major hit, but it set the stage, literally, for another type of Yiddish play, the domestic drama. More practical and "realistic" than the musical comedies, and easier to relate to then the classics, these plays touched upon Jewish culture. They were about working people, butchers, factory workers, firefighters and seamstresses. They were about typical Jewish families and the desire of the younger generation to better assimilate into the American mainstream. They were about coming from the old country and missing relatives and customs they had left behind. They were about weddings and celebrations, as well as sadness and tragedy. They played on the emotions of an audience that related to the storylines and identified with the characters.

As the new wave of immigrants that came to America from 1905 through 1908 became more sophisticated and grew to seek more than just the "light" musical genre, Gordin's writings and Adler's performances would once again be in vogue as well as the domestic "slice of life" domestic dramas. Pretty soon, all three types of plays would encapsulate Yiddish theater.

As for Goldfadn, the man who started it all, his reputation preceded him when he came to New York City in 1887. He was a folk hero. His songs were sung in Russian and Hungarian as well as in Yiddish. Despite great adoration by the masses, he remained poor, unable to build and sustain a successful company in London, Paris or New York City. By the time of his arrival in America, Yiddish theater, beginning with his play *The Witch*, had logs of its own and stars leading their own companies. Goldfadn was unable to make a dent in the already established American medium that he had created in Europe over a decade earlier. His penchant for control and his steadfast ways were unwelcome among the new breed of performers, and before long he was on his way back to Europe, not to return until 1902, some two decades after the birth of Yiddish theater in America.

Not unlike a silent film star returning to the business in the era of "talkies," Goldfadn was out of step with the changes in the genre. His efforts to get a company off the ground or a show produced were futile. Finally, in 1907 he was able to convince Thomashefsky to produce his play *Ben-Ami*. The play was a success. Goldfadn died shortly after opening night. His funeral drew some 30,000 people to pay their respects to the father of Yiddish theater. Following his death, the play lasted for several months playing to sold out audiences. Years later, The Goldies would be established as awards given out by the Hebrew Actor's Union in his honor to celebrate excellence in the theater.

Yiddish theater would continue to draw an audience, with several variations, including patriotic shows during World War I. In the 1920s, another artistic form prevailed, namely Vaudeville. As the second generation of immigrants became Americanized and the influx of new immigrants slowed considerably, Yiddish as a spoken language began to disappear. The children of the early immigrants spoke English, and they were gravitating to vaudeville and to the stages of Broadway. Through the years, special projects, like that of Tilson Thomas, Thomashefsky's grandson, as well as museums and numerous books, such as that of Nahma Sandrow, have chronicled the golden age of Yiddish theater. They have educated several generations of Jews, providing them with a glimpse of this important and highly influential period in Jewish American culture.

Meanwhile on Broadway

At the turn of the century (the 20th, that is), the Broadway theater district was primarily centered between Union Square (14th Street) and 24th Street, just north of what came to be known as the Yiddish Broadway. It would be during the early 1900s that the Broadway theater district began moving north to Herald Square (West 34th Street) and continued on to 42nd Street, and above. George M. Cohan's classic lyric echoed the movement of "Broadway" as he wrote: "Give my regards to Broadway, remember me to Herald Square, tell all the gang at 42nd Street that I will soon be there." The subway and better streetlights made it easier and safer to get around at night, allowing for expansion of the theater district. The Times Building on Longacre Square opened in 1902, and the name was officially changed to Times Square. Theaters, including the Victoria, Republic, Lyric and the New Amsterdam, were among the new venues built on 42nd Street between 1899 and 1905.

It was during these early years of the 20th century that several key Jewish entrepreneurs drove the expansion of the Broadway theater district. They included Charles Frohman, Oscar Hammerstein and the Shuberts, all of whom are Broadway legends thanks to their "off-stage" contributions to what would become known as the Great White Way.

Charles Frohman, who moved with his family from his birthplace in Ohio to New York City in 1864, went from a career in the newspaper industry to a booking agent, producer and theater owner. His production of *Shenandoah* in the late 19th century was his breakthrough success. He followed that show with Clyde Fitch's *Masked Ball,* and his producing career was off and running. By the time he died aboard the Lusitania, which was torpedoed and sank in 1915, he had produced over 700 shows. Additionally, he had opened his own theater, The Empire, and had become part of the theater syndicate that would control the industry through their own booking/management system for the first 15 years of the century. He ran six New York theaters and controlled numerous others around the country as well as some in London. Along with his influence in bringing shows and stars to Broadway, Frohman is probably best remembered for producing an adaptation of the Barrie novel, which became the original *Peter Pan* starting Maude Adams. His brother Daniel teamed with Charles for a while, before going off on his own to help develop road companies, which would tour the country with popular shows. Daniel did, however, also keep his hand in Broadway activities as manager of the Lyceum Theater.

The Shubert Brothers, Sam, Jacob and Lee, were also Jewish immigrates who came to the United States with their parents in the late 19th century. Settling in Syracuse, New York, they found themselves fascinated by the theater, particularly the inner workings. As teenagers they worked diligently to pull themselves out of poverty, and before long, they were all theater managers. However, it was together that they would become a force to be reckoned with in the business.

Shortly after the turn of the 20th century, the Shubert brothers moved to New York City, borrowed money, and purchased their first venue, the Herald Square Theater. It was from that point forward that they would build an empire. Sadly, in 1905, however, they would lose Sam, at the age of 30, who died from injuries sustained in a train wreck in Pennsylvania. The remaining two brothers, spurred on by the callous response from the syndicate to their brother's death, would forge ahead to become one of the most significant driving forces in theater history, booking over 600 shows under the esteemed title "Shubert Presents." Known initially for their operettas, the brothers saw the mass appeal of revues and used their theaters to present many up and coming performers, some of whom, like Al Jolson, emerged as major stars. *Maytime* (1917), *Blossom Time* (1921) and *Big Boy* (1925) were among the most successful early musicals to come from the Shubert brothers.

The Shubert Organization, now run by the non-profit Shubert Foundation, continues to play a major role in theater today, owning 17 theaters on Broadway plus several Off Broadway theaters and actively producing new shows, including many on Broadway. The numerous productions of the Shuberts and the Shubert Organization began with *The Night of the Party* in 1902 and have continued through the decades with shows such as revivals of *Hamlet, Romeo and Juliet,* and *The Merchant of Venice;* and original productions of *Grand Hotel, Hooray for What, Ziegfeld Follies of 1936* and *1943, Dancin', Ain't Misbehavin', Children of a Lesser God, City of Angels, Spamalot, School of Rock,* and *The Humans.* The Shuberts have also featured special Broadway performances over the years ranging from Sarah Bernhardt to Gilda Radner.

Oscar Hammerstein was also one of the premiere impresarios at the turn of the 20th century, later opening opera houses and theaters in Philadelphia and London, while producing a few shows and operettas at his own New York theaters. A jack of all trades, Hammerstein was an inventor, writer, editor, publisher, composer, speculator, designer, builder, promoter, showman and one of the most prominent forces in American theatre.

Having made a fortune in the cigar industry, Hammerstein started out by moonlighting as a theater manager at venues showing German operas, and in some cases presenting some of his own plays. Near the end of the 19th century, he built the first of two theaters in the largely unsettled Harlem area, the Harlem Opera House on 125th Street. He would then move downtown with the opening of the Manhattan Opera House on 34th Street. In what would become Times Square, he opened the lavish Olympia Theater, followed shortly thereafter by the Victoria and the Republic. A few years later, both the Victoria and Republic would have roof gardens.

Despite some failures along the way, Hammerstein's theaters would become some of the premiere show palaces on Broadway for many decades. Even though his own personal passion was opera, his theaters would become venues for all genres of theatrical shows. Hammerstein would later become known as the Father of Times Square. (More on both Hammerstein and the Shuberts, in the next chapter on vaudeville.)

The other significant Jewish theater family, the Nederlanders, first established their presence in 1912 when David Nederlander acquired the lease of the Detroit Opera House. They would soon move to Broadway where their impact would be felt for the rest of the century and beyond. James M. Nederlander, known in and around the industry as Jimmy, headed until his death in 2016 the organization that now controls not only several Broadway theaters but theaters in other U.S. cities as well as in London. Jimmy started in theater at the age of seven, sweeping floors in his father's theaters. He would grow to learn the business inside and out and later on become a theater owner, with nine venues on Broadway, and as a producer bringing numerous shows to the stage, including *Whose Life is This Anyway?*, *Peter Pan*, *Woman of the Year*, *Nine*, *Noises Off*, *The Will Rogers Follies*, and revivals of *The King and I* and *Fiddler on the Roof*, among others.

Jimmy also played a major role in the development of outdoor theaters in various parts of the country while staying true to New York. At one point, he even owned part of the New York Yankees with George Steinbrenner and received a World Series ring to go with his numerous theatrical awards.

Jimmy was involved in the family business since the 1940s, with some 300 shows and a Tony Award for lifetime achievement in 2004, and is rightly recalled as one of the luminaries of the business. I had the pleasure of knowing Jimmy, working with him, and being his partner in the Palace Theater for more than 30 years.

Today, Jimmy's son, James L. Nederlander (the "L" stands for Lawrence), is president of The Nederlander Organization. This includes not only the Broadway and London theaters, but those in other parts of the United States, including Los Angeles, Chicago, San Diego, and San Jose. His production credits include a range of shows, including *West Side Story*, *Movin' Out*, *La Cage aux Folles*, *The 25th Annual Putnam County Spelling Bee*, *Spider-Man: Turn Off the Dark*, and revivals of *Grease* and *Fiddler on the Roof*. James has also brought celebrities to Broadway and other venues, including Yanni, Raffi, Adele, Billy Joel, Harry Connick, Jr., Neil Diamond, and Sting. Together Jimmy and James were the first father and son to be named New York City Living Landmarks, in 2012, which was the centennial anniversary of David Nederlander's first theater acquisition.

THE EARLY SHOWS

And then there were the shows and the stars of the early years of the 20th century. *Florodora* was the hit of the era, running for over 550 performances, while *The Wizard of Oz* debuted onstage in 1903 for nearly 300 performances and was followed shortly thereafter by *Babes in Toyland* which ran for 192 performances. But it was Shakespeare's *Hamlet* that drew significant attention for the casting of the world-famous actress Sarah Bernhardt, who performed the show in French. Bernhardt had appeared on Broadway before, as Roxanne in Edmond Rostand's *Cyrano de Bergerac*, as well as in some French productions.

The French-born Bernhardt, of Jewish heritage, was baptized and raised in a convent. In her teens, she would try her hand at comedy and tragedy as well as burlesque before emerging as a star in France in the 1860s. For the next four decades, she would perform in a wide variety of plays worldwide, making some appearances in United States. While she was heralded as a brilliant actress, her Broadway presentation of *Hamlet*, she was not a favorite of the critics or the audiences. Frustrated, Bernhardt would return to France. She would come back to the United States and Broadway several years later in various roles, including a brief stint in vaudeville. More than just a legendary stage performer and queen of the tragic dramatic roles, Bernhardt was also a promoter, producer, sculpture, artist and, like Bessie Thomashefsky, a woman who transformed the role of women in theater to a higher level than that of the many showgirls in the popular follies.

Alla Nazimova was another Jewish actress of the era who made an impact on Broadway. The daughter of Russian-Jewish immigrants, Nazimova was already a theatrical star in Moscow, and in other parts of Europe, when she first appeared in productions on the Lower East Side, but not in Yiddish. Instead, she performed in Russian, in a theater she helped establish.

As Yiddish theater grew and embraced the classics of Henrik Ibsen and George Bernard Shaw, among other playwrights, Broadway theatergoers would soon follow suit, and it was Nazimova who would star in *Hedda Gabler* in 1906 and *A Doll's House* the following year. While she would later emerge as a major star of the silent film era, making a weekly salary of $13,000, unheard of for that time period, Nazimova would return to Broadway to reprise the two Ibsen shows as well as appear in Anton Chekhov's *The Cherry Orchard* and later on in *The Good Earth*. So powerful were her performances that the Shuberts named one of their theaters The Nazimova, in her honor, until she signed with their rivals, the syndicate.

It was also during the early years of the 20th century that a talented Jewish playwright came upon the scene in New York City. His name was David Belasco, and he grew up in San Francisco as a Sephardic Jew. Over the span of 46 years, starting in the 1880s, he would write, produce and/or direct over one hundred Broadway plays including *Madame Butterfly*. While Belasco was never a part of the Yiddish theater (although his father-in-law Morris Gest was a producer), he did bring some of the real-life experiences depicted in Yiddish theater to the Broadway stage.

Belasco was also a theater manager and owner, taking over Hammerstein's Theatre Republic in 1902. He later sold the theater and it was once again named the Republic. He later went on to build more theaters in New York and in other cities.

The Influence of Yiddish Theater on Broadway

While Broadway theater had been around before the emergence of Yiddish theater in America, the latter would have a significant influence on English-speaking theater. It was the playwright Gordin, along with actor Jacob P. Adler, who brought the classics of Ibsen, Tolstoy and Shaw to America in Yiddish theater before they emerged on Broadway. Shakespeare and other classic works had been performed, but a broader scope of "sophisticated" works shined on the Yiddish stages and drew the attention of American producers and theater owners, many of whom were Jewish and were very tuned into what was happening on Yiddish Broadway. The domestic dramas would also find their home on Broadway in the form of timely plays about social and political issues.

Although the language barriers prevented many of the Yiddish theater stars from successfully making the crossover to Broadway, some did find ways of making the transition. Jacob P. Adler, as mentioned earlier, proved that it could be done, and done well, when he took the character Shylock to Broadway (in Yiddish) in *The Merchant of Venice*. Meanwhile, Bertha Kalish was able to use her powerful singing voice and multi-lingual ability to enjoy success on both stages, while the diminutive Molly Picon, who became a legend in vaudeville and on the English-speaking stages for decades, learned Yiddish at a young age and was able to criss-cross back and forth between the two genres. Actor Paul Muni would also make his start in Yiddish theater in 1907, at the age of 12, under his given name Moony Weisenfreund. He would later make the transition to Broadway in a 1926 in a play entitled *We Americans* and just a few years later would embark on a film career that would extend over three decades.

The most profound influence of Yiddish theater upon Broadway, however, came not only from the performers on stage but from those watching from the audience or in the wings, experiencing and learning about theater. A young

Stella Adler and a boy named Lee Strasberg were both influenced by their early Yiddish theater experiences. Many Jewish performers, especially those who later became stars of vaudeville, saw their first shows in Yiddish theaters while growing up on the Lower East Side. While they eventually emanated toward the American theater, many were heavily influenced by these early experiences on Second Avenue. The Jewish humor—personal, relatable and typically based on day-to-day encounters—became commonplace in vaudeville and in comedies on Broadway for generations, as well as in various media from *The Goldbergs* on radio in the 1930s to *Seinfeld* on television in the 1990s

The music of Broadway and what became known as Tin Pan Alley also had underpinnings from the klezmer music and operettas brought over from Eastern Europe and first heard on the Yiddish stages. The likes of Irving Berlin and George Gershwin, among other noted composers (discussed in Chapter 3, on the great Jewish composers and lyricists), also benefitted from their early Yiddish theater experiences.

For the Jewish people, theater became part of their American culture, with Yiddish theater expanding into the other boroughs of New York, as well as around the country. For the Jewish immigrants who had been chased from their homelands, whose cultural and religious institutions had been shut down, theater was a rare opportunity for freedom of expression, an opportunity to communicate that which was stifled in so many parts of the world. On stage, they could not only retell the stories of pain and suffering, but rejoice in song and laugh at life's many foibles. Whether one spoke Yiddish or not, the theater was a cultural resource and it provided the glue that held a poor, somewhat destitute, immigrant community together. That community grew stronger and future generations of Jewish performers emerged, wanting to take to the stage and communicate through music, lyrics, comedy and/or dramatic presentations. It was this Yiddish community that served as the foundation for the many years of Jewish involvement in theater that would follow.

2

Part of the Melting Pot: From Vaudeville to Broadway

It's not uncommon for teenagers to find new and invigorating forms of entertainment, including those that might be considered objectionable by their parents. Such youthful rebellion was just as common a century ago as it is today. In the early years of the 20th century, the Jewish immigrants toiled away, working long hours to put food on the table while living in overcrowded ghetto conditions in Manhattan's Lower East Side. For them, Yiddish theater remained a sanctuary second only to temple, a place to grasp the culture brought forth from Europe and a means of embracing the rich traditions that make up Judaism. It was an opportunity to celebrate freedom, having seen many of their theaters shut down under oppressive foreign rule.

Yet, while Yiddish theater thrived, a newer temptress began to seduce the younger generation, with the lure of glamour, fame and money, in this, the land of prosperity. The allure was vaudeville, a term culled from a phrase popularized in France during the 15th century, "Un chanson du Vau de Vire," meaning "A Song of the Valley of Vire." This phrase referred to popular drinking songs and songs with barbed satire and topical humor. By the end of the century the term "vaudevire" had emerged, which later became vaudeville.[1]

Unlike the traditional and secular works found on the stages of Yiddish theater, vaudeville was the epitome of the great American melting pot, welcoming immigrants of all nationalities. The phenomenon had begun in the late 1870s and had gained enormous acceptance throughout the United States. Vaudeville was culled from various sources including the Barnum and Bailey Circus, with the idea of presenting numerous, diverse acts of all types in one show. There were vestiges of minstrel shows, complete with blackface and street performers, who had sung and danced for coins, now earning money and having a roof over their heads.

Having moved much of mainstream entertainment out of saloons and into respectable theaters, vaudeville was billed as entertainment for the masses. It was run by shrewd entrepreneurs who served as managers and knew how to work the "bottom line" and make money by giving the public a bevy of performers on one bill. Between seven and fifteen acts might perform on a given night, including jugglers, acrobats, song and dance teams, musicians, solo singers, comedy teams, novelty acts, and even the occasional animal act. In recent memory, the entertainment closest to mainstream vaudeville harkens back to *The Ed Sullivan Show,* which ran on CBS television from 1948 through 1971, presenting a similar diverse mix of variety acts.

For the second generation of Jewish immigrants, vaudeville offered an opportunity to assimilate into the mainstream. The potential payoff was greater than Yiddish theater as vaudeville had a wider presence with many more venues all throughout the country. Vaudeville theater had opened in cities such as Boston, Chicago and even out west in San Francisco. It was the ideal place in which to sing and/or perform comedy, and both music and humor were (and remain) staples of Jewish life and Jewish culture.

Music and Laughter Lead to Vaudeville

The study of music was part of the Jewish upbringing in Europe and was emphasized from an early age in America as well. Song was part of Jewish festivals, religious gatherings and of Yiddish theater. Even a young Oscar Hammerstein, who had left Germany, running away from his family in 1863 at the age of 16, was already versed in piano, flute and violin when he landed on American shores.

By the age of nine or ten, most of the Jewish soon-to-be vaudevillians were fluent on a musical instrument, and many sang as well. Jewish humor, meanwhile, was unique unto itself, exploring life as it unfolded, while often helping to ease the brunt of persecution and in America, ghetto living conditions. Jewish humor often asks the question "Why?," as in, "Why do we act in a particular manner or behave in such a way?" or "Why must we suffer?" Self-reflective and even self-deprecating, such humor would translate well into mainstream vaudeville. However, unlike the Jewish monologists of years to come, with their exploration of family, of life, love, relationships and of simply "being Jewish," vaudeville humor was largely based on stereotypes, most of which would be considered anything but politically correct today.

In vaudeville, each ethnic group had their own stereotypical characters, or caricatures, and they were not always portrayed by performers of that ethnicity. The Jewish characters in vaudeville were taken in part from characters in other literature, such as Shakespeare's Shylock, and in part from the ghetto, with an exaggerated Yiddish accent. Being dishonest and frugal when it came to dealings with money, for example, would manifest itself onstage in a humorous routine or a comedy skit, as they were called. While the depictions of Jews in this manner perpetuated the stereotypes, the Jewish entertainers were welcomed into prominence as part of American culture. Jews, as well as other minorities, were accepted, largely through their own derogatory caricatures, as part of what was widely received as the comedy of the era. Although the patriarchs of Yiddish theater snubbed their noses at such humor, the younger generation of Jewish performers saw it as "good clean fun." The young up-and-coming vaudevillians argued that the best performer to play a Jew was a Jew, and self-mocking was part of their assimilation process. In some ways it was not unlike hazing at a fraternity. This was a rite of passage, a way of "Americanizing."

Of course the question has often been asked regarding whether the effects of such depictions encouraged anti–Semitism or not. While religion was not a factor on stage, some will argue that such depictions reinforced the negative image of the Jewish people. Of course, the contrary argument is that the familiarity with actual Jewish people through their presence in vaudeville, albeit using stereotypical characters, actually lessened the fear that spurred such hatred by showing that the Jewish people were able to "fit in," laugh at themselves and entertain, like everyone else. While this is not a focal point in this book, it is worth mentioning that there is little, if any, evidence that anti–Semitism increased because of vaudeville. It is also worth noting that several Jewish performers, including Eddie Cantor, Al Jolson and Fanny Brice, emerged as some of the most renowned, best loved stars of their time, admired by non–Jews as well as Jews.

It should also be mentioned that many Jewish vaudevillians, as well as other performers of the era, donned blackface. While far from politically correct today, this was customary at the time. The most notable blackfaced performer was Al Jolson, who rose to enormous stage and film notoriety while behind the dark makeup.

Jewish Vaudevillians

The routines of the Jewish performers left an indelible mark on vaudeville, and later on many of these performers would go on to great success on the Broadway stage.

For Fania Borach, better known as Fanny Brice, vaudeville was one of several stops on the way to a successful career that would include radio, film and Broadway. Like most of the Jewish entertainers of that time, she was born on Manhattan's Lower East Side, the daughter of European immigrants. Although her family moved to Newark, New Jersey, when she was young, she grew up determined to return to New York City, on stage. With that as her goal, she entered talent contests, winning some while also impressing one of Broadway's most distinguished gentlemen, Irish-born composer, lyricist, director and performer, George M. Cohan, for whom she auditioned at the age of 16. Cohan put her in the chorus of the show *Talk of New York.* Inexperienced, however, she was fired before the show opened.

Undaunted, and still determined, Brice, still known as Fania Borach, went into burlesque, touring with *The Transatlantic Burlesquers* (1907–1908) as a chorus girl. Considered a notch below vaudeville, by "respectable" audiences, burlesque had grown with its own circuit, featuring a bevy of chorus girls and similar, yet racier, performers to those typically found on the vaudeville stages. It was on this circuit, however, in a show called *The Girls from Happyland,* that Brice would make the transition from "back row" chorus girl to lead performer. Relegated to only singing, and often from off-stage, Fanny, who changed her name to Brice because it was less ethnic sounding (which would prove ironic in her later comedy career) knew she had to learn to dance to get her feet firmly planted back on the main stage. With that in mind, she would take her mother's lacy garments, go backstage at the burlesque theaters and spend some of the money she had earned to bribe the chorus line dancers to teach her the steps. Eventually, she became an understudy to one of the lead dancers. It was fortuitous that she would get the opportunity to go on stage when the lead got ill, and Fanny made the most of that opportunity by wowing the crowd.

In years to come, she would also make the transition from singing to comedy, using a Yiddish accent to capitalize on the nation's penchant for ethnic comedy on both circuits, burlesque and vaudeville. Because of her knack for parody and her lanky appearance, Brice was not about to compete for the same attention garnered by the chorus girls. However, she was determined. If she was not going to be the prettiest girl on the stage, she would be the funniest. It wasn't long before she achieved that distinction, thanks to a song by a young, still relatively unknown composer named Irving Berlin. The song, "Sadie Salome, Go Home," which Brice described as a "Jewish comedy song," parodied the enormously popular "Dance of the Seven Veils," which had become a hallmark of both the vaudeville and burlesque circuits. Brice had legitimate singing ability, but the combination of a Yiddish accent (although she didn't actually speak Yiddish) and a mock "veils" dance was a tremendous crowd pleaser, winning her standing ovations night after night.

It was at this time, still at the age of just 17, that the real "Funny Girl" was born, breaking into a male-dominated field, with impeccable comedic timing and an aptitude for drawing laughter with her facial expressions as well as her material. As influential as any Jewish performer of the 20th century, Brice legitimized comedy for women, particularly Jewish women. Her insights into American and Jewish culture were the perfect cornerstone for comedic expression. She encapsulated the women with whom she had grown up on the Lower East Side, and their plight became part of her dramatization, not in mockery, but as a foundation for her routines, which epitomized strength. Brice, whose career spanned 40 years, not only played Broadway, but would have her career portrayed in a successful Broadway show *Funny Girl* (and later two films, *Funny Girl* and *Funny Lady*) starring Barbra Streisand.

At the same time that Brice was making her transition from burlesque to vaudeville, little Molly Picon was also emerging on the scene from the Lower East Side of Manhattan. Picon was born Margaret Pyekoon in 1898, to Russian-immigrant parents.

After her father left, Margaret and her two sisters moved with their mother to Philadelphia where she would win her first talent contest at the age of five. From that point forward, there was no turning back. Taking the stage name of Molly, she was a versatile performer, honing every skill she could, from acrobatics and gymnastics, to musical instruments to comedy. At just 4'10" the diminutive Picon won over the hearts of vaudeville audiences who, after seeing her portray many roles as a young boy, would later be wowed by her "All-American girl" image. And yet, she never let go of her cul-

The multitalented Molly Picon captured the hearts of several generations of theatergoers from Yiddish theater to Vaudeville to Broadway. She also appeared in films, including *Fiddler on the Roof*, and both radio and television shows, such as *Car 54, Where Are You?* (Museum of the City of New York).

ture, also performing in Yiddish theater productions and in a Yiddish repertory troupe. In fact, at 15, she did several shows, including performances of *Uncle Tom's Cabin*, in both Yiddish and English. Picon would go on to tour the world as a performer, still somersaulting her way across the stage well into her 50s and performing into her 80s, gracing Broadway in a variety of shows. She championed both Jewish and American causes, all after honing her skills as part of that legendary vaudeville community.

Meanwhile, another female star of the era, Lenora Goldberg, better known as Nora Bayes, was making a name for herself on the vaudeville circuit in Chicago. Just after the turn of the century, Bayes would marry and team up with Jack Norworth, her second of five husbands. Norworth had migrated to vaudeville from the minstrel circuit. Yet, it was Bayes as the main attraction, as noted from their billing: "Nora Bayes, Assisted and Admired by Jack Norworth." Bayes, a singer and songwriter, would team with her husband to write a string of hit songs, also making some of the earliest popular recordings for Columbia Records in the late teens and early 1920s. Her penchant for comedy made her a double threat, and audiences adored her ability to milk every laugh out of a comedic song lyric. Her diverse repertoire of songs, coupled with her comedy routines and royalties from her recordings, soon had her bringing in upwards of $100,000 a year, astounding at the time, making her one of the highest paid performers of the era. Along the way, she would also appear on Broadway in the Lew Fields' hit, *The Jolly Bachelors* which ran for 165 performances in 1910.

While Bayes' career extended beyond vaudeville, it was on the vaudeville circuit that she rose to stardom singing everything from tear-jerking ballads to ragtime ditties to her comedic melodies. However, unlike her peers, Bayes had neither an "ethnic look," nor act. In fact, she was far less Jewish than her contemporaries. Although she had grown up in an Orthodox Jewish family, Bayes was very secretive about her upbringing, and while she did not renounce her Judaism, she did not make it a part of her stage persona.

Conversely, Eddie Cantor was very much a Jewish comic at every turn. Born Israel Iskowitz, his start in show business was much like that of Picon and Brice, beginning on the Lower East Side, where his Russian-immigrant parents settled. Orphaned at an early age, Cantor was raised by his maternal grandmother. Like Picon, he won his first talent show at the age of five and was destined to be a performer. He held down a variety of jobs including a stint as a singing waiter in Coney Island, with a young piano player named Jimmy Durante accompanying him. Cantor would find his way onto the Broadway stage as a teenager doing routines of other Jewish comics and blackface performances while discovering his knack for playing characters based on his own

Lower East Side experiences. Known as the performer with the "banjo eyes," Cantor accentuated his comedy with wide eyes and plenty of energy. He brought a comic sensibility and a sensitivity to the stage as a likable "nebbish" that contrasted with the more familiar slapstick routines found in vaudeville.

While Cantor did depict the stereotypical characters of the time, he was shrewd, and his characters, often vulnerable, were the inspiration for latter day Jewish comics from Woody Allen to Billy Crystal. Cantor would go on to become one of the era's most successful performers. Despite falling into debt during the stock market crash of 1929, he would rebound in film, radio and even with a very successful book entitled *Caught Short! A Saga of Wailing Wall Street.*

Also building an esteemed reputation in vaudeville was Al Jolson, whose routines were less "Jewish" by nature than those of Brice or Cantor. Born in a small Jewish village in Russia sometime around 1886 (there is no documentation), Asa Yoelson would come to the United States with his parents shortly before the end of the 19th century. The son of a cantor, he and his brother Hirsh were trained to sing from a very young age, with the anticipation that they too would follow in their father's footsteps. However, when their mother died in 1895, she left the two very young boys without their closest bond. From

this painful beginning, Asa and Hirsh would grow up quickly, learning toughness and immersing themselves in American culture, especially show business.

Together, changing their names to Al and Harry and a less ethnic surname, Jolson, they broke into the business as a team, performing comedy routines, such as a crude ethnic act called *The Hebrew and the Cadet,* while taking occasional solo billings when they came along. By 1901, however, Al was getting more work on his own, singing in a traveling circus and making his way into both the burlesque and vaudeville circuits.

While he's largely remembered for donning blackface in the movie *The Jazz Singer,* Al Jolson's numerous stage skills and vaudeville performances made him one of the most sought-after headliners of his time (Museum of the City of New York).

It was shortly afterwards that Al Jolson would don the blackface for which he became so famous. Despite the obvious offensive overtones seen today, blackface by the early 1900s had been a part of stage performing for nearly seven decades and was viewed, at that time, as just another form of ethnic humor. For many performers, including Jolson, it was also seen as a mask to work behind, allowing the performer to boost his or her confidence. In the case of Jolson, his confidence grew as he became a full showman, singing, dancing, doing comedic vaudeville routines and whistling while wearing white gloves and white makeup to accentuate his hands and his mouth. On stage he engaged his audiences in a full theatrical experience while growing to become one of the nation's leading performers. Off-stage his ego grew enormously along with his fame. His constant pursuit of chorus girls would end each of his three marriages, but his devotion to the stage remained undying. In fact, he proceeded to headliner status in venues from San Francisco to Hammerstein's Victoria Theatre in New York City.

If Jolson had any impact upon the Jewish performers of his time, it was evident in the fact that he did not make an impact as a "Jewish" performer per se. He was a non-sectarian entertainer, pulling material from a wide range of resources and performing in a manner that would win over mainstream audiences. He was a showman first and foremost.

Brice, Cantor, Bayes, Picon and Jolson each amassed a significant following through vaudeville. They were headliners and heralded as the most popular stars of their era along with Sophie Tucker, with her Red Hot Mama sensuality and the rapid-fire comedy team of Weber and Fields, who included everything from slapstick to clog dancing in their act. Another star of the era, Ed Wynn, born Isaiah Edwin Leopold, ran away from home at 15, used his middle name and proceeded into a vaudeville career that would lead him to the Ziegfeld Follies in 1914 on Broadway. As a writer, producer, director and multi-faceted performer, Wynn would move on to a career that spanned over 50 years and included radio, film and television success.

As vaudeville continued, it became the venue for every type of performance imaginable, ranging from the amazing illusions of Harry Houdini (who was born Jewish, but changed his name to the more Italian sounding Houdini, since, at the time, the Italian Catholic immigrants were more widely accepted) to unique performers of all backgrounds including the Keaton family, tossing around their five-year-old son Buster, and the racy performances of Mae West. It was a form of variety entertainment that ran the gamut from bawdy to sophisticated to simply intriguing, and everyone took part including Babe Ruth, explorer Captain Cook and Helen Keller who lectured through an interpreter. "Vaudeville audiences were not passive observers. They were vocal and sometimes physical participants in performances. Their cheers, jeers or painful silences would make or break an act," adds John Kenrick in his "A History of the Musical. Vaudeville—Part II."[2]

While vaudeville and burlesque were the "movies and cable television" of the era, New York's Broadway theaters were drawing an increasing number of stylish, "higher-end" patrons. And while a few vaudeville performers were tapped for various Broadway shows, for many of the Jewish vaudevillians, the best was yet to come.

FLO ZIEGFELD

While Flo Ziegfeld was not Jewish, he had an integral role in boosting the careers of many Jewish stars of the early 20th century. Florenz Ziegfeld was born to be a promoter. From his childhood, he had a knack for drawing the attention of the public. In fact, he once got into trouble for taking money from local kids to see his invisible fish. He showed them a bowl of water. He also had a penchant for publicizing anything and everything.

During his early years as a manager and booker, Ziegfeld developed a knack for discovering and promoting new and unique talent, and it wasn't long before he was taking his performers on extended tours on the vaudeville circuit. By the 1890s, Ziegfeld's magic touch for finding talent took him to Broadway, where he produced musicals to showcase several talented performers at one time. However, it wasn't until 1907 that Florenz Ziegfeld would reach the pinnacle of his esteemed career when he took the Ziegfeld Follies to Broadway for the first time.

The Shubert Brothers were already enjoying success on Broadway at the Hippodrome Theater with revues featuring popular song and dance numbers. Ziegfeld, however, had bigger plans. While Ziegfeld possessed no skills as a singer, dancer or performer, he had a keen eye for finding beautiful women, a talent that would later be the downfall of his several marriages.

In his quest to discover great talent and his penchant for exploring new and innovative means of promoting the "next great performer," Ziegfeld had amassed a considerable amount of knowledge when it came to distinguishing which acts would attract and entertain the general public. Pageantry, comedy, sexuality and song and dance were all part and parcel of the public's penchant for performances. With that in mind, he introduced elements of vaudeville and burlesque, plus a line of chorus girls, reminiscent of the Parisian Folies-Bergère, into what he would call his own follies. He then added elaborate sets, dazzling costumes, original songs by various composers, choreography by the best in the business, Julian Mitchell, and *The Ziegfeld Follies of 1907* was born, using thirteen letters in the title (after his name), because he was superstitious. Coincidently, the show also cost $13,000.

Opulent production numbers, political and topical satire and of course the ladies, billed as "Glorifying the American Girl," were all hallmarks of what would emerge as the longest running Broadway series of shows, with nearly two-dozen renditions until the 1930s (not to mention four additional versions after Ziegfeld's death).

One of Ziegfeld's star performers was his first wife, Anna Held, of Polish-Jewish descent, whom he had brought back with him from France. In fact, Held, on whom he worked his publicity magic turning her into an immediate star, was credited in part for the idea of staging an American revue, featuring more than 60 Anna Held Girls, who marched around the theater beating snare drums in the original '07 revue.

Held had made her stage debut in the Yiddish theaters of London in companies run by Goldfadn and actor-manager Jacob P. Adler. It was in Paris, however, that she had generated attention by singing in local cafés. In fact, she was so enamored by the French, that she would go to great lengths for many years to perpetuate the myth that she was French. She even converted to Catholicism, which was also because she was fearful of being Jewish in Europe, having been among those chased from her native Poland along with her family when she was a child.

It was during one of Held's European performances in London, in 1896, that Ziegfeld discovered her, offering her $1,500 a week to appear on Broadway. It was an exorbitant amount of money at the time, but Ziegfeld was convinced she could become a star, and she did. Ziegfeld publicized that she had such clean, pure skin because she bathed in milk every day. While the story was fictitious, it landed in all of the celebrity gossip columns, started a brief fad and made Held the talk of the entertainment business. Held forever became known as the girl in the milk baths.

THE STAR-MAKING FOLLIES

It was the Ziegfeld Follies that brought Brice, Bayes and Cantor to Broadway. Bayes joined the 1907 revue and introduced the classic song "Shine On, Harvest Moon" in 1908. Cantor would be a comic regular on the Broadway revues, working with performers of all ethnic backgrounds, such as W.C. Fields and Will Rogers, among others. Brice, a staple of the Follies, would become a show favorite through both her comedy and her songs, including "Second Hand Rose," playfully lamenting her early years in the Jewish ghetto. On one particular night, Brice added an unexpected twist to the show. After being accused by co-star Lillian Lorraine of trying to steal her boyfriend, the two performers began brawling in the wings of the theater. The fight culminated with Brice knocking Lorraine to the ground and dragging her by the hair across the stage to a stunned, but amused, audience. No, not even the shocked Ziegfeld himself dared to even attempt to work the scene into the regular show.

For Cantor, Brice and Bayes, the transformation from second-generation immigrants to mainstream entertainers was complete. They never lost sight of their Jewish roots or heritage, as exemplified by Brice, who after a few years away from the Follies returned as *The Yiddish Bride*.

Jewish performers were now accepted into the mainstream entertainment community as part of Ziegfeld's world, a world that turned a blind eye toward ethnic and racial discrimination. In fact, Ziegfeld refused to cave under pressure to oust Bert Williams from the Follies. Williams was the first African American to co-star with white performers on the Broadway stage, and Ziegfeld held firm that whoever did not want to work with Williams did not have to be part of the show. Few, if any, performers left.

Sophie Tucker was also in the Follies for a short time, but left, reportedly over disputes regarding her songs and her billing. Ed Wynn was also one of the notable Jewish performers who gained attention in the Follies. Meanwhile, the music was supplied by a variety of songwriters including Irving Berlin, while a 19-year-old piano player named Gershwin accompanied rehearsals in later renditions of the ongoing show.

One notable exception, who was not part of the Ziegfeld universe, was arguably the most highly acclaimed performer of the era, Al Jolson. In 1908, Jolson left vaudeville to become part of a successful traveling minstrel troupe, which drew rave reviews when they hit New York. It was at this point that Ziegfeld asked Jolson to audition for his upcoming Follies. Jolson, however, refused to audition for anyone. This was the beginning and end of his connection with the long-running follies. Nonetheless, the Shubert Brothers had other plans for Jolson to make his Broadway debut.

THE SHUBERTS BRING JOLSON TO BROADWAY

It was a lavish Broadway production entitled *La Belle Paree* in 1911 that brought Jolson to Broadway at the new Winter Garden Theatre. After an inauspicious start, the show, trimmed from a painful four hours to a more manageable three, was also rearranged to feature more Jolson. In fact, over time, his comedy and music took center stage. And that was just the beginning. Jolson would go on to star in a number of Broadway shows, including *Vera Violetta*, *The Honeymoon Express*, *Robinson Crusoe, Jr.*, and perhaps the best known, *Sin-*

bad, in 1918. All of the shows, featuring Jolson in blackface, became vehicles to showcase the star's talent, which continued to grow until the Shuberts began billing Jolson as "America's Greatest Entertainer," a title which at the time he had arguably achieved.

Jolson would have more than a light hand in each show, rewriting scripts and lyrics, while launching into musical numbers that weren't initially even part of the show. Much to the chagrin of the playwright, librettist or the remaining cast, he would typically ask the audience if they wanted to see more of the show, or hear him sing. They would typically opt for more of Jolson. His command of the stage and the sheer presence and magnetism of Jolson would influence numerous performers for decades, even long after his death in 1950.

Meanwhile Back on the Vaudeville Stages

As one generation forged ahead to Broadway and soon to the newer media, such as radio and film, the years following the First World War brought the next breed of Jewish talent to the numerous nationwide stages of vaudeville.

The format remained much the same, with performers now being booked on well-established circuits while traveling from one city to the next. However, the "shtick" that was once very ethnic was now giving way to a more diverse mix of song and hijinks, much of which focused on the social and political climate of the post–World War I era.

It was during this time that four of five Jewish brothers would emerge as one of the funniest comedy troupes to ever take the stage. This was largely due to the persistence of their mother, who served as their manager. Minnie Marx, who immigrated to the United States with her family as a teenager in 1888, was part of a show business family. Her brother Al Sheen was a comic, her father a ventriloquist, her mother a harpist and Minnie herself was a singer. Only her husband was not in the business, instead working as a somewhat unsuccessful tailor, one who refused to measure anything or anyone.

Minnie's boys, later the name of a Broadway show (in 1970), began as a singing group called The Nightingales. In time, they would take on various configurations and change their stage name, as other performers would come and go (even mom and their aunt would join the act), but most significantly, the Marx Brothers would start to improvise and introduce comedy into the performances.

Soon, the brothers, all of whom had musical talent, would switch from a musical show to what was primarily a comedy show with some music. By the

1920s the vaudeville shows of the Marx Brothers were second to none. With the help of their uncle Al Sheen, now a vaudeville star, the Four Marx Brothers, as they were billed, created and established their own identities and played off one another with impeccable timing. Although Jewish, the Marx Brothers' on-stage personalities belied their ethnic background. In fact, Chico had such a thick Yiddish accent, that he, like Houdini, opted to go Italian, taking on the character that would forever be his stage persona. In time, thanks to Chico's Italian accent, Groucho was quoted as saying, when asked about being Jewish performers, "Most people think we're Italian."

In the 1920s the Marx Brothers took their madcap comedy routines to Broadway with three shows, *I'll Say She Is*, *The Cocoanuts* and *Animal Crackers*, the latter two also becoming a couple of their celebrated films. With music by Irving Berlin and a book by George S. Kaufman, *The Cocoanuts* was probably the most celebrated of the three musicals and ran for nearly 300 performances at the Lyric Theater.

During their formative years, the Marx Brothers crossed paths, in 1911, with a young violinist, the son of Jewish immigrants from Lithuania. He happened to be playing in the same theaters as the "then" singing brothers. The young performer, Jack Kubelsky, would become close friends with Zeppo Marx and in time accompany him to a family Passover Seder where he would meet, and later marry, the Marx Brothers' cousin Sadie. Changing his name to the less ethnic Jack Benny, he would soon enjoy his own vaudeville career, which evolved much in the same manner as the Marx Brothers', from music to comedy. By the 1920s the fiddle would play second fiddle to his comedy routines. Along with Sadie, who changed her name to Mary Livingstone, Benny would go on to vaudeville success that launched his illustrious comedy career.

At the same time that Benny was taking his mild-mannered approach to success on the vaudeville circuit, another son of a Jewish immigrant was teaming up with an Irish clog dancer to form one of the most prolific comedy teams of all time. George Burns and Gracie Allen met in 1922 and within five years not only became husband and wife, but the toast of the vaudeville circuit, with Burns as the good-natured straight man and Gracie as the befuddled blonde. Benny and Burns were not only very good friends, but both depicted the Jewish persona in a new light, without the shouting or using the thick Yiddish accent that had become so familiar to the earlier vaudevillians.

While neither Benny nor George Burns made significant strides onto the Broadway stages, both were among the Jewish stars to evolve from vaudeville and go on to legendary status. And there were others, such as George Jessel and Milton Berle who would emerge from this era and make their mark on stage for years to come.

One of the younger of the Jewish performers to make his way into vaudeville was George Jessel. Born in 1898, in the Bronx, Jessel was earning money for his family, following the death of his father, by the time he was ten. He would soon team up on comedy sketches with Al Jolson, among others, while also building up his solo act. While comedy was his forte, Jessel did a little of everything, which included writing songs, such as the 1920 hit (which he co-wrote) called "Oh! How I Laugh When I Think How I Cried About You." Jessel also got to step out of the vaudeville circuit and take on significant roles in Broadway musicals, the most successful of which was the lead role in *The Jazz Singer*, which opened at the Fulton Theater in 1925 and ran for 303 performances, before a brief revival in 1927 and a major hit film, remade three times. Jessel was offered the role in the initial film, but declined because Warner Brothers would not meet his salary demands. His career would move primarily to film and television, continuing through the 1960s. It also opened the door for Jolson to star in the film version of *The Jazz Singer*.

Milton Berle, born Mendel Berlinger in Harlem in 1908, started his career at the age of five by winning a Charlie Chaplin look-alike contest. Berle would make his way to silent films and establish himself as a very successful child actor. By 1921, he was ready to move into vaudeville and debuted at the prestigious Palace Theatre. For years, Berle was a headliner on the vaudeville circuit. Then, in 1932 he would take part in *Earl Carroll's Vanities*, an ongoing revue that ran in new renditions for most of the '20s and into the early '30s. The risqué revue, featuring sexy showgirls, was also known for crude humor and some major stars such as W.C. Fields and Sophie Tucker. Berle would also be seen on Broadway in *Saluta!* in 1934 and as part of *New Faces* of 1937, at which time he was far from actually being one of the "new faces" in show business. From his child acting days to his years in vaudeville, to film, radio and television, Berle's career spanned over 80 years!

ABIE'S IRISH ROSE

While little fuss was ever made publicly about George Burns and Gracie Allen being a real-life interfaith couple, at a time when such pairings were far less common than they are today, there was quite an uproar over an Anne Nichols play called *Abie's Irish Rose*. The play featured the unlikely romance between an Irish Catholic woman and a Jewish man. They would fall in love and get married, but hide the marriage from their fathers who were depicted as the traditional (and somewhat stereotypical) Jewish and Irish patriarchs who would not bless such a union. Unable to hide their ethnicities for long, the truth comes out about the interfaith couple, and their insistence on remaining together leads to two more weddings, one by a rabbi and one by a priest, both of whom had learned a great deal about tolerance from serving together in World War I and witnessing the hardships that can unite even the most dissimilar individuals. By the end of the play, thanks to the birth of twins, one named for each father, harmony is achieved in this diverse family.

The significance of *Abie's Irish Rose*, however, moved beyond the obvious ethnic controversy. It was, in fact, among the first plays to shift the ethnic tone and portrayals of characters away from the "caricatures" and very pronounced stereotypes found in vaudeville and toward a more realistic portrayal of how Jewish and Irish families acted in the real world. There was also a message associated with the play, which, in a post war era, was that of tolerance and acceptance. This was presented in a light, whimsical manner.

Despite the play's inherently positive message, Nichols could not get the play produced, as she was met with constant resistance over the subject matter. So, she mortgaged her home for $5,000 and produced the show herself. The initial reviews were anything but encouraging, and, in fact, some critics were even offended at the idea of such an ill-conceived marriage. Nonetheless, audiences showed up to see it. They were intrigued, entertained and even educated. And, they kept on coming to see the unlikely hit show.

Abie's Irish Rose, which opened in May of 1922, would close 2,327 performances later in October of 1927, after becoming the longest running Broadway show to date, a record it would hold for more than a decade. Two movies were later made based on the play and a television show in the 1970s, *Bridget Loves Bernie*, was also inspired by *Abie's Irish Rose*. Ironically, some 50 years after the opening of the play, the lighthearted sitcom would once again raise the same issues of interfaith marriage and once again spark controversy. Apparently, some things never change. As it turned out, unlike the play, CBS would cave under a mountain of protest letters and cancel the show after just one controversial season.

Kosher Kitty Kelly (1925) and *The Cohens and the Kellys* (1926) were among several "copycat" shows that followed *Abie's Irish Rose*, focusing on the Jewish-Irish theme. Along with *Partners Again* (1922) and several other mildly successful shows of the 1920s, the image of the Jewish character on stage matured to illustrate a more well-rounded individual, able to make an audience laugh at his or her foibles without resorting to "shtick." The second- and third-generation Jewish performers were no longer "unkempt" on stage or portraying ghetto life. Instead they were now seen as successful American Jews. They had businesses, fought as U.S. soldiers in a major war, were now part of the American culture and able to appeal to the wider range of theatergoers, while still being seen as "Jewish" on stage. They had succeeded in softening the Jewish stereotype and creating introspective, yet entertaining, characters that would remain an integral part of Broadway shows for years to come.

To define the Jewish impact, and transformation, in the vaudeville era, one has to look only as far as *The Jazz Singer*, circa 1925, starring George Jessel on Broadway, and later Al Jolson in the classic film. *The Jazz Singer* was symbolic of what had been transpiring throughout the first quarter of the 20th century. In the play, the young Jessel does not wish to follow in the steps of his Orthodox family and become a cantor like his father. Instead he wishes to become a jazz singer, which was exactly the saga played out by many of the second generation of Jewish immigrants as they entered show business instead of family business, or, in many cases, opted to be vaudeville performers (as opposed to jazz singers) rather than cantors.

In the next chapter, we'll take a look at some of the musical giants of this same era, many of whom had careers that spanned decades, including the legendary Irving Berlin. These composers and lyricists had an unparalleled impact on musical theater.

3

The Music of Broadway:
Classic Composers,
Legendary Lyricists

While vaudeville flourished during the first three decades of the 20th century, so did the Broadway musical, thanks in large part to a handful of Jewish composers and lyricists who would later emerge as icons. The son of a cantor, Israel Baline, better known as Irving Berlin, went from dabbling in Yiddish theater to writing for vaudeville. However, it was one breakthrough hit song, "Alexander's Ragtime Band" written in 1911, that launched a remarkable career. Berlin would go on to establish himself as one of America's foremost songwriters, while penning the music and lyrics for a dozen Broadway shows and revues beginning with *Watch Your Step* in 1914. And while much of the focus of American entertainment was on *Ziegfeld's Follies*, by the late 1920s, Jerome Kern, the son of a furniture and piano salesman, would also establish himself as one of Broadway's most prolific composers.

By the 1930s, American music, and especially that of the Broadway musical, was the beneficiary of this wealth of great Jewish composers and lyricists. In this chapter, we explore and feature the early musical influences and the legacies of Berlin, Kern, George and Ira Gershwin, Richard Rodgers, Oscar Hammerstein II, and Lorenz Hart as well as the brilliant writing of humorists and playwrights George S. Kaufman and Moss Hart. Yes, these were the children of the first wave of Jewish immigrants who left their indelible stamp on American musical theater forever. These masters of lyric and melody composed hundreds of hit songs over the span of several decades, but the 1930s were particularly intriguing as a time in which they were all part of American music at the same time, combining their talents to build a legacy.

Life During the Depression

Before focusing on the composers and lyricists themselves, it's important to take a look at the atmosphere in which they were living and working. The stock market crash of 1929 and subsequent depression years of the 1930s were felt throughout the entire nation. It was, however, particularly hard on the Jewish people.

In his articles "America Was Different. America Is Different," Jerry Klinger, president of the Jewish American Society for Historic Preservation, points out that "the Bank of the United States was a Jewish bank. In fact, almost all of its 400,000 depositors were Jews. This meant that the bank held the assets of ⅕ of New York City's Jewish population and ⅒ of all American Jews. The failure of the Bank wiped out most of the assets of the Jewish immigrant generation."[1]

Some of the blame for the depression was pinned on the Jewish people and, as a result, anti–Semitism rose significantly during the early 1930s. American anti–Semitism was further fueled by the CBS radio broadcasts of Father James Coughlin, who had a huge following. He actually blamed the Jews for everything from the depression to the Russian Revolution. His sympathy for the policies of Adolf Hitler and Benito Mussolini, plus his blatant anti–Semitic messages, were dismissed by many, but still spearheaded the rising wave of anti–Semitism. In fact, when his radio show was cancelled in New York, two thousand of his followers gathered in protest, chanting "Send Jews back where they came from" and "Wait until Hitler comes over here!"[2]

Among the anti–Semitic notables of the time were Henry Ford, Charles Lindbergh and well-known poet Ezra Pound. In fact, during World War I, Ford wrote a series of viciously anti–Semitic articles for *The Dearborn Independent*. The newspaper proceeded to print such articles for 91 issues, even beyond those written by Ford. In 1942, nearly two decades later, Ford reportedly did apologize in a letter to Sigmund Livingston, then Anti-Defamation League national chairman, writing, "I do not subscribe to or support, directly or indirectly, any agitation which would promote antagonism against my Jewish fellow citizens."[3]

Meanwhile, jobs were hard to find, especially for Jewish and African American workers. Even Jewish and African American doctors had a hard time finding work. Few Jewish physicians were hired in any hospitals other than the 40 Jewish hospitals in the country. By 1938, an American Jewish Congress report noted that anti–Jewish restrictions in want ads had reached their highest level in history.[4]

The theater world, however, was still largely populated by Jews, and the Shuberts had a firm hand on what was taking place on Broadway. In fact, many theater historians claim that if it weren't for the Shuberts, Broadway would never have made it through the depression years. Departing from their usual hard-line business approach, during the early depression years, the Shubert Brothers helped bail out small producers and did what they could to keep their own employees working as long as possible. After a couple of years with their own business in receivership, the Shuberts were able to buy back the organization under the name Select Theaters and come back strong, thanks to the Ziegfeld Follies productions.

The Jewish people knew about persecution, and this new generation was not about to let the theater suffer because of it. A generation earlier, actors and playwrights had fled Eastern Europe to enjoy the freedom of the United States. This generation was determined to withstand any adversity they might face. The children of the immigrants had largely assimilated into the American mainstream, and while they would still embrace their Jewish culture, they were far more secular than their ancestors. For many, theater remained a safer haven than more traditional industries, one in which skills and talent largely overshadowed religious affiliation and one in which the Jews had already gained a foothold through the many Jewish theater owners. While attendance fell off during the depression years, theater remained a place to escape and enjoy entertainment, much as it was during the heyday of Yiddish theater. No matter how bad things got, theater always had its place in Jewish culture.

A LIGHT IN DARK TIMES

Throughout the 1930s, the Jewish composers wrote up-tempo music in a very somber time. The lyricists, meanwhile, wrote about love, about life and about country in patriotic songs. If nothing else, they used their musical talents to compose songs of hope and dreams, and in some cases significant shows about minority acceptance such as *Show Boat* and *Porgy and Bess*. Often poignant messages about social acceptance showed up in both the storyline and the music itself, but guised in another framework, and not about Jewish acceptance, especially during the 1930s. Nonetheless, these composers and lyricists wrote timeless melodies and intimate lyrics for musicals that grew richer in storylines and away from the revues and follies of the 1920s.

While the number of shows opening on Broadway each year during the 1930s dropped, there was still quite a disproportionate number of musicals featuring Jewish composers and/or lyricists. One explanation for the many Jewish composers was that traditional Jewish religious music was typically led by a single singer, a cantor, while Christian music was usually sung by a chorus. In fact, many of the composers were the sons, or grandsons, of cantors, some emanating from several generations of cantors, and most had pianos in their homes. "Jewish homes had pianos and the children learned how to play. That was standard, no matter what the economic situation," says Ellen Adler, of life in the 1930s.[5]

Many of the composers and lyricists of this era honed their skills in what was known as Tin Pan Alley, from which sheet music and later recordings originated and were hawked by shrewd salesmen. It all took place in the area of Manhattan around West 28th Street, a neighborhood that music publishers called home from the late 19th century up through the 1930s. It was there that the Jewish musical legends of Broadway worked and collaborated, including Irving Berlin, George and Ira Gershwin, Jerome Kern and Vincent Youmans, as well as non–Jewish musical geniuses such as Cole Porter.

Irving Berlin

Irving Berlin (born Israel Baline) may very well have been the most influential American songwriter of the 20th century. Unlike some of his contemporaries, Berlin, who rose to fame in 1911, remarkably never faded from prominence. Like many of the composers in this section, it's difficult to condense the accomplishments of Irving Berlin, especially considering that his career spanned many decades. Nonetheless, we'll try to encapsulate some of his many accomplishments.

Berlin and his family arrived in America in 1893, when he was just five years of age, escaping the persecution of the Jewish people in Russia. He was the youngest of eight children. Like so many immigrant families, the Balines lived on the Lower East Side of Manhattan. His father was a cantor, but unable to find full-time work in the United States, he also worked at a local market.

When Israel's father passed away, he took to street-singing for money while only eight years of age. Later, while in his teens, he became a singing waiter at several local cafés where he generated attention and in a short time became very popular. It was during this time that Israel teamed up with a pianist on a song called "Marie of Sunny Italy." The song was published but the printer, in error, wrote the name Berlin on the page, and Israel Baline adopted the new name.

In the early years, Irving Berlin mostly wrote lyrics, while other composers wrote the music, since he did not play the piano. In time, he would start coming up with melodies and have arrangers turn them into songs. One of his earliest lyrics was "Sadie Salome, Go Home," made popular by Fanny Brice, and a huge hit in 1909. But it was a couple years later that *Alexander's Ragtime Band* would follow, and Irving Berlin was immortalized.

By 1914, Berlin would write the first of more than 20 Broadway scores for a show called *Watch Your Step* starring the dance team of Vernon and Irene

Castle, who were quite well known at the time. The show opened at the New Amsterdam Theater and ran for 175 performances.

At nearly 30 years of age, Berlin was drafted into the army in 1917. He was, however, stationed in New York where he composed an all-soldier review called *Yip Yip Yaphank*, including the hit song "Oh! How I Hate to Get Up in the Morning." The show raised thousands of dollars for an army camp service center, and the grand finale had actual United States soldiers literally marching from the stage to the troop carrier to depart for destinations worldwide. While the show was a success, Berlin decided not to use one of the songs he had written, a tune that would become an American classic some 21 years later.

By the mid–1930s, Irving Berlin was a household name. He even had a Broadway theater, The Music Box, built in his honor, where he staged several *Music Box Revues*, writing tunes not unlike those he had written for the *Ziegfeld Follies* earlier in his career. The '30s were also unique in that Berlin teamed with a couple of the greatest Jewish talents of the century. Berlin would collaborate with Moss Hart and George S. Kaufman on *Face the Music* and again with Hart on *As Thousands Cheer*.

As the decade neared an end, with tension escalating overseas, Berlin was asked if he had a patriotic song for Kate Smith to celebrate Armistice Day. He provided the song that had been left out of *Yip Yap Yankhank*, called "God Bless America." Of the nearly 1,500 songs written by Berlin, "God Bless America" would become the most

America's beloved songwriter Irving Berlin, left, poses with Sgt. Ezra Stone during the run of *This Is the Army*, one of a number of Broadway roles in which Stone, a Jewish actor, would appear. Stone's career also took him from the hit radio series *The Aldrich Family* to directing television shows, including *The Munsters*, *Lost in Space*, and *Love, American Style* (Museum of the City of New York).

significant of his 60-year career. It originated as a prayer of sorts, emanating from his mother's frequent words "God bless America," in thanks for providing her family with a home after fleeing Russia. All of the royalties from the song were given to the Boy Scouts of America. Once the war began, Berlin would stage a 12-week run of *This Is the Army*, which opened on Broadway on the Fourth of July and then moved to Washington, D.C., before going on tour around the world. The money raised was used to help support the Army Emergency Relief Fund. So committed to the cause was Berlin, that he would appear on stages worldwide and sing "Oh! How I Hate to Get Up in the Morning." Over 350 military personnel were included in the 100-plus performances of the musical. Ironically, the integrated cast was the only integrated unit in the army at the time.

Berlin would also go on to team with Rodgers and Hammerstein, who served as producers, on *Annie Get Your Gun*. The classic musical featured the show biz anthem "There's No Business Like Show Business," which, like "God Bless America" in 1917, was almost left out of the show. Opening in May of 1946, *Annie Get Your Gun* became the third-longest-running musical of the 1940s, with more than 1,100 performances. Then, while writing the music and lyrics, Berlin would team with Moss Hart as co-producers on *Miss Liberty* at the end of the '40s, a show with choreography by Jerome Robbins. Yes, Berlin, in his extended career, would have the pleasure of working with many of the premiere talents of the 20th century. He would also pen numerous hit songs through the 1940s and '50s, some for films and none bigger than "White Christmas." As his friend Jerome Kern once noted, "Irving Berlin has no *place* in American music—he *is* American music."[6]

Ironically, Berlin did not profess the same musical talent as many of Broadway's other musical icons. As Alec Wilder noted in his book *American Popular Song*, "I heard Berlin play the piano, back in vaudeville days and found his harmony notably inept."[7] Yet, those who worked with him over the years recall that he had the melodies in his head, knew exactly what he was looking for, and wasn't satisfied until the right chords were found.

In his personal life, Berlin's first marriage in 1912 was to a Jewish woman, Dorothy Goetz. Tragically, she caught typhoid fever on their honeymoon and died shortly thereafter. Berlin's heartfelt love song "When I Lost You" was written for her. Nearly a decade later, Berlin would fall in love again, this time to heiress Ellin MacKay, who was not Jewish. In fact, her wealthy and influential father, Clarance MacKay, did everything he could think of to stop the wedding of his daughter to the already famous Jewish songwriter. Even with the tabloids following their every move, the relationship continued despite his efforts. At one point in an effort to appease her father, Ellin suggested that a Catholic priest preside over the wedding ceremony. Berlin would not go along with this, so a justice of the peace at City Hall in New York City married them.

Despite MacKay's dislike of his son-in-law, it was Berlin who helped MacKay when, following the stock market crash of 1929, he was in need of a "bailout" so to speak. Even that only softened MacKay's dislike of Berlin.

For more than 60 years, the interfaith marriage would flourish, and Ellin's father would eventually grow to accept Berlin and love his four granddaughters, who were raised to learn about both religions and both sets of holidays. And yes, the man who wrote "White Christmas" and "Easter Parade" took his wife and children to a Reform Jewish temple and celebrated Passover and Yom Kippur with his family throughout the rest of his 101 years.

If anyone assimilated into the American mainstream, it was Irving Berlin. While he never lost touch with his Jewish roots, Berlin symbolized patriotism and American pride. Along with raising millions of dollars for the Boy Scouts and Girl Scouts, his contribution to the United States Armed Forces was immeasurable. For his contribution to troop morale, Berlin was awarded the Medal of Merit by President Harry S Truman.

But his patriotism was also a form of gratitude. Like his mother, Irving Berlin was deeply thankful that America was here to welcome his family and the immigrants who had no place else to go. "God Bless America," when released in 1938, became a prayer for the nation as well as a personal prayer for the Jewish people as news from Nazi Germany became increasingly frightening to American Jews. Even one of Berlin's daughters would later recount that her father was terrified for the safety of his daughters who were half Jewish.

Jerome Kern

Like his good friend Irving Berlin, Jerome Kern was also the son of immigrants, although in his case of German descent. At an early age, his family would leave New York's Lower East Side and settle across the Hudson River in Newark, New Jersey, where Kern started piano lessons at an early age. By the time he was a teenager, he was already proficient at musical composition and skipped his last year of high school to enroll in the New York College of Music.

It was evident early in Kern's life that he was destined to be in the music business. Besides his great talent, he demonstrated that a more traditional job was not in his best interest when he was hired by his father to work in a furniture store. On his first day of work, Kern, with music on his mind, was asked to order two pianos. He accidentally ordered 200 pianos, and while the deliverymen carried them into the soon-to-be grossly overcrowded store, Jerome and his dad agreed that he was best pursuing a career playing piano rather than ordering them.

Like many other up and coming composers, Kern wanted to write music for shows "in development" for Broadway, which was one of the best ways to break into the business. However, without credits it was hard to launch such a career, so Kern took off for London where he found work writing for music hall shows.

Still not even 20 years old, he returned to the States and was asked to write music for a British production called *Mr. Wix of Wickham*. The production was being altered slightly for Broadway and was in need of some "American" songs. While *Mr. Wix of Wickham* was not a hit, Kern launched a successful career writing additional songs for shows. Some of these shows, such as *An English Daisy, The Catch of the Season, The Little Cherub, The Doll Girl* and *The Girl from Utah*, among others, made it to Broadway in the early years of the 20th century. Kern was the composer while various lyricists, such as Schuyler Greene, penned the words. Greene teamed with Kern on one of his earliest hit shows, in 1915, a musical called *Very Good Eddie* which ran on Broadway for 341 performances. Then two years later, Kern teamed with P.G. Wodehouse for an even longer running musical called *Oh, Boy!* which played on Broadway for 463 performances, becoming the third longest musical of the 1910s. Over the next few years, Kern and Wodehouse would turn out other hit shows, all staged at the Princess Theater. Pretty soon Kern became *the* composer for the Princess Theater, penning the music for such light musicals.

It was in the late 1920s, however, which Kern would team with Oscar Hammerstein II for one of Broadway's groundbreaking musicals, *Show Boat*, produced by Florenz Ziegfeld, based on Jewish novelist Edna Ferber's story about life along the Mississippi River. Ferber, born in Kalamazoo, Michigan, in 1885, was a reporter in Wisconsin by the age of 17. But her true talent was in creating stories, rather than reporting on them. Thus her days as a novelist began several years later with *Dawn O'Hara*, in 1910. She would go on to win a Pulitzer Prize in 1924 for *So Big* and proceed to write books for some 50 years, including *Cimarron* in 1929, the film adaptation of which won Best Picture honors at the Academy Awards in 1931. She would also collaborate with George S. Kaufman on several plays including *Dinner at Eight* and *The Royal Family*.

Ferber's *Show Boat*, once made into a musical, featured the classic "Ol' Man River," among other American standards. It was groundbreaking as it sharply contrasted with the typical light musicals, a style that was becoming all too familiar to theatergoers. Ferber's story was rich and the Kern and Hammerstein songs were significant and deeply woven into the fabric of the show, which covered a span of over 40 years and touched upon relationships and cultural realities of the era. The issue of racism was brought to light at a time when African Americans were not accepted into most of white American culture.

Show Boat opened at the Ziegfeld Theatre on December 27, 1927. It was proclaimed, the following day, by the *New York Times* as "an American masterpiece." The audience left the theater thinking about the story as well as humming the tunes. As a result it was revived several times on Broadway, as well as at the New York City Opera house and three times on film.

The 1930s would see a number of other Jerome Kern musicals make it to Broadway, including *The Cat and the Fiddle,* in which he teamed with lyricist Otto Harbach, *Music in the Air* with Oscar Hammerstein II, and *Roberta,* again with Harbach and featuring the ageless hit "Smoke Gets in Your Eyes."

Kern's melodies were described as pure, timely and timeless. He did not use rhythmic or harmonic contrivances, but instead sought out a beautiful, and simple, single melody line. He was also a perfectionist, steadfast in his melodies and was not one to change his tune, literally, to fit his lyricist's wishes. Nonetheless, he collaborated with some of the finest lyricists in the history of Broadway musicals.

Oscar Hammerstein II

Oscar Greeley Clendinning Hammerstein II, the grandson of the legendary opera and theater impresario who built much of Broadway, was born in the summer of 1895 in New York City. His father, William, managed the Victoria Theatre, where the senior Hammerstein had built a roof garden on top of the stately structure. Despite being a vaudeville producer, and despite the family's great theatrical history, William Hammerstein did not want his son Oscar taking part in the rough show business lifestyle. However, after his father's death in 1914, the 19-year-old Hammerstein II began writing and performing in variety shows at Columbia University, where he was attending as a pre-law student. Determined to be part of the theater, and get out of attending law school, Oscar II urged his Uncle Arthur, also a Broadway producer, to give him a job as an assistant stage manager. Arthur, however, did not want to go against his brother's wishes. After some convincing, Arthur saw the determination of the young Hammerstein and conceded, giving him his first job in the theater.

By 1919, Hammerstein had gotten married and been promoted by his uncle to production stage manager. It was in this role that he met, and began working with, Otto Harbach. Their first success came with composer Vincent Youmans, who was coming off a relatively unsuccessful show called *Little Girls in Blue,* with lyrics by a young Ira Gershwin. Youmans hired Harbach and Hammerstein to write the lyrics for a show called *Wildflowers,* produced by Arthur Hammerstein. The musical would premier on Broadway in 1923 and run for 477 performances. From there, it was on to an even bigger hit, also produced by Oscar's uncle, called *Rose-Marie.*

By 1925, Youmans had moved on to write *No, No, Nanette,* while Berlin and George S. Kaufman were working with the Marx Brothers on *The Cocoanuts.* Hammerstein and Harbach teamed on the show *Sunny* with composer Jerome Kern. Opening in September of that year, *Sunny* ran for over 500 performances. It was the first time Hammerstein and Kern had worked together, and they would follow this debut with the legendary musical *Show Boat* just two years later, which opened at the Ziegfeld Theatre just two days after Christmas.

While Ziegfeld produced *Show Boat,* the next venture for Hammerstein was truly a family affair. *Sweet Adeline* ushered in the 1930s at the Hammerstein Theater with book and lyrics by Oscar Hammerstein. It was produced by Arthur Hammerstein and directed by Reginald Hammerstein. The music came from Kern, who was becoming part of the Hammerstein family. In the early '30s, the team of Kern and Hammerstein, famous both individually and together, would not only handle the music, lyrics and book, but would also serve as co-directors on the hit show *Music in the Air.*

As the decade progressed, however, Hammerstein was drawn to the silver screen and the grandeur of Hollywood and motion pictures. For the rest of the 1930s Oscar Hammerstein II was notably missing as one of the major contributors to Broadway. He would, however, return to theater in New York, to work on an all–African American opera called *Carmen Jones,* which was favorably received. It was shortly thereafter that he would meet up with his former Long Island neighbor, and fellow Columbia University alumnus, Richard Rodgers.

Together, Rodgers and Hammerstein would become the most influential American musical team of the century. Their pairing began with a musical adaptation of the book *Green Grow the Lilacs,* written by Lynn Riggs. The musical, initially called *Away We Go!,* would be ready in March of 1943, and open at the St. James Theater under a new name, *Oklahoma!* It featured songs such as "Oh What a Beautiful Mornin'" and "People Will Say We're in Love." Some 2,122 performances later it closed on Broadway, setting a record at the time as the longest-running musical in Broadway history. *Oklahoma!* would subsequently tour for over a decade. But it was more than a major hit musical. Like *Show Boat,* 15 years earlier, *Oklahoma!* was a landmark show, changing the face of Broadway musicals again. The combination of serious drama and music carefully integrated into the story once again set the show aside from the more familiar light Broadway fare. Additionally, the cast was largely comprised of singers who could also act, rather than the reverse, bringing some of the best musical performances ever to Broadway. The show garnered many awards, perhaps none greater than a special Pulitzer Prize. *Oklahoma!* was obviously adapted for the screen and once again enjoyed tremendous success.

While it would be a challenge to follow up on such a masterpiece, Rodgers and Hammerstein would enjoy great success with *Carousel* in 1945 and *Allegro* in '47. But it was in 1949 that they would procure the rights to the best-selling James Michener book *Tales of the South Pacific*, which they would combine with Michener's *Our Heroine* to create the musical *South Pacific*. Rodgers and Hammerstein also shared producing credits. Featuring timeless standards like "Younger Than Springtime" and "Some Enchanted Evening," and with Mary Martin in the starring role, *South Pacific* played over 1,900 performances in its initial run and would be revived to tremendous success on Broadway. Like *Oklahoma!*, it would be staged by touring companies and in regional theater forever. It would also bring the team of Rodgers and Hammerstein their second Pulitzer Prize.

The next show was based on *Anna and the King of Siam*, a 1944 book from the diaries of a British governess in the Royal Court of Siam (now Thailand) in the mid–1800s. The book had been made into a dramatic film in 1946. This time it would become a blockbuster musical (the only kind of musicals written by Rodgers and Hammerstein) called *The King and I*, featuring the songs "Getting to Know You," "Shall We Dance?," "I Whistle a Happy Tune," and "Hello, Young Lovers." *The King and I* opened at the St. James Theater and ran for 1,246 performances.

Again Rodgers and Hammerstein also produced the show, which starred Gertrude Lawrence and Yul Brenner, with choreography by Jerome Robbins, who had conceived and choreographed *On the Town* just seven years earlier, thus launching his own Broadway career. By the time he first worked with Rodgers and Hammerstein, Robbins had already worked with Leonard Bernstein and Sammy Cahn and was established in a career that would continue for decades, with numerous hit shows. More about Jerome Wilson Rabinowitz, better known as Jerome Robbins, in upcoming chapters.

If *Oklahoma!, Carousel, South Pacific* and *The King and I* were not already enough to hang their hats on, the team of Rodgers and Hammerstein would have one more mega-hit show, this time based on the singing von Trapp family's true story of escaping the Nazis in World War II by climbing over the Alps. *The Sound of Music*, like their other hugely successful shows, was a story of significance. It included beautiful and joyous music that served as an integral part of the show and the storyline. The songs, including "Do-Re-Mi," "Edelweiss," "My Favorite Things," "Climb Every Mountain," and of course the title song, "The Sound of Music," not only evoked images of the show, but took on a life of their own.

Unfortunately, Hammerstein would have little time to enjoy the remarkable impact of *The Sound of Music*, which ran for 1,443 performances and has since been revived for Broadway several times. Hammerstein passed away in August of 1960, at the age of 65. On a night in September of 1960, the lights on Broadway were turned off in memory of the great lyricist, who was called "the man who owned Broadway."

Richard Rodgers (and Lorenz Hart)

Richard Rodgers was born in 1902 in Queens, New York, to a wealthy Jewish family. His father was a doctor and his grandfather had become wealthy in the silk trade. Rodgers took to the piano at the age of six. While vaudeville and Yiddish theater were the impetus for many young Jewish writers, composers and performers, Rodgers was weaned on Broadway musicals and operettas, which his family took him to see often as a youngster.

By the time he was 17, Rodgers had a published song and was writing amateur musical revues. It was during his family's summer vacations on Long Island that he got to know Oscar Hammerstein II, who encouraged the young Rodgers to keep on working toward his musical goals. And Rodgers did just that, teaming up with a school friend, Lorenz Hart, or Larry, who wrote lyrics for Rodgers' melodies.

Rodgers and Hart first teamed up at the age of 18, while they were both attending Columbia University in upper Manhattan. They started out by writing songs for several variety shows at the school, thus honing their skills and familiarizing themselves with each other's style while generating the attention of some professional composers. It was through such networking that they met Lew Fields, formerly of the famous vaudeville comedy team, Weber and Fields. At the time Fields was in need of songs for an upcoming show called *Poor Little Ritz Girl*. So, in 1920, Rodgers and Hart had their first Broadway writing assignment. The show only lasted for three months on Broadway and was quickly forgotten, but it was a huge step for the young songwriting duo. In fact, Fields was so impressed with Rodgers that when he went on tour in Europe with Fred Allen and Nora Bayes, he asked Rodgers to come along and conduct the orchestra. Only 19 years old at the time, Rodgers left school and went on the tour.

Rodgers and Hart would continue together for years to come. Hart, like Rodgers, came from a Jewish family with money. He attended private schools prior to Columbia University. Hart had a strained relationship with his strict father, and after his father's death, he spent several years living with his mother. Far less grounded than his partner, Hart spent time traveling, partying and drinking. In a closeted era, he was fairly open about his homosexuality but was forever seeking someone with whom to share his life.

His emotional ups and downs were reflected in his lyrics, at times being sarcastic or caustic, while at other times simply longing for love. In the classic

"My Funny Valentine," Hart writes about wanting someone who, not unlike him, was not particularly attractive, and then responds with the words he wants to hear, a request not to change. His personal life was reflected in many of his songs, such as "I Wish I Were in Love Again." Despite his inner turmoil, and because of it, Hart's lyrics were considered among the most touching, and sometimes most biting, of the era between the two world wars.

Rodgers and Hart would hit their stride with the 1926 sketch comedy *The Garrick Gaieties,* featuring several stars and an actor named Lee Strasberg, who would later change the craft of acting. The show was unique in that it was a satirical revue based on the popular "Follies," poking fun at the very business in which they would thrive for some 26 Broadway shows.

Along with the New York Yankees, Rodgers and Hart were probably the most successful team from 1925 through 1943, sometimes writing three or four Broadway shows in a single year. Among their many musicals was a second version of *The Garrick Gaieties* in 1926, as well as *A Connecticut Yankee* in 1927, *Present Arms* in 1928 and several hits in London including *Evergreen,* which ran for over 250 performances in 1930. After a five-year stint writing for films, Rodgers and Hart returned to the theater with *Jumbo* in 1935 starring Jimmy Durante and *On Your Toes* in 1936, starring Ray Bolger, which ran for over 300 performances on Broadway. *Babes in Arms,* in 1937, would become one of the team's biggest hits, featuring "My Funny Valentine" and "The Lady Is a Tramp." Like Irving Berlin and Jerome Kern, Rodgers and Hart, while writing songs integral to the script, also had a knack for penning popular hits that had a life of their own outside the theater walls, songs that would ultimately became classics.

Five Broadway shows later, they would usher in the 1940s with their most significant musical, *Pal Joey,* starring Gene Kelly and featuring "Bewitched, Bothered and Bewildered." Despite some mixed reviews by critics, the show was a success and an even bigger hit when brought back again in 1952 and in subsequent revivals. Together Rodgers and Hart would write *By Jupiter* as their last play together in 1943. By this time, Hart's drinking, his emotional turmoil and frustrations were taking a toll on the collaboration. Hart was no longer as reliable or responsible as he had been, and the team suffered. Supposedly Rodgers would also have his own bout with alcohol, but he kept it under wraps, and it did not take a toll on his career.

Rodgers and Hart were offered the opportunity to write the score for *Oklahoma!,* but at this point Hart was neither emotionally or physically up to the task. Thus began the teaming of Rodgers and Hammerstein, as discussed under the career of Oscar Hammerstein II (above). Hart did return to write another song with Rodgers for the revival of the show *A Connecticut Yankee,* but shortly thereafter he disappeared from Rodgers' life and then from the public eye. Hart passed away of pneumonia shortly after the opening of *Oklahoma!* in 1943.

Amazingly, Rodgers and Hammerstein were able to follow up one triumphant show with another, from *Oklahoma!* to *Carousel* to *South Pacific* to *The Sound of Music.* Collectively, the Rodgers and Hammerstein musicals earned 34 Tony Awards, 15 Academy Awards, two Pulitzer Prizes, two Grammy Awards and two Emmy Awards. *Time* magazine and CBS News cited Rodgers and Hammerstein in 1998 as being among the 20 most influential artists of the 20th century. Yet, their pairing was one of two amazing collaborative unions in the career of Richard Rodgers, which spanned some 50 years.

Following his lengthy partnerships with Hart and Hammerstein, Richard Rodgers wrote another show called *No Strings* in 1962 in which he attempted to be his own lyricist. While the show was not very successful, it did include the hit song "Love Makes the World Go Round." He would then try to team with a few other lyricists but could not find anyone the likes of the two composers with whom he had worked for so long. Rodgers died in late December of 1979.

During his long illustrious career, Rodgers married Dorothy Belle Feiner and had two daughters, Mary and Linda. One of Rodgers' grandsons, Adam Guettel, apparently following the musical lineage, was a boy soprano at the Metropolitan Opera at the age of 13 before switching his career to that of a composer. His score and orchestrations for the 2005 Broadway hit *The Light in the Piazza* won him two Tony awards. Another grandson, Peter Melnick, served as composer for *Adrift in Macao*, which debuted at the Philadelphia Theatre Company in 2005 and was produced Off Broadway in 2007.

George and Ira Gershwin

The sons of Russian-Jewish immigrants, Israel and then George Gershowitz were born in the late 1890s and grew up on New York's crowded Lower East Side. George was the first of the brothers to show interest in music when he began playing the piano that was originally supposed to spark musical interest in his older brother Israel, better known as Ira. It was George who would leave school as a teenager to pursue his songwriting career in Tin Pan Alley while Ira would remain in school and go on to college. George would also be the first to get his work published, in his late teens, with songs such as the "Rialto Rag" and his first big hit, at the age of 21, "Swanee," with lyrics by Irving Caesar. At roughly the same time, Ira was asked to write lyrics for a show called *Two Little Girls in Blue*, co-produced by Vincent Youmans, which he wrote under the name Arthur Francis. It was while on their way to Broadway that the

Gershowitz brothers would change their name to the less ethnic-sounding Gershwin.

George first saw Broadway success as he began writing the music for George White's *Scandals*, in 1922, part of the ongoing series of less spectacular, but highly entertaining Ziegfeld-esque revues. George Gershwin wrote for the first five of the thirteen reviews that would include performers the likes of W.C. Fields, Alice Faye, Bert Lahr, Ray Bolger, Rudy Vallee, Ethel Barrymore and Ethel Merman. His "Rhapsody in Blue" was among the songs written for one of George White's *Scandals*.

It was in 1924, when the brothers teamed up on the first of 14 Broadway musicals. It was a musical comedy called *Lady Be Good* starring Broadway's newest song and dance team, Fred and Adele Astaire. Cashing in on the popularity of vaudeville, the show was about vaudevillians. The 1925 follow-up, *Tip Toes*, featured the same creative team, except for a change of directors. Having enjoyed two hits in a row, the creative team (including director, John Harwood) went for the trifecta, and *Oh Kay!* was born. While this show was not at all about vaudeville, it was nonetheless another hit musical, starring Gertrude Lawrence.

The Gershwins were off and running and would work again with Fred and Adele Astaire in *Funny Face*, which also included a young Betty Comden (see Chapter 4) in the cast. By the start of the 1930s, the Gershwin brothers were synonymous with Broadway hit musicals. *Girl Crazy* not only launched the decade for the Gershwins, and featured the hit song "I Got Rhythm," but it also became the first musical comedy to win a Pulitzer Prize. Three film versions were made of the popular show.

Following *Strike Up the Band* and *Of Thee I Sing*, the brothers would team on their final show, adapted from the 1925 novel *Porgy* by DuBose Heyward. In what would be billed as a "folk opera," George, Ira and DuBose Heyward (as librettist) would ultimately create a Broadway show about African American life in the Deep South called *Porgy and Bess*. Set in Charleston, South Carolina, at the turn of the century, in an area called Catfish Row, the story is about Porgy, a crippled beggar who travels about in a goat-drawn cart, and falls in love with Bess, a woman of questionable reputation. Bess, however, is the mistress of Crown, a gambler, who kills a man in a fight that erupts from a craps game. He flees, but returns to Bess, only to find she is with Porgy. A fight ensues and Porgy kills Crown and lands in jail. By the time he gets out of jail, Bess has left for New York, and Porgy sets out to find her.

The show's gambling, murder and drug-dealing portrayed African Americans in a manner that offended some, and there has long been controversy around the show. Conversely, the show was also heralded for drawing attention to the struggles and difficulties of life in the Deep South. *Porgy and Bess* was a show about a world the white theater-going audiences of the 1930s knew nothing about. It was a ground-breaking story that also brought a fusion of musical styles together in one show including blues, gospel, jazz and that of Tin Pan Alley.

Ironically, the Gershwin brothers almost never got to write their most culturally significant work. The Metropolitan Opera had commissioned George Gershwin to write a grand opera back in 1930. Gershwin wanted to write the show based on the book *Porgy* and have an all–African American cast. However, the Met was open only to white performers. Meanwhile, Oscar Hammerstein and Jerome Kern, also interested in bringing *Porgy* to the stage, suggested using Al Jolson in blackface to make a musical comedy. Ultimately, Gershwin decided to decline the Met's offer and instead teamed with Heyward to write the show for Broadway where he was able to assemble an all–African American cast.

Porgy and Bess opened in the fall of 1935. Many critics heralded it, but audiences in a segregated world did not flock to see the performances. The show closed after just 125 performances, and a frustrated George Gershwin headed to Hollywood. Sadly, he would die just two years later.

Over time, the show, featuring the songs "Summertime" and "It Ain't Necessarily So" had many renditions worldwide featuring star performers from Cab Calloway to Sidney Poitier to Sammy Davis, Jr., to Maya Angelou all taking roles. While the musical gained greater acceptance, segregation would still persist, making it difficult to stage *Porgy and Bess* in many communities for years to come. It was, however, revived for over 300 performances on Broadway in 1953. Interestingly, it opened at the Ziegfeld Theatre. This was fitting, considering that Ziegfeld was one of the Broadway producers of his time who did not succumb to racism or segregation in his shows. Yet, even when *Porgy and Bess* was restaged in parts of the country to celebrate the 75th anniversary of its opening night on Broadway, there was still quite a bit of controversy.

Three years after his brother's death, Ira Gershwin would once again begin writing lyrics. He would collaborate with Kurt Weill and Jerome Kern and then in 1954 with Harold Arlen on *A Star Is Born*.

Harold Arlen

Born and raised in Buffalo, New York, Hyman Arluck would later change his name to Harold Arlen and enjoy a brilliant career as a composer and lyrist. Arlen's father, Samuel, a renowned cantor in Buffalo, introduced his son to music by having him join the synagogue's choir at the age of seven. Within a few years, Harold started learning piano, catching on quickly. While he was learning and enjoying classical compositions, he also gained an appreciation for popular music, including jazz and ragtime.

By the time he was in his teens, Arlen was so engaged in his passion for music that he would drop out of school, much to his parents' discontent. Arlen would spend several years in various bands, including the Nappy Trio, the Yankees Six, and a local favorite, the Buffalodians. At one of the band's many bookings, Alren met a dancer from Boston named Ray Bolger, and the two would become good friends. Little did either of them know that years later they would both be immortalized in *The Wizard of Oz*.

Once Arlen had earned enough money from the success of the Buffalodians, who went out on tour, he would settle in New York City to work mostly as a piano player and musical arranger. His musical prowess would soon lead to work on the vaudeville circuit and eventually to Broadway, writing the music for *Earl Carroll's Vanities* in 1930 and again in 1932, *George White's Musical Varieties* in 1932 and 1933, and several other musical revues. Arlen had a knack for popular musical numbers, and as result he would team with a number of lyricists, including Ira Gershwin, Ted Koehler, and even Truman Capote. One lyricist he would often team with was Yip Harburg. Together it was Arlen and Harburg who would write the music and lyrics for the 1939 film classic *The Wizard of Oz*. Ironically, "Over the Rainbow," the most notable of the many Harburg–Arlen songs, was cut from *The Wizard of Oz* three times before finally being included in the version of the film the world has come to know and love. The song went on to win the Academy Award for Best Song in 1939 and was considered one the greatest songs of the twentieth century.

Among Arlen's other famous tunes you'll find "Get Happy," "Let's Fall in Love," "Fun to Be Fooled" with the Gershwin brothers, "Stormy Weather," "I've Got a Right to Sing the Blues," "That Old Black Magic," and the Judy Garland classic "The Man That Got Away."

As for Broadway, Arlen's post–World War II musicals included *St. Louis Woman, Bloomer Girl,* and *Jamaica.* His music has also been included in *Mostly Sondheim, Swing!, After Midnight,* and a show I produced featuring the songs of Sinatra, with the dances of Twyla Tharp, called *Come Fly Away.*

Yip Harburg

Words make you think a thought. Music makes you feel a feeling. A song makes you feel a thought.

These are the words of legendary songwriter Yip Harburg, who was forever immortalized by his songs for the 1939 film *The Wizard of Oz,* including "Over the Rainbow," with music by Harold Arlen. The team of Harburg and Arlen would go on to provide the music and lyrics for several films and Broadway musicals. One of their most popular tunes, "It's Only a Paper Moon," actually preceded *The Wizard of Oz* by several years and included Billy Rose, who worked with Harburg on the lyrics.

Born just before the turn of the century, Isidore Hochburg, another in a long line of successful songwriters from New York's Lower East Side, would become known as E. Y. Harburg. Because of his constant energy, he adopted the nickname "Yip," which in Yiddish means squirrel.

Harburg was raised in an Orthodox Jewish family that provided him with a rich cultural background. As he grew up, he became quite conscious of the social and political issues in the world around him. As a result, he would write for the Townsend Harris Hall High School newspaper, along with Ira Gershwin. After working as a journalist abroad and unsuccessfully trying to navigate his own business through the start of the Depression era, Harburg, with some help from Gershwin, would find his way into songwriting.

His first venture onto Broadway was with Arlen on the musical revue *Earl Carroll's Sketch Book of 1929*. His ability to write songs in a variety of styles made Harburg a natural for revues that did not follow a linear storyline and incorporated various musical genres. In the early '30s, Harburg would write for a number of other popular revues, including *Garrick's Gaieties, Earl Carroll's Vanities, Ziegfeld's Follies, Ballyhoo of 1932,* and *Americana,* to name a few. It was for the show *Americana* that he would pen perhaps the most apropos lyric of the Great Depression, "Brother, Can You Spare a Dime?"

From the Great Depression to World War II, during which time he wrote lyrics for the 1937 anti-war musical *Hooray for What!*, Harburg was frequently driven to shows in which he could exercise his social conscience. Even the 1947 hit *Bloomer Girl,* a historical musical about a girl who, during the Civil War, refused to marry her suitor until he released his slaves, was a musical with a message. As it was at that time anyone with a social conscience would be scrutinized by the House Un-American Activities Committee (HUAC) during the McCarthy hearings of the 1950s. Harburg was targeted by the HUAC, but the allegations didn't slow him down, at least not until after he was able to write the lyrics for *Finian's Rainbow,* which hit Broadway in 1947 and ran for 725 performances, followed by three revivals over the next 62 years.

Harburg was eventually blacklisted from films and television for nearly 12 years. In 1957, he was still hired by David Merrick to write the lyrics to the musical *Jamaica,* starring Lena Horne and Ricardo Montalban. While he had only a few more Broadway credits before his death in 1981, Harburg's lyrics would be heard in several other shows, including *Mostly Sondheim* and *After Midnight.*

Ervin Drake

Songwriter Ervin Drake may be best remembered for his song "It Was a Very Good Year" (a hit for Frank Sinatra), but for Drake, it was a very good 95 years in which he enjoyed a long and diverse career. Born in New York City, Drake was the middle of three brothers, the oldest of whom was also a songwriter while his younger brother wrote for DC Comics. Erwin meanwhile took to songwriting at an early age, publishing his first song at the age of 12. But it would not be until his mid–20s that his songwriting career would really take off with the English lyrics to the unlikely hit Brazilian instrumental "Tico Tico," It was the beginning of a long string of hit songs, some of which became classics, such as "I Believe" and "Good Morning Heartache." Drake's songs were recorded by the likes of Frank Sinatra, Barbra Streisand, Billie Holiday, Perry Como, Diana Ross, Frankie Lane, and other legends. Along with songwriting, Drake took to producing in the early days of television, mostly variety shows. From the late '40s into the early '60s, Drake produced hundreds of programs, including several for the *Merv Griffin/Betty Ann Grove Show*, *The Mel Torme/ Teresa Brewer Show*, and the *Timex Comedy Hour*, along with numerous specials.

As for Broadway, Drake had an inauspicious start with a month-long run of an original comedy called *Heads or Tails* in 1947. After his television career, his luck would improve with the show *What Makes Sammy Run* in 1964, for which he wrote the music and lyrics. Later, his music and lyrics would be featured in *Sophisticated Ladies* in 1981 and in *Motown the Musical* in 2013.

While Drake enjoyed success in television and Broadway, his greatest passion was songwriting, and he held the position of president of the American Guild of Authors and Composers. Always an activist, Drake would lead a successful campaign for the passage of the U.S. Copyright Law of 1976.

SIGNIFICANT WRITERS

Musicals need storylines and plays need to be about something. With that in mind, various writers would contribute to the Broadway stage in the 1920s and '30s. Along with the many Jewish composers and lyricists, there were also a number of important Jewish playwrights during this time. Two of the most significant were George S. Kaufman and Moss Hart.

Kaufman, born in Pittsburgh to a Jewish family in 1889, was an avid reader, with a great wit. He enjoyed reading plays and in an era long before blogs, began putting his own witty remarks on paper. After moving to New York at the age of 20, Kaufman would utilize his writing skills to land jobs as a drama desk reporter for the *New York Tribune* and eventually as the drama reporter for the *New York Times*. In this capacity, Kaufman would not only build a significant following, based on his humorous observations, but would become part of what was known as the Algonquin Round Table. Meeting at the restaurant in the Algonquin Hotel in midtown Manhattan, the group, which included writers Dorothy Parker and Robert Benchley, playwrights Robert E. Sherwood and Edna Ferber, plus Harpo Marx, Irving Berlin and Tallulah Bankhead, among others, became known for their endless stream of ongoing droll banter, while playing various games and unleashing inventive practical jokes upon one another. They became an unofficial club of sorts, including only the sharpest and wittiest participants. The Algonquin Round Table also established a bond that drew them into working together on occasion. In fact, in one instance, in 1922, they teamed up to stage a one-night parody of the popular European revue *Le Chauve-Souris*, calling their show *No Siree!* The satire received raves from those lucky enough to see it. Having enjoyed the process of "putting on a show," they would attempt another satirical revue called *The Forty-Niners* for the public later that year, but it lasted for only two weeks on Broadway. The Algonquin Round Table, however, lasted nearly a decade, through the 1920s up until the stock market crash of '29. After the crash, although many lifelong friendships had formed, they no longer met at their own table. One member reportedly knew it was over when she went to the customary table in the Rose Room of the hotel in 1932 and found a family from Kansas sitting there.

From their many hours spent at the infamous round table, Kaufman and writer Marc Connelly would collaborate on several shows in the early 1920s, including *Dulcy, To the Ladies* starring Helen Hayes, and *Merton at the Movies,* Kaufman's first parody of Hollywood. Producing more than two shows a year, the duo enjoyed great success. However, in 1925, two other round-tablers, Irving Berlin and Harpo Marx (along with his famous brothers), would team up with Kaufman and Morrie Ryskind on a hit musical, *The Cocoanuts,* which would later become one of the Marx Brothers' classic films. Kaufman would work once more with the Marx Brothers, writing the book for *Animal Crackers,* while Ryskind would go on to write with the Marx Brothers on some of their movies, including *A Night at the Opera,* one of the Brothers' biggest hits.

Much like Kaufman, Ryskind was also quite politically minded. After being booted from Columbia University for referring to the dean as Czar Nick in a humor publication (essentially because the dean would not let the nephew of Leo Tolstoy speak at the college), the Brooklyn-born Ryskind would go on to write political sketches for *Garrick Gaieties* in 1925 and subsequent revues prior to teaming with Kaufman. While Ryskind would later get more deeply involved in politics, eventually swinging from the left in his younger years to the right in his later years, he made his mark as a writer with Kaufman. He would also earn one of two Academy Award nominations by writing a film adaptation of a Kaufman collaboration with Edna Ferber called *Stage Door*, starring Katharine Hepburn and Ginger Rogers and featuring Lucille Ball, Eve Arden and Anne Miller.

By the 1930s Kaufman had hit his stride, with help from Ryskind, who was asked to tone down Kaufman's satirical anti-war play *Strike Up the Band* to make it more mainstream. The addition of music and lyrics by the Gershwin brothers helped make the edgy satirical show about war more appealing to the mainstream market. Theatergoers were seeking out more upbeat entertainment during the depression years. Considered ahead of its time, the humor, and the music, played by an orchestra that included Glenn Miller, Benny Goodman and Jimmy Dorsey in the pit, made *Strike Up the Band* one of Kaufman's most significant early Broadway accomplishments. Meanwhile, the always-prolific Kaufman was also contributing to revues by providing sketches, such as those he wrote for Max Gordon's show *The Band Wagon* in 1930, a show that ran for 260 performances starting in 1931, featured Fred and Adele Astaire, and was very highly acclaimed.

Since success is known to breed success, Kaufman would team again with the Gershwins and Ryskind the following year for another satirical musical comedy entitled *Of Thee I Sing*. Compared by Stanley Green, in his book *Broadway Musicals Show by Show*, to a Gilbert and Sullivan opera in its construction and style, the show outlasted *Strike Up the Band*, posting 441 performances at the Music Box Theater. This time Kaufman broadened his range from political satire, which was still the impetus of the show, to also poke fun at the institutions of marriage, beauty pageants and motherhood. *Of Thee I Sing*, which later went on tour for several years, won a Pulitzer Prize. It also sparked yet a third musical in the same style called *Let 'Em Eat Cake*, featuring the same creative team. This time, however, it might have been better to quit while they were ahead. Kaufman's humor was a bit too acerbic, and the show was less mainstream than its predecessors. As a result, *Cake* grew stale quickly and closed in just three months.

Prior to the third satirical sequel with Ryskind, Kaufman had also co-directed a show written by Moss Hart entitled *Face the Music*, with music and lyrics by Berlin. Unlike many of the early Jewish theatrical talents, Moss Hart was not born in a tenement on the Lower East Side of Manhattan, but was instead born in an Upper East Side tenement on 105th Street, another immigrant neighborhood.

It was Hart's Aunt Kate who first introduced him to theater as a young boy, and he would forever owe her his gratitude, as it would become his life's ambition. While honing his skills as an actor and director, and working with theater troupes, Hart began writing plays throughout the 1920s, with minimal success at best. Finally, at the end of the decade, his play *Once in a Lifetime* drew the attention of a Broadway producer who introduced him to George S. Kaufman, who was already established. Together they would turn *Once in a Lifetime*, a spoof about the new era of talkies in Hollywood, into their first collaborative Broadway hit comedy.

While both were city boys, born in Pittsburgh and New York City, respectively, Kaufman and Hart each owned farmhouses in an area known as Bucks County, Pennsylvania. The rural enclave, which also became a retreat for Oscar Hammerstein II, Stephen Sondheim, James Michener, Dorothy Parker, Pearl Buck and S. J. Perlman, served as a quiet locale for Kaufman and Hart to write. It was there that they penned one hit show after another throughout the 1930s. It was also at the now-famous Bucks County Playhouse that the duo could have their works staged, often directing or even performing in the shows, which helped them hone their final drafts. Occasionally celebrity friends, such as Harpo Marx, would join them.

The offbeat comical 1936 Kaufman-Hart hit, *You Can't Take It with You*, played for almost 850 Broadway performances and won the Pulitzer Prize for Drama. It was also during that same year that they teamed with the other Hart, Lorenz, and Richard Rodgers on the musical *I'd Rather Be Right*, featuring George M. Cohan playing President Franklin D. Roosevelt. A "light" plotline served as a structure in which to satirize everything from the fireside chats and presidential conferences to FDR's seeking a third term. The comedy hit *The Man Who Came to Dinner* would follow shortly thereafter. This time the focus was on a dinner guest, Sheridan Whiteside, who, in the weeks prior to Christmas, falls and injures his hip just outside the home where he is about to dine. He then proceeds to be attended to by a confused small-town physician, while driving everyone in the house crazy. The concept for the show was reportedly based on the behavior of Alexander Wollcott, a drama critic and radio star whose temperament made him an unappreciated house guest. *The Man Who Came to Dinner* not only went on to Broadway success but became a standard, staged time and time again in local theater companies and universities for many years.

Through eight collaborations, the wit of George S. Kaufman and Moss Hart set a standard for comedy on stage, whether in a musical or straight play. Although their final collaboration, *George Washington Slept Here*, was not very successful, the two remained friends as they continued their individual careers.

While Hart and Kaufman enjoyed their greatest success together, Kaufman collaborated with several other playwrights including his second wife, Leueen MacGrath, a beautiful, much younger actress who had enjoyed success on the stages of London. They teamed on a couple of shows that went to Broadway, but were essentially flops.

Kaufman would move from theater and journalism to Hollywood where he would direct films and appear on television. He was forever known as one of America's greatest humorists and satirists, poking fun at politics, American culture and the idiosyncrasies that made up daily life. He was one of the few writers that the Marx Brothers, Groucho in particular, truly respected and admired. Thus, Kaufman became a part of American folklore.

"At his best, he was the best of playwrights, and more. He was part of a good time Americans were once able to enjoy—when they dared to laugh at themselves, rather than yield that privilege to others," wrote Robert Gottlieb in his 2004 *New Yorker* magazine article "The Hitmaker" about Kaufman's career and personal life, which included two wives, a reputation as a womanizer, a Hollywood scandal and a daughter named Anne from his first wife, Beatrice Bakrow. George was married to Beatrice, who had penned an unsuccessful Broadway show called *Divided by Three*, for 28 years until her sudden death in 1945. According to Gottlieb's article, after her death Kaufman thought he'd never write again, but he did.

Moss Hart, meanwhile, would go on to enjoy Broadway success with *Lady in the Dark* in 1941. The show evolved into a musical comedy with Ira Gershwin writing the lyrics. It ran for 305 performances and starred Gertrude Lawrence, Victor Mature and Danny Kaye. Hart would later enjoy success as a director, winning a Tony Award for his direction of *My Fair Lady*, which ran on Broadway for years starring Julie Andrews and Rex Harrison. Hart was also known for marrying actress Kitty Carlisle in 1941. Both Kaufman and Hart died in 1961.

SIGNIFICANT STORIES AND SATIRES

Along with Irving Berlin's patriotism, the Jewish composers and lyricists were not strictly thinking musically, but were challenging themselves to broaden the horizons of what was traditionally thought of as the Broadway musical. Just as Gordin and Jacob P. Adler had introduced more sophisticated works to the Yiddish stage, Rodgers, George Gershwin and others were seeking material from books of substance with stories that evoked thought and sometimes even controversy. *Show Boat, Oklahoma!* and *Porgy and Bess* were among the most significant works of the '30s and early '40s, and the most substantive. These shows remain classics.

Jewish humor, especially political satire and humor about both domestic and world news, was also offering a broader, more thought-provoking theater experience to audiences. From the Broadway stage to the late-night television talk shows, political humor would outgrow its origins in newspaper columns and become a staple of American humor thanks largely to the work of George S. Kaufman and Moss Hart, who were among the forerunners of the genre.

CHANGING TIMES

The composers, lyricists and satirists of this era were the sons of immigrants who were clearly not interested in learning or speaking Yiddish and had instead quickly assimilated into American culture.

After the doors were essentially closed to immigration in 1924, the immigrant culture was no longer sustained by a steady influx of "greenhorns," a term that referred to each new wave of immigrants. Native-born Jews soon outnumbered their first-generation ancestors. The new generation was now part of middle class respectability, while retaining a strong Jewish identity. In the mid–to late–1930s, as news from overseas continued to generate fear among Americans, especially Jews, assimilation became less of a cultural shift and more of a means of self-preservation. Few lyrics or even books were written about Jews, and the Broadway hits, featuring the music of the Jewish composers and lyricists, had few to no Jewish characters or references. There was no Shylock spouting Yiddish or Fannie Brice parodying Sadie with a Yiddish accent. Anti-Semitic groups became visible, and some even voiced their support of Hitler. As a result, many Jewish composers and lyricists, while not necessarily hiding their identities, were not bringing their Jewishness into the open for fear of repercussions. Yet, many supported Jewish causes, and most Jews in theater, like those throughout America, had their concerns regarding the frightful situation in Europe.

While this chapter focused on the musical legends of the era (and beyond), the next chapter will focus on the dramatists of the time and the growing political involvement of many Jewish performers and writers as World War II grew near.

4

Group Theater, Acting Teachers and Life During Wartime

While the depression era and pre-war years of the 1930s brought together many of the legendary composers and lyricists of the century, as featured in the previous chapter, it was also a time for great dramatic works and a period in which the innovative concept of group theater was born. The depression years caused many Americans to re-think their views on politics and question their belief in the security of the nation. After all, the nation had let the banks collapse, and with it the hopes and dreams of many Americans. While the upbeat song and dance musicals were still a source of entertainment, escapism and optimism, many writers, particularly those who were Jewish, explored the effects of the Great Depression upon American life. Theater could be a source for calling attention to current social issues and conflicts, and not only those from history or from the stories found in classic literature. Playwrights were now putting down on paper stories that reflected the pulse of the American people.

In 1931, three young Jewish idealists, determined to invigorate the American theater and present shows of significant social and cultural impact, joined forces. Their concept was to stage original plays that reflected contemporary American life during this difficult time period. They wanted American theater to not only provide entertainment, but also be used as a powerful form of expression, as was the case for centuries in other parts of the world. The result of their efforts was called Group Theater, which was founded by Harold Clurman, Cheryl Crawford and Lee Strasberg.

Clurman had grown up in an immigrant Jewish family on the Lower East Side where he was exposed to Yiddish theater as a child. The passion and vitality of the shows featuring performers the likes of Jacob Adler (whose daughter Stella he would later marry) inspired Clurman to become an actor, while the community atmosphere of Yiddish theater inspired the communal concept of

Group Theater. Clurman would go on to study acting in France before returning to New York, where he found small parts in shows while also serving as a stage manager and reader for the Theater Guild.

Lee Strasberg, also of Jewish descent, came to New York in 1909 when his family immigrated to America and, like Clurman, settled on the Lower East Side. His first acting experience was in a Yiddish theater production staged by a drama club. He would later enroll in the Clare Tree Major School of Acting. But it was upon seeing Constantin Stanislavski's Moscow Art Theatre in 1923 that his life would change. Strasberg was so impressed by the performers and their commitment to their craft that he would go on to study with Stanislavski and in time create his own "method" of acting. In 1925, Strasberg would make his first professional appearance in a show called *Processional* produced by the Theater Guild. It was also through the Theater Guild that he would begin to teach his method-acting techniques while also directing plays.

Cheryl Crawford, meanwhile, was born in 1902 in Akron, Ohio, where she grew up. She later attended Smith College and majored in drama. Despite performing in many college plays and taking acting classes in New York City after graduation, her dream was not to perform, but instead become a theatrical producer. With that in mind, she took a job as an assistant director at the Theater Guild prior to being one of the three co-founders of Group Theater.

Years later, after the era of Group Theater, Crawford would be the co-founder of the American Repertory Theater and one of the founders of The Actors Studio. She would also emerge as a very successful Broadway producer, bringing *Brigadoon, Paint Your Wagon, Sweet Bird of Youth* and *Mother Courage and Her Children* to the stage.

It was this trio—Clurman, Strasberg and Crawford—that was determined to go beyond the limitations of the Theater Guild and form their own complete theater ensemble, including actors and crew. Based on the Moscow Art Theater, such an ensemble would create, perform and grow together as one single theatrical entity. The relationships within the group would flourish, and the hope was that the familiarity would extend to the stage, resulting in more convincing, real, onstage interactions than those typically found in most theatrical productions. There were no individual stars, but instead a group of actors, writers, directors and so on. Thus the concept of Group Theater was born. The next step was to find the performers who understood this new concept and embraced it. Pooling their resources and reaching out to many talents whom they knew individually, Clurman, Strasberg and Crawford brought together 28 actors who understood the idea of a collective entity and wanted to be part of plays that presented social issues on stage. Among the performers in the group were Stella Adler, Luther Adler (Stella's half-brother and son of Jacob), Harry

Bratsburg (who later rose to acting fame as Harry Morgan), Lee J. Cobb, John Garfield and Elia Kazan. The group also included writer Clifford Odets and composer Kurt Weill.

For Luther Adler, the group experience was just part of a career that spanned five decades, starting with his acting debut in 1908, at the age of five, in the Yiddish play *Shmendrik*. His Broadway career began with a 1921 play called *The Hand of the Potter*, in which he was billed by his birth name of Lutha J. Adler. His final performance would be a most appropriate and triumphant conclusion to a magnificent career, as he took over the role of Tevye in the original production of *Fiddler on the Roof*. Throughout his long career, Adler never lost his Jewish roots, playing Moe Axelrod in *Awake and Sing!*, Sam Katz in *Paradise Lost,* and Shylock in *The Merchant of Venice*. The hard-working actor would also find time for Off Broadway productions, plus several films and many television roles in the 1960s.

While largely Jewish, the participants in Group Theater were diverse in their cultural makeup and in their various skills. Writers, directors, producers and actors all gave of their time and abilities in an effort to create a unified vision that would manifest itself in a very high quality of theater. Their efforts would indeed pay off. Group Theater would stage 20 productions over a period of 10 years, some of which were box office hits, most of which were highly acclaimed and all of which spoke to the human experience of the generation.

"They were the next generation of actors after Yiddish theater and vaudeville. They wanted to be very realistic so they set out to build a unified group," explains Ellen Adler. "They would train together, eat together and do everything together and they would not go to casting calls or auditions outside of the group," adds Adler, also recalling that the greatest challenge for the group was raising funds. "They had to raise the money for each show, at a time when there wasn't much money available for theater, especially for doing serious political plays," notes Adler.[1]

The first play staged by the group, at the Martin Beck Theater in 1931, was called *The House of Connelly*, written by Paul Green who had already won a Pulitzer Prize for his play *In Abraham's Bosom,* and his works were already highly anticipated. A native of Lillington, North Carolina, Green wrote *The House of Connelly* about the struggles and decline of a southern family. While Green was not particularly pleased with the upbeat ending tacked on by the group, the play and the performers, influenced by Strasberg's method acting, won critical acclaim for the work.

In 1933, the group would enjoy their first box office hit, along with critical acclaim, when they staged Sidney Kingsley's first play, *Men in White*, about surgical practices in a hospital and the very real trials and tribulations of the doctors who work there. The play also brought attention to the issue of illegal abortion. Like most of the group members, who championed social issues from a left-wing political perspective, Kingsley would speak out on legalizing abortion, which would occur some 40 years later. Directed by Strasberg, *Men in White* would go on to win a Pulitzer Prize for Drama.

Among the other notable plays performed by the group was Clifford Odets' *Awake and Sing!* One of the great dramatists of the 1930s, Odets wrote this story about a middle-class Jewish family in the Bronx. It was unique in that Jewish characters had rarely been seen on Broadway since the days of vaudeville, and those were typically stereotypes for the sake of laughs. This kitchen sink drama about the family's struggles through the depression years, from their cramped Bronx tenement, touches on their hardships, their courage and their dreams of a brighter future. The original group production won rave reviews and would be revived on Broadway several times, including a 2006 version that would win a Tony Award for Best Revival of a Play.

The following show, a Paul Green and Kurt Weill anti-war show entitled *Johnny Johnson*, gave the group a new challenge as the three acts of the play were different in genre, ranging from comedy to satire to tragedy. Once again the results were critically acclaimed. Another Odets classic, *Golden Boy*, in 1937, would emerge as the group's most successful show, running for 250 performances at the Belasco Theatre. Ironically, the success of the show was due in part to bringing in Frances Farmer to appear. Farmer was already established as a box office draw from her film career. This was out of character for the group, which took pride in unity and self-contained collaborative efforts. The group, however, was having financial difficulties and was hopeful that by bringing in an established star they would generate enough income to continue. Farmer received mixed reviews but was able to help Group Theater continue a while longer. Nonetheless, she later explained in interviews that she felt she had been used, particularly when she was not asked to be included in subsequent group shows. Farmer was, however, linked to one member of the group in the press, as she was having a widely publicized affair with Clifford Odets.

By the end of the decade it was becoming clear that it would also be the end of the first era of Group Theater. Funding was hard to come by, the lure of Hollywood was siphoning off talent, and friction between various members was taking its toll on the group. In 1941, after a ten-year run, featuring primarily critically acclaimed dramas, but only a few box office hits, Group Theater came to an end. It would, however, have a considerable impact on American theater. Several of the group members, including Strasberg and Stella Adler, would go on to teach acting and become the most respected instructors in the industry. Crawford, Kazan and Robert Lewis went on to form the Actors Studio where they would train a future generation of performers in the style of Group Theater. Repertory theaters from coast to coast would also utilize much of the group's concept for decades, working together to stage performances.

John Garfield

One of the most notable acting careers launched in the days of Group Theater was that of John Garfield. He was another of the many Jewish performers to emanate from the Lower East Side of Manhattan, where he was born Jules Garfinkle in 1913. After his mother's death, when Jules was seven, he would grow up in Brooklyn and then in the Bronx, where he was raised by various relatives. A troubled youth, he was constantly in trouble as a youth. In an attempt to give him some direction in life, he was introduced to acting and boxing, both of which would steer him away from trouble, provide some discipline, and ultimately set him on a more positive course.

After appearing in his first Broadway show, called *Lost Boys*, he was cast in the 1932 production of *Counselor-at-Law*, and join the group shortly thereafter. Known for playing the brooding and "tough guy" characters, Garfield took on challenging lead roles in *Waiting for Lefty* and *Awake and Sing!* before playing the boxer in *Golden Boy* in 1937, all plays written by Clifford Odets. He was also offered the lead role in the film *A Streetcar Named Desire*, before Brando, but it did not come to fruition because contract negotiations failed.

Garfield would go on to change his name from Jules to John in 1938 at the request of Warner Bros., who felt the name Jules was "too Jewish." Name changing was becoming more commonplace as news from overseas, coupled with growing anti–Semitism in the United States, was creating a stigma around being Jewish. He would, however, maintain his Jewish identity and settle in Hollywood where he took on a number of leading film roles all through the 1940s, bringing the Strasberg Method, first utilized in Group Theater, to Hollywood.

Martin Balsam

One of the earliest members of Actor's Studio was 22-year-old Martin Balsam, who made his way from the Bronx to Broadway in 1941 in a little-known play called *Ghost for Sale*. Later on, after serving in the military, he switched uniforms and took a job as an usher at Radio City Music Hall, whetting his appetite even more to be on stage and screen. Balsam amassed a number of major film credits, including *On the Waterfront, 12 Angry Men, Breakfast at Tiffany's, Tora! Tora! Tora!, Psycho, All the President's Men, Little Big Man, The Taking of Pelham One Two Three,* and *Murder on the Orient Express,* along with taking on many television roles.

Some nine Broadway shows after his debut in *Ghost for Sale,* Balsam not only starred in three of the four short plays that made up Robert Anderson's *You Know I Can't Hear You When the Water's Running,* but also won a Tony Award for his efforts. By the time he retired, the Russian-Jewish Balsam had won over many audiences while drawing critical acclaim.

The Teachers: Strasberg and Adler

Starting in the 1920s, and for some 60 years until his death in 1982, Lee Strasberg would train actors in his own version of method acting culled from the great Stanislavski. Following the decade of Group Theater, he would spend a short time in Hollywood before joining Elia Kazan at Actors Studio in New York City. Strasberg would become known as one of the most prominent acting teachers of the 20th century, and in 1969 opened the Lee Strasberg Theater and Film Institute in New York City and in Hollywood. Still going strong today, the institute has taught "The Method" to thousands of actors for nearly 50 years.

While there have been many success stories that emerged from the Strasberg methodology, which included concentration and the use of sensory and affective memory, his method also generated criticism. Critics contended that Strasberg's Method, and his teaching techniques, which delved into the emotional recollections of students, were overly psychoanalytical. They contended that such methods could prove harsh and in some cases damaging to the young actors. His supporters countered that so many of his students had gone on to great success using his methods that they were clearly effective. Ultimately, Strasberg was considered both a genius and a madman, depending on which side of the argument you took.

Strasberg's primary competitor as an acting teacher, Stella Adler, was said to have asked for a moment of silence in her class upon news of Strasberg's death. While she had great respect for Strasberg, she then followed the moment of silence by saying that it would take a hundred years to undo the damage he had inflicted upon the acting world.

Nonetheless, the Strasberg alumni are more than a little impressive, including Alec Baldwin, Anne Bancroft, Ellen Burstyn, Jill Clayburgh, James Dean, Sally Field, Jane Fonda, Dustin Hoffman, Marilyn Monroe, Paul Newman, Al Pacino and Shelley Winters.

Stella Adler, meanwhile, was the daughter of the legendary Yiddish theater stars Jacob and Sara Adler. She was born in 1901 in New York City. One of a number of performers in the family, Stella would make her acting debut on stage with her father at the age of four to an adoring crowd. Although she was on stage during some shows with her parents, she mostly watched the Yiddish theater performances from the wings and was heavily influenced by these early experiences.

At the age of 18, she headed to Great Britain to study, while also appearing for a year in her father's production of a show called *Elisa Ben Avia*. It was, however, back in the United States that she would be most influenced by seeing the Moscow Art Theatre and, like Strasberg, learning about the work of Russian actor-director Constantin Stanislavski. By 1925, Adler had become a student of Stanislavski in the American Laboratory Theater School. Even after becoming part of Group Theater in 1931, she took a brief hiatus to go with Harold Clurman to train with Stanislavski in Paris. This trip abroad helped help her resolve questions she had about his methods, as often presented by Strasberg, with whom she had an opposing view. Strasberg would emphasize the use of all of the senses to pull from past emotions and use those emotions in the role. "Think of something that made you happy or sad," comes from the Strasberg method, while Adler believed that acting was about the character and that the actor must research the character and use his or her imagination. "What would he or she (the character) do in this situation?" comes from Adler's method.

After an acting career that included many roles in the group presentations on Broadway and a few years working under the name Stella Ardler, while appearing in three films in Hollywood, Adler began teaching acting at the Drama Workshop, part of the New School for Social Research in New York's Greenwich Village. Then, in 1949, she opened her own acting school, The Stella Adler Conservatory, which still thrives today under the leadership of her grandson, Tom Oppenheim, artistic director since 1994 of what is now called the Stella Adler Studio of Acting. Oppenheim recalls spending time with his grandmother, sitting with her in her home, and how easily she could teach you something important about acting. "I had given her a single red rose. At a certain point in the visit she said to me, 'I will show you something about this rose. You can hold it this way so the audience sees it, or this way so that it's your secret.' The revealed rose says something entirely different from the concealed rose. By showing me this, she was giving me access to an aspect of the craft unique in the world of acting ... the vocabulary and language of props," explains Oppenheim.[2]

In the early 1950s, Adler performed on Broadway in a few shows, but she was more dedicated to, and passionate about, teaching a new generation of actors. One of her earliest students, taking his very first acting classes, was a young man named Marlon Brando, who would later praise Adler's work with him and with her students in general. Other students included Robert De Niro, Melanie Griffith, Harvey Keitel, Warren Beatty and Martin Sheen as well as other film and Broadway actors.

Adler would later become an adjunct professor at the Yale School of Drama and head the undergraduate drama department at New York University. Her work extended the lineage from her own early influences of Yiddish theater to that which she contributed while in Group Theater, on to her teachings and on to current and future generations of actors. In the end, those early Yiddish theater influences were impacting performers two generations later. Clearly the Adler family would prove to have one the most significant influences on acting, and on Broadway, in the 20th century.

As noted on the Stella Adler Studio of Acting web site, "The spirit that has animated the Adler family for over one hundred years stems from the insight that growth as an actor and growth as a human being are synonymous."[3]

Activism

THE BERGSON GROUP

Stella Adler, like most of the Group Theater participants, was not only concerned about bringing social issues and injustice to the stage, but was also an activist. She would join the Committee for a Jewish Army of Stateless and Palestinian Jews, which became known simply as the Bergson Group, based on the pseudonym of its leader, Hillel Kook, who took the name to keep his identity and his family in Palestine safe. The Bergson Group was dedicated to spreading the word to Americans about the atrocities taking place in Europe at the hands of the Nazis.

The winds of war were already blowing fiercely throughout much of Europe by the late 1930s, but the United States media provided few details of the horrors that were taking place. At this point, the government was editing reports of the mass murder of two million Jews. The stories were relegated to small articles, such as one found on page ten in the *New York Times* and a three-inch article on page six in the *Washington Post*. The public at large was not apprised of what was going on overseas, as these atrocities were not making the headlines. Additionally, the United States president at the time, Franklin D. Roosevelt, remained conspicuously uninvolved in the overseas activities.[4]

Many celebrities joined the Bergson Group to publicize these atrocities and generate public support, urging the United States to "get involved" in saving the Jewish people. At first, most of the participants were Jewish, such as Stella Adler and her brother Luther, as well as Eddie Cantor, composer Kurt Weill, Milton Berle, Carl Reiner and both Groucho and Harpo Marx. Soon, however, many non–Jewish performers also joined the cause, such as Marlon Brando, Frank Sinatra, Perry Como, Vincent Price and Count Basie. Full-page ads placed by the Bergson Group in major newspapers were designed to bring greater awareness to the plight of the European Jews. They also mentioned not only the celebrities involved but also the names of political figures and labor leaders who were supporting this important Jewish and humanitarian cause.

Determined not to sit idly by while such atrocities were taking place daily in Europe, the Bergson Group held rallies to accompany the newspaper ads, many of which were written by *Gone with the Wind* screenwriter Ben Hecht. A journalist, author of more than 30 books, award-winning screenwriter and play-wright, Hecht, a Zionist, was very active in political issues in the 1930s and a strong believer in the formation of a Jewish state.

While their efforts began prior to the war, in hopes of getting America involved, the Bergson Group would get stronger during the war. In the summer of 1943, they challenged the Roosevelt administration, wanting to know why the efforts to win the war did not extend to rescuing the Jewish people in Europe. At a conference in New York City, some 1,500 delegates joined forces to try to figure out ways in which the government could help the European Jews. The presiding bishop of the Episcopal Church, the Rev. Henry St. George Tucker; former president Herbert Hoover; newspaper impresario William Randolph Hearst; New York City Mayor Fiorello La Guardia; and NAACP president Joel Spingarn were among the many non–Jewish partici-pants. Clearly the messages of the Bergson Group transcended cultural and religious lines.

Also in 1943, Hecht's original play, *We Will Never Die,* opened at Madison Square Garden in New York City and toured the nation bringing the stories of the European Jews to more than 100,000 Americans. Hecht would later write another Broadway show in 1946, after the war, called *A Flag Is Born* to draw attention to the millions of displaced Jewish people and the need for the State of Israel. Many Jews had fled Germany only to be murdered in Poland or unwel-come in other European nations.

The American League for a Free Palestine, basically another name for the Bergson Group, produced the play. The three-member cast, Celia Adler (Stella and Luther's half-sister and a star of Yiddish theater in the 1920s and '30s), Paul Muni and Marlon Brando received praise for their work, and the group's efforts were sponsored by many luminaries, including Leonard Bernstein and even Eleanor Roosevelt. In the end, *A Flag Is Born* went out on tour and helped raise money for the millions of Jews displaced during and after the war.

In time, the pressure from the Bergson Group and the support of Treasury Secretary Henry Morgenthau, Jr., would finally convince FDR to create the War Refugee Board, which was reportedly responsible for saving roughly 200,000 Jewish people. While the Bergson Group is little more than a footnote

Cecil, left, and Luther Adler, center, both children of Yiddish theater legend Jacob Adler, co-starred in *A Flag Is Born*. The production raised awareness of the plight of the thousands of Jewish people in Europe displaced after the war. The actor at the rear is unidentified (Museum of the City of New York).

in American history, they worked tirelessly in an effort to bring awareness to the American people and the government of the plight of the Jewish people in Europe. Sadly, the loss of life during the late 1930s and through the war years grew to epic proportions. The Bergson Group members and their followers believed that earlier involvement in the war by the United States and the support of the FDR administration might have saved thousands of Jewish people.

And More Teachers: Meisner and Berghof

Another founder of the Group Theater, Sandy Meisner, became an extremely successful and highly regarded acting teacher. Like Adler and Strasberg, Meisner developed his own methodology, with an emphasis on being truthful on stage, and encouraged his students to act with other actors, not against them.

The son of Hungarian Jewish immigrants, Meisner learned piano at an early age and studied to become a concert pianist before having to take on other jobs to help support his family. But acting became his dream, and he would perform in Lower East Side productions directed by Lee Strasberg, which had a significant influence on his development as a performer and subsequently as a teacher.

By the age of 19, the Brooklyn-born Meisner would land a role as a farm hand in the original comedy *They Knew What They Wanted*. He went on to appear in numerous shows ranging from the Rodgers and Hart revue *The Garrick Gaieties* in 1926 to the Group Theater productions of *Awake and Sing!*, *Paradise Lost*, *Waiting for Lefty*, and *Golden Boy*, among others in the 1930s. Finally, in 1959, he would finish his four decades on Broadway with *The Cold Wind and the Warm*.

It was in 1935 that Meisner began teaching at New York's Neighborhood Playhouse School of the Theatre, which had originally opened in 1915. It was there that he taught his students that acting is rooted in acquiring a solid organic technique. This was a cornerstone of his teaching process, which featured a lot of give and take within the classroom. Mesiner would later head the program for the next two decades and remain involved in the Playhouse until the age of 90. The Neighborhood Playhouse School of the Theatre, featuring the acting techniques of Sandy Meisner, is still going strong today.

Notable alumni include James Caan, Robert Duvall, Lee Grant, Jennifer Grey, Jeff Goldblum, Grace Kelly, Christopher Lloyd, David Mamet, Steve McQueen, Gregory Peck, Amanda Plummer, Sydney Pollack, Tony Randall,

Mary Steenburgen, Brenda Vaccaro, Eli Wallach, Jessica Walter, and Joanne Woodward, among many others.

Another legendary Jewish acting teacher was Vienna-born Herbert Berghof, who studied under Max Reinhart before fleeing the Nazis and making his way to America in 1938. Seven years later, together with his wife, actress Uta Hagen, he opened his HB Studio on Bank Street in New York City. Not unlike other great American Jewish acting teachers, the work of Russian director and teacher Constantin Stanislavski influenced his teaching methodology. Practicality was emphasized by Berghof, who said, "If what you're doing doesn't make you want to walk and talk, you're in trouble." He also believed that the best moments in a performance are intuitive, perhaps the result of previous work, but not "planned."

Berghof first made it to Broadway by staging the musical revue *From Vienna* in 1939. His first appearance as a performer followed a year later in *Reunion in New York,* and from there, he found himself in the groundbreaking *Oklahoma!* After several other roles as a performer, Berghof would make his directorial debut on Broadway with the 1952 drama *Waiting for Godot,* staring Bert Lahr and E. G. Marshall. Berghof would conclude his Broadway career with a show called *Charlotte,* which he translated and adapted.

Today, HB Studio is still going strong, developing new performers in the style of the legendary founder. On the roster of this famous acting school you'll find F. Murray Abraham, Debbie Allen, Carroll Baker, Anne Bancroft, Candice Bergen, Peter Boyle, Matthew Broderick, Jill Clayburgh, Claire Danes, Robert De Niro, Faye Dunaway, Rita Gardner, Judd Hirsch, Carol Kane, Harvey Keitel, Jessica Lange, Linda Lavin, Jack Lemmon, Marsha Mason, Steve McQueen, Liza Minnelli, Sarah Jessica Parker, Christopher Reeve, Jason Robards, George Segal, Rod Steiger, and Sigourney Weaver.

The Dramatists

The Jewish people have long needed to be conscious of that which was taking place in the world around them. Perhaps the many oppressors forcing them to flee from many parts of the world created a need to be socially and/or politically aware. Often outnumbered, many Jews of the era learned to "sleep with one eye open" as the saying goes. The dramatic writers of the 1930s and '40s were among those who were aware of the struggles of both Jews and Americans. They absorbed as much as they could from the political and social climate and tried to express their observations on paper. Some were part of Group Theater, while others worked independently. Many took part in social and political activities, and several made a significant impact upon American literature and on Broadway. Here are a few:

Clifford Odets

Born in 1906 in Philadelphia to a middle-class Jewish family, Clifford Odets would write dramatic works featuring characters of various cultures and ethnicities. He would become widely considered the greatest dramatist of the 1930s.

After his family moved to New York during his youth, Odets continued his education into high school but then dropped out to pursue his interest in theater, performing in small repertory groups. Troubled and often alone, Odets reportedly made several suicide attempts while trying to find his own voice and struggling with his identity. In the 1930s, as mentioned above, he became a prominent member of Group Theater. However, he was always seeking some greater sense of order, and with that in mind he was inspired to join the Communist Party while evolving from an actor to a playwright.

It was during the 1930s that Odets would write *Waiting for Lefty* about a labor union strike, along with *Awake and Sing!*, and *Paradise Lost*, three of his most powerful works, all staged by the group and all written about struggles of the poor or downtrodden.

Odets' works featured bold characters. The dialogue was that of the working class, gritty and real. His early writing also focused heavily on social and political concerns. However, in *Golden Boy* he dealt with inner turmoil between the desire for financial success and that of striving for personal fulfillment and love. Much of this epic drama was thought to have stemmed from Odets' inner conflict. While Odets' Communist ties were evident in some of his work, they came to the forefront in *Till the Day I Die*, in which he wrote about the Communists and the Nazis, and their differences.

While his works remained brooding and engaging, Odets' plays of the 40s lost the anguish and passion of the earlier years. His stories dealt more with personal issues and human psychology. Nonetheless, Odets, who died in 1963, is best remembered for writing about social injustice and the struggles of the working class.

Irwin Shaw

The Bronx-born, Brooklyn-raised novelist, playwright, and screenwriter Irwin Shaw (originally Irwin Gilbert Shamforoff) began his writing career penning scripts for the *Dick Tracy* and *Andy Gump* radio programs in the 1930s. It was from there that the son of Russian Jewish immigrants would make his mark, while still in his early 20s, with a one-act anti-war drama called *Bury the Dead*. The play drew high critical acclaim and ran for nearly 100 performances on Broadway.

While writing short stories that appeared in high-profile magazines, including the *New Yorker, Esquire, The Saturday Evening Post,* and *Playboy,* as well as penning his original plays, Shaw would become acquainted with the Group Theater, with whom he shared a similar political ideology. Toward the end of their decade-long run, the Group produced two of Shaw's plays on Broadway, *The Gentle People* in 1939 and *Retreat to Pleasure* in 1940.

After serving in World War II, Shaw brought *Sons and Soldiers* to Broadway and *The Talk of the Town,* starring Cary Grant and Ronald Colman, to the big screen. He would also pen the first of his many novels, *The Young Lions,* based on his experiences in the war. The novel was published in 1948 and lead to a film a decade later starring Marlon Brando, Montgomery Cliff, and Dean Martin. Meanwhile, Shaw landed four more plays on Broadway, each for a very limited run. However, his career would be interrupted by blacklisting after his 1951 novel *The Troubled Air,* which focused on McCarthyism. Labeled a Communist, Shaw took off for Europe where he remained for the better part of the next 25 years. That did not stop him from writing his most commercially successful novel, *Rich Man, Poor Man,* which would later become a television miniseries. While Shaw had limited box office success on Broadway, his plays, novels, and short stories were rich in characterizations, themes, and observations from a very full life that took him from Brooklyn to the Group Theater to Hollywood, through a war and off to Paris.

Elmer Rice

Born to poor second-generation Jewish immigrants in 1892, Elmer Leopold Reizenstein grew up in New York City. He took an early interest in theater as a child, reading plays, taking part in school productions and going to shows with his parents, when they could afford to take him.

Rice was a good student and went on to law school from which he graduated in 1912. However Rice did not pursue the practice of law as he was disenchanted by what he considered the hypocrisy of the profession, which had lawyers making compromises on what they believed in order to win a case. Instead, much to the displeasure of his family, he decided to try his hand at writing a play based upon that which he learned while in law school. The result was his first play called *On Trial,* which was produced on Broadway in 1914. The show was an instant success, drawing critical acclaim and running for 350

performances. It was also just the beginning for one of the most prolific dramatists of the 20th century.

After a couple less successful plays, Rice wrote a tragic/comedy called
The Adding Machine about a bookkeeper who is replaced by an adding machine
and goes on to murder his boss. The play, staged in 1923, became a big hit, as
did *Street Scene*, in 1929, which would win Rice a Pulitzer Prize. He then wrote
Counselor-at-Law, a play that would return him to writing based on his legal
training.

The work of Elmer Rice reflected rebellion and earned him a reputation
as a crusader. He was always fighting for freedom of speech and reflected such
challenges in his work, depicting the struggles of tenement life in *Street Scene*
and addressing Nazism in America in *American Landscape*. While the critics
were often harsh, claiming his work to be too avant garde, Rice was never one
to conform, continuing to write some 50 plays on a wide range of subjects in
a career that spanned 50 years. Although he did not have the blockbuster hits
nor the great American classic dramas, his works, often reflecting his Socialist
beliefs, were innovative, experimental and pushed the idea of uncensored freedom of expression. As a result, Rice, while not a household name, was often
one whose works were discussed and debated in theater and drama classes.

LILLIAN HELLMAN

Lillian Hellman was born in New Orleans in 1905 to Jewish parents. At
the age of five, her family moved to New York City. However, she still spent
part of her childhood years at a boarding house in the South run by her aunts.
Like many other writers, performers and musicians of the era, Hellman
attended Columbia University, and, also like many writers, performers and
musicians of the era, she would not graduate. Instead, at the age of 20, she was
hired as a book reviewer for the *New York Herald Tribune*.

After heading to Hollywood and back, her playwriting career would take
off at the age of 29 with *The Children's Hour*, about a child who accuses her
teachers of being lesbians, a very controversial theme for the time. Hellman,
however, made the point that the overriding theme of the play, based on a true
story from Scotland, was the power of a lie to ruin the careers of these two
women. The outcome for the controversial drama was a run of 700 performances on Broadway, making it one of the most successful dramas of 1935.

Although Hellman would write only 11 more plays, among them was *The
Little Foxes* about the deception, mistrust and greed of a southern family, the
Hubbards, at the turn of the century. The show opened on Broadway in 1939
and was a major hit, leading to the movie adaptation, the same year. Starring

Bette Davis, the film was nominated for nine Academy Awards, but didn't win any in the year of *Gone with the Wind*, *The Wizard of Oz* and *Mr. Chips Goes to Washington*. She would later write about the Hubbard family again in her 1946 drama, *Another Part of the Forest*. Hellman moved to screenwriting throughout the '40s, and her works included *Watch on the Rhine*.

Throughout her life, Lillian Hellman remained active in social causes, and although she claims she never officially joined the Communist or Socialist parties, like many of the Jewish writers and performers of the thirties and forties, she remained very much to the political left. Hellman took part in, or supported, the activities of groups with liberal agendas. This would later catch up with her during the Communist witch-hunts of the early 1950s.

SIDNEY KINGSLEY

Another Jewish playwright from New York City, Sidney Kingsley was born in 1906 and grew up with an interest in theater. At Cornell University in the 1920s, he pursued his interest by writing for the school's drama club.

Kingsley's first play, *Men in White*, as noted earlier, was performed by Group Theater in 1933 and became one of their earliest hits. The show also garnered Kingsley a Pulitzer Prize. His next several plays would focus on social issues that included ghetto housing and anti-war sentiments. His historical drama, while the United States was engaged in World War II, called *The Patriots*, opened in 1943 and was highly acclaimed. The play, chronicling the rivalry between Thomas Jefferson and Alexander Hamilton at the turn of the 19th century, was well received by audiences at a time when the nation was focusing on patriotism, democracy and seeking the strength necessary to achieve victory in World War II. *The Patriots* ran on Broadway for 173 performances.

After a brief post-war stint in Hollywood, Kingsley would return to write for Broadway in the 1950s. His dramatic works included *Darkness at Noon*, based on Arthur Koestler's novel about the Moscow Show Trials of 1938 and Communism.

Broadway During the War Years

Clearly, the war years took their toll on Broadway as many young men were called into military service and many women were doing their part to help the war efforts at home. Funding for Broadway shows was hard to secure and, still reeling from the depression years, more and more people were opting for a less expensive form of entertainment, the movies. What was at one time over 250 productions staged in the late 1920s was now down to 72 Broadway shows in the 1940–41season. Some theaters were even forced to shut down, while others were transformed into movie houses and even used promotions like "free dish nights" to attract customers. This promotional idea lasted through the war years and on into the 1950s and featured one piece from a set of dishes given away to each paying customer. To make matters worse, the area around Broadway, particularly 42nd Street, was featuring burlesque shows and becoming a haven for prostitution, gambling and other undesirable activities, making it less appealing for theatergoers to attend shows at night.

The war nonetheless brought together the people of the United States, including the left and right-wingers, who stood behind their nation. More than half a million Jewish soldiers were part of the United States Armed Forces and fought in World War II. In support of the war effort, the American Theater Wing recruited numerous volunteers, many from the Broadway shows. The Shubert Brothers donated their 44th Street Theater, and this became home to the Stage Door Canteen, which was opened by the Theater Wing to provide food and entertainment for the servicemen on leave from the war. Thousands of servicemen from all over the world visited the famed Stage Door Canteen, and many of the Broadway performers of the era donated their time to sing, dance or put on sketches. In time, there were nine stage door canteens operating in several cities and in three countries, all helping lift the spirits of the Allied troops. By late 1945, after the war, when the stage door canteens ran their final shows, it was estimated that some 20 million servicemen and personnel helping the war effort had been entertained by the dedicated volunteers while having a meal or at least a cup of coffee.

A series of sketches presented to factory workers, also doing their part for the war effort, was another part of the Theater Wing's dedication to helping during the war years. Featuring Broadway actors, along with various other singers, dancers and comics, these shows, called *Lunchtime Follies*, became very popular. The shows, while entertaining, also served to rally workers behind the common cause. Moss Hart was one among a number of Broadway writers to volunteer to write for the *Lunchtime Follies*.

Across the country, the Hollywood Canteen was also providing servicemen with food and entertainment. John Garfield and Bette Davis were instrumental in launching this West Coast version of the Stage Door Canteen. Garfield had attempted to enlist in the military on two occasions but was turned down due to heart damage.

The United Service Organization (USO) was also instrumental in providing the servicemen with entertainment, starting with Camp Shows in 1941, and the government gave ample support to the cause. Many stage and screen performers joined in on these performances staged in various parts of the world.

While some of Broadway's finest were doing what they could to entertain the servicemen in these difficult times, others were serving in the military. Among the half-million Jewish troops serving in World War II were several names that would be featured prominently in Broadway's future, including Mel Brooks (*The Producers*), who saw action de-activating mines in the Battle of the Bulge, Neil Simon (who wrote more than 20 Broadway hits including *Biloxi Blues* about his World War II military training) and Sid Caesar (*Little Me*).

Meanwhile, despite the falling number of shows, there were still nearly 11 million people, including many servicemen on leave, taking in Broadway shows in 1943. Along with Irving Berlin's patriotic hit, *This Is the Army,* another show featuring a significant number of military personnel was called *Winged Victory.* Written and directed by Moss Hart, *Winged Victory* ran for 212 performances at the 44th Street Theater. *Something for the Boys*, featuring plenty of singing and dancing designed to boost the morale of American troops, saw nearly 450 performances before being made into a film. Of course there were also mainstream favorites, such as another version of Ziegfeld's perennial follies, which in 1943 starred Milton Berle. At age 35, Berle was in the prime of his long career and provided much-needed comedy during a very stressful time. The 1943 version of the Follies played over 550 performances.

Daniel Kaye Kominsk, the son of Jewish-Ukrainian immigrants, better known as Danny Kaye, was also making audiences laugh on Broadway in the early '40s in the Kurt Weill, Ira Gershwin, Moss Hart comedy *Lady in the Dark,* which ran for more than 450 performances at the Alvin Theater. Kaye then starred in the Cole Porter, Herbert and Dorothy Fields comedy *Let's Face It,* which delighted audiences for more than 550 performances. The show included some songs written by Kaye's wife, songwriter Sylvia Fine, who became well known for writing very witty, extremely fast-paced songs for her husband and other performers.

Coming off his classic role as the cowardly lion in *The Wizard of Oz,* Bert Lahr was another Jewish performer from New York City who entertained audiences during the war years. Born Irving Lahrheim, the young actor dropped out of school at 15 to make a name for himself on the burlesque circuit in the 1920s and soon made it to Broadway in the 1927 show *Harry Delmar's Revels.* He was in a number of revues in the 1930s including some of Ziegfeld's, and in the 1940s, he was featured in *Seven Lively Arts, Meet the People* and *Make Mine Manhattan.* While he would forever be immortalized as the cowardly lion,

Lahr was regarded as one of the all-time great clowns of American theater, continuing the Jewish humor of the early days of Yiddish theater and certainly of vaudeville as well as the Jewish clowning that had been prevalent in Europe in the previous century. Later on in his long career, Lahr would also take on some serious roles, such as appearing in *Waiting for Godot*. However, he was best remembered on Broadway for his comedy.

A musical talent to make his mark on Broadway during the war years was composer Kurt Julian Weill, born in the Jewish quarter of Dessau, Germany, in 1900. By the age of 15, Weill was adept at the piano and already studying music composition, music theory and conducting. By the early 1930s, he had established himself as a successful composer in Germany. Being Jewish, however, Weill was forced to flee from Nazi rule in 1933 and settled in Paris. Just two years later Weill and his wife made their way to New York City, where he adapted his works to suit the American style of musicals.

Weill's string of Broadway hits would begin in the late '30s with *Knickerbocker Holiday* opening at the Ethel Barrymore Theater. He would follow with several successful shows through the '40s including *Lady in the Dark*, with Ira Gershwin and Moss Hart, *One Touch of Venus, Street Scene* by Elmer Rice and *Love Life* and *Lost in the Stars*. Sadly, Weill, who, like many others, joined in the volunteer efforts during the war years, died of a heart attack in 1950. It was a few years later that his *Threepenny Opera* would emerge as a huge Broadway hit. The show had made its way to Broadway very briefly in 1933 after being triumphant throughout Europe. It opened in March of 1954 and ran for some 2,611 performances, making it, at the time, the most successful musical of all time. The show featured the "Ballad of Mack the Knife."

While Weill and other Jewish composers, lyricists, playwrights, directors and performers teamed up in many configurations throughout the '30s and '40s, there was one successful show during the war years that brought together four highly significant new talents to the Great White Way. *On the Town*, which opened during the end of the year holiday season of 1944 and introduced the writing team of Betty Comden and Adolph Green, the music of Leonard Bernstein and the choreography of Jerome Robbins to Broadway.

COMDEN AND GREEN

The musical writing team of Betty Comden and Adolph Green stepped into the spotlight with *On the Town*, only they did it from offstage, both having had less than stellar acting careers. It would serve as the debut for one of the greatest musical teams in Broadway history. While many thought they were married on one another, they were not. Comden and Green were essentially a

New York–born writing team who met in 1938 through mutual friends and went on to write numerous hits for Broadway and later on for Hollywood.

Both frustrated by their lack of acting roles, they formed their own acting troupe that performed in Greenwich Village at a club called the Village Vanguard. While their shows were well received, they both became tired of trying to find material that they wanted to perform on stage. Therefore, they decided to try their hand at writing music and lyrics for their own shows. At some of their shows, Green invited his musician friend Leonard Bernstein to accompany them on piano. It was Bernstein, however, who invited them to work on the book for his ballet entitled *Fancy Free*, which he had composed with a young choreographer named Jerome Robbins. From this ballet, a Broadway musical emerged with a simple plotline about three sailors on shore leave pursuing three young women around New York City. This simple show, renamed *On the Town*, featured music, dancing and an optimistic love of life that made it the triumphant musical hit of 1945 at the Adelphi Theater. The show also featured the classic song "New York, New York" and had Comden and Green performing on stage as part of the original cast. *On the Town* would enjoy two revivals and become a major motion picture as well.

Comden and Green would go on to write *Billion Dollar Baby* in the same year, 1945, and collaborate with Bernstein again in 1953 on *Wonderful Town*, also about life in New York City, with an un-credited Jerome Robbins handling choreography along with the legendary George Abbott. *Wonderful Town*, starring Rosalind Russell, ran for over 550 performances at the Winter Garden Theater. Among the subsequent Broadway musicals from the team of Comden and Green were *Two on the Aisle, Peter Pan, Subways Are for Sleeping*, and the huge 1956 hit *Bells Are Ringing*, in which they once again teamed with Robbins on a show set in New York City. *Bells* rang for over 900 performances at the Shubert Theater. Comden and Green will be discussed again in later chapters, as I had the honor of teaming with them on the 1991 musical *Will Rogers Follies*.

LEONARD BERNSTEIN

On the Town also brought a 27-year-old Leonard Bernstein to Broadway. The son of Russian-Jewish immigrants, Bernstein, born in 1918, learned to play piano in his early teens. Despite lack of encouragement from his father, who wanted his son to pursue other interests, Bernstein followed his dream and honed his musical talents, studying at Harvard and other universities. Encouraged by Aaron Copland among others, he wrote his first symphony, *Jeremiah*, in 1943. He would soon land a job at the New York Philharmonic as an assistant conductor. However, in late 1943, Bernstein got his break, filling in one evening for conductor Bruno Walter, who took ill. Conducting the New York Philharmonic orchestra over network radio in a critically acclaimed concert made Bernstein an overnight sensation.

Bernstein went on to become a legendary conductor, but also received his fair share of well-deserved critical acclaim for composing several Broadway musicals. Following *On the Town*, Bernstein wrote the music and lyrics for a musical version of J. M. Barrie's *Peter Pan*. Then came *Wonderful Town* for which Bernstein won a Tony Award, and a musical version of Voltaire's satire *Candide* that came and went quickly in its initial run on Broadway before returning for a successful revival in 1974. Of course *West Side Story* would immortalize Leonard Bernstein on Broadway and in film, rounding out what would be one of the most significant musical careers in American history.

Leonard Bernstein never lost touch with his Jewish identity that was instilled in him at an early age through his parents. His 1943 symphony, *Jeremiah,* was about the story of the Jewish prophet who wrote about the destruction of the first temple and the exile of the Jewish people into slavery. In 1945 he was commissioned by the Park Avenue Synagogue in New York City to write a liturgy for the Sabbath service, which was entitled *Hashkiveinu,* and in 1961 he wrote a symphony called *Kaddish.* While he maintained a secular quality in most of his compositions, Bernstein's work was influenced by Jewish history and stories from the Old Testament.

JEROME ROBBINS

The fourth of the luminaries to emerge from *On the Town* as a major Broadway force was Jerome Robbins, who today is considered by many as the first and foremost name associated with Broadway choreography. Robbins would move with his family at an early age to Weehawken, New Jersey, where his father and uncle opened a corset business. In a short time the corset business became known to the show business community, especially the vaudeville circuit. The young Jerome, however, was not interested in the family business but instead studied at the New Dance League, learning ballet, modern dance and Spanish dancing with the renowned Helen Veola, as well as dance composition and choreography under the great Bessie Schonberg.

In 1940, Robbins became part of the Ballet Theater, now known as the American Ballet Theater. This began a 12-year dance career in which he would join the New York City Ballet. It was also during this time that he would choreograph *Fancy Free* for Ballet Theatre and then make his foray onto Broadway with *On the Town*.

Robbins would go on to fuse classical ballet with the exuberance and energy of Broadway dance as he worked on a host of shows through the late '40s including *Billion Dollar Baby, High Button Shoes* for which he won a Tony Award, *Miss Liberty, Call Me Madam* and *Look Ma, I'm Dancing.* In the '50s, he would join forces with Rodgers and Hammerstein on *The King and I* and became known as the choreographer for some of Broadway's all-time classic shows including *West Side Story, Fiddler on the Roof, Gypsy* and *Funny Girl.* He won critical acclaim time and time again for bringing a dynamic energy and something new to the dance sequences in each of these shows. "He was," as the *New York Times* dance critic Anna Kisselgoff wrote, "the first major American-born classical choreographer."[5]

Interestingly, while the name Rabinowitz translates to "son of a rabbi," Jerome elected to change his name. Robbins felt that the name made him known as the son of an immigrant. From breaking down in tears at his Bar Mitzvah unable to finish, to entering into ballet, which was not a very Jewish world, Robbins was, according to his biographers, uncomfortable being Jewish. Like Bernstein and many other performers of the era, he was also at odds with his father over his choice of career, choosing dance over more "practical" options.

However, unlike Bernstein, Robbins spent years moving away from his Jewish heritage. For many years he struggled with his Jewish identity as well as with his own sexual orientation. In time, Robbins would eventually come to embrace his Jewish background, leading to his enthusiasm for bringing *Fiddler on the Roof* to the stage and embarking on Jewish works for the New York City Ballet. In fact, in his travels throughout the 1950s he went to Israel where he played an important role in strengthening the nation's dance scene. He also became comfortable with his sexuality and being openly gay.

Broadway After the War

The neighborhood around the theater district continued to deteriorate after World War II. Many young, naive American soldiers had returned with newfound sexual prowess having been in parts of Europe and Asia where young prostitutes were eager to please American servicemen. As a result, the area on and around 42nd Street became a haven for pornography and prostitution, which certainly did not help the legitimate theaters in the area. In addition, the newfound popularity of television gave potential theatergoers a form of no-cost home entertainment. The result was bleak for Broadway. Despite the enormous success of *Annie Get Your Gun,* which opened in 1946 and played for more than 1,100 performances, the theater district was struggling. Shows were costly to stage, with a musical running up a bill of over $200,000 for a full-scale production. As a result, more theaters opted to show movies. By 1948 there was an 80 percent unemployment rate for Broadway actors and the respective employees who worked in the theaters. By 1949, the number of new shows hit a three-decade low of 57.

One manner in which Broadway drew some attention was by establishing the Tony Awards. Named for actress, director, producer and co-founder of the American Theater Wing, Antoinette Perry, who had recently died, the awards commenced in April of 1947 with a ceremony held at the Waldorf Astoria hotel, later to be moved to Radio City Music Hall. While the Tony Awards did not bring instant attention to a widespread audience, as they became a prestigious annual event and they gave the theater community confidence that Broadway would be on the rebound very soon.

With *South Pacific* enjoying phenomenal success, the 1940s drew to a close. It was a devastating decade with a war the likes of which the world had never seen. The war did, however, bring America together in a united effort, which was unparalleled in the nation's history. The patriotism of Irving Berlin, the Jewish performers rallying the country through their participation in the Bergson Group and by volunteering their time and effort during the war years, and of course the half-million Jewish-American soldiers, stemmed the tide of anti–Semitism that was growing in the 1930s. The children of Jewish immigrants had indeed assimilated into mainstream America. They had fought side by side with soldiers of all nationalities, while also helping with the war efforts on the home front. The "children of immigrants" label had finally disappeared.

Numerous second-generation American Jews had also made a major impact upon Broadway as composers, lyricists, writers and performers. While many had changed their names, most still embraced their Jewish heritage, and many continued, in the years after the war, to provide assistance to the millions of displaced families and veterans who served.

As Broadway ushered in the 1950s with the mega-hits *Guys and Dolls* and *The King and I*, another battle was emerging within America. Despite being allies with the United States during the war, Communism once again took center stage as the ideology in the Soviet Union. As a result, anti–Communism moved to the ideological center of American politics.

As author Ellen Schrecker wrote, "The Cold War transformed domestic Communism from a matter of political opinion to one of national security. As the United States' hostility toward the Soviet Union intensified, members of the Communist party came increasingly to be viewed as potential enemy agents."[6] Such intense scrutiny would impact the careers of numerous celebrities, including many Jewish writers and performers whose liberal views came under attack. In the next chapter, we look more closely at the effects of McCarthyism and the anti–Communism crusade on the Broadway community.

5

From Communism
to the Catskills

"Are you now, or have you ever been, a member of the Communist Party?"
From politicians to performers to average Americans, people throughout the
United States were being questioned and in some cases accused of being Communist sympathizers in a nation that had succumbed to a new wave of post–
World War II paranoia. The Soviet Union, in the early 1950s, was now emerging
as a powerful rival in its quest to challenge the United States as an economic,
military and political world leader. Since the Soviet Union was a Communist
nation (with China soon to follow), a rising fear in the late 1940s grew among
American citizens and by the 1950s it had swept over the nation with the misguided belief that, like a disease, Communism could spread quickly and take
over American ideology. The mere idea that anyone living amongst us could
be a Communist sparked fear and panic. Young Republican senator Joseph
McCarthy, from Wisconsin, took it upon himself to lead a crusade in hopes of
finding and weeding out those who were Communists. The result was a witch
hunt in which anyone who was believed to have subversive ideas, or be associated with left-wing political organizations, was called in to testify before the
anti–Communism committee. In fact, in 1951 Senator McCarthy even charged
that President Truman was a Communist agent.

Caught in this frenzied hunt for Communism were both writers and performers primarily in Hollywood, but also in New York. Among them were
many Jewish celebrities who had been outspoken in their criticism of the government, and some of whom were followers of Communist ideas, if not actually
members of the Party. These were idealists, not extremists, who challenged
the norms and spoke out, as the Jewish people had been known to do for centuries. They spoke out against intolerance and social injustice. Communism
was initially a socioeconomic ideology, which was later used in foreign countries as a means of strict government control, as was the case in the Soviet

Union. This was not part of the agenda of those who believed in the basic ideology. Nonetheless, many people were branded as Communists, and as a result they were blacklisted and unable to find work. Among the names listed as Communist sympathizers were Leonard Bernstein, composer Mark Blitzstein, John Garfield, Arthur Laurents, Arthur Miller, Zero Mostel, Edward G. Robinson, Lillian Hellman and several of the Group Theater members including Luther and Stella Adler, Henry Morgan, Clifford Odets and Elia Kazan. In all, over 300 performers, writers, composers and others in show business were blacklisted. Some returned to their careers in a few years, while others lost their careers entirely, some of whom died in poverty after resorting to alcohol.

It was Lillian Hellman, in particular, who attracted a great deal of attention from the House Un-American Activities Committee (HUAC), which, although established in the late 1930s, had risen to great prominence in the early '50s because of the widespread pursuit of Communists. Today, Hellman's body of work remains highly respected, and she maintains her place as one of the most significant playwrights of the 20th century. However, her strong liberal views made her a primary target in the Communist witch hunt. In fact, her FBI files, reportedly, consisted of 307 pages. As it turned out, Hellman was never officially tried, nor was there evidence that she ever posed a threat to the United States government in any manner. Nonetheless, prior to World War II, according to her FBI files, Hellman was under surveillance. The books and magazines she read, the organizations she belonged to and whom she associated with were all being monitored. Obviously her plays were also dissected for their underlying social meaning. *Watch on the Rhine*, which enjoyed a run of 378 performances on Broadway, was among the plays most carefully scrutinized, as well as *The Little Foxes* and some of her screenplays. And, as was the case with the Communist pursuit of the time, phrases, nuances and even characters could be easily misconstrued in favor of the argument the FBI and "Red hunters" wished to make. Even her memoirs would infuriate the extreme anti–Communists, reporting on whom she talked to and the organizations she supported. To make matters worse, *The Daily Worker*, the Communist Party newspaper, gave a very favorable review to *Watch on the Rhine*. Of the numerous positive reviews, the play, and subsequent film, received in newspapers coast to coast, this was the one that J. Edgar Hoover, the FBI and the Hellman haters would acknowledge. Hellman made it clear in a letter to the House Un-American Activities Committee that she was not about to change who she was or what she believed. She stated in her letter, "I cannot and will not cut my conscience to fit this year's fashions."[1]

Of course, it was more than just Hellman's work being scrutinized. There were some 50,000 members of the Communist Party in the United States in the 1940s. It was not illegal to join, nor was there great objection in the 1930s or during the war years of the '40s when the United States and the Soviet Union were allies. Conservatives were distrustful of those who aligned with the Communist party, even if they were not members, but by and large, most Americans remained indifferent until McCarthy began his crusade.

In 1947, HUAC began calling witnesses from Hollywood, believing some to be planting the seeds of anti–American activities in their work. The majority of those questioned refused to name names. Others who were summoned, such as Walt Disney, testified to HUAC that the threat of Communists in the film industry was indeed a serious one. Meanwhile, Danny Kaye was among several actors who started a group called the Committee for the First Amendment. The group protested in Washington against the attacks on the entertainment industry.

While McCarthyism and the paranoia that surrounded this dark period in American history would last only a short time in the early 1950s, the results would have lasting effects on many people in the entertainment industry. For playwright Arthur Miller, the Communist pursuit was very reminiscent of those

"THE WORLD OF
SHOLOM ALEICHEM"
(IN ENGLISH)
——— NEXT WEEK ———
LUTHER ADLER in "A VIEW FROM
THE BRIDGE"
BY ARTHUR MILLER

TICKETS ON SALE NOW!   Write or Phone GE 1-4555
TUES. THRU SUN. EVES. $3.85, 3.00, 2.00   SAT. EVE. $4.20, 3.40, 2.40
THURS. SAT. MATS. $2.20, 1.65, 1.10   REDUCED RATES FOR THEATRE PARTIES
                                        BOOK NOW!

AMPLE FREE PARKING

Arnold Perl's *The World of Sholom Aleichem*, which has been referred to as a grab bag of shtetl folklore, features stories from beloved Yiddish writer Sholem Aleichem. The play first opened in 1953, cast almost entirely with actors who had been blacklisted. Many productions later, it would eventually make it to Broadway, briefly, in 1982 (Museum of the City of New York).

that he recalled from American history classes. The Salem witch hunts of the 17th century were also spurred on by a growing paranoia and misguided beliefs that witches were actually living amongst the people of Salem, Massachusetts. Not unlike what was happening in Washington, D.C., the people of Salem were being found guilty on minimal evidence and hearsay. For Miller these similarities proved to be the impetus for the classic and very timely play, *The Crucible*, first brought to the Broadway stage in 1953. Of course the guise of the Salem witch hunts didn't get past the devout anti–Communists. In 1956, Miller was called in for questioning by HUAC. He refused to go along with the modern-day witch hunt and was convicted of contempt of Congress for not giving the names of peers who were assumed to be Communists.

Arthur Miller

Born in 1915 to Polish-Jewish immigrants in New York City, Arthur Miller grew up in East Harlem and later in Brooklyn before going off to the University of Michigan. It was in college that Miller wrote his first two plays, *The Villain* and *Honors at Dawn*, both of which garnered awards.

After college, Miller took on several jobs while writing his first Broadway play, *The Man Who Had All the Luck*, which opened and closed in 1944. While the play essentially bombed on Broadway, it did win a Theater Guild Award. It was Miller's second play, *All My Sons*, that generated significant attention as his first Broadway hit. The play, based on a true story, focused on an imprisoned man who, along with his partner, had sold faulty cylinders to the United States Army, resulting in the crashing of 21 planes. The story illustrated how his family, partner and others in his life coped with his actions, including his son who killed himself rather than living with the knowledge of what his father had done. The dramatic/tragic play not only ran on Broadway for 328 performances, but also won a Tony Award. In addition, it drew the attention of HUAC, concerned about the story of a traitor to the American cause.

Miller's next play, *Death of a Salesman*, emerged as one of the greatest American dramas ever written—if not *the* greatest. Opening in 1949, *Death of a Salesman* would not only enjoy an initial run of 742 performances on Broadway, but would also be performed at all levels of theater, from professional productions to high school presentations, for decades to come. It was the first play to win a Tony Award, New York Drama Circle Critics' Award and Pulitzer Prize for Drama. Willy Loman would become a household name as the tragic play later showed up on the reading lists of schools coast to coast. Miller even directed *Death of a Salesman* at the People's Art Theatre in Beijing, China, in

The

PLAYBILL

for the Morosco Theatre

Death of a Salesman

Arthur Miller's *Death of a Salesman* opened in February of 1949, with Lee J. Cobb introducing the role of Willy Loman to Broadway theatergoers. The classic drama would return to Broadway five times, while remaining a staple in regional theaters and school productions (courtesy Playbill Inc.).

1983. On Broadway, the play would return four more times, as of 2012, and Willy Loman would be played by Lee J. Cobb, George C. Scott, Brian Dennehy, Phillip Seymour and Dustin Hoffman.

When Dustin Hoffman stepped into one of the most noteworthy roles in American theater, as Willy Loman in the highly received 1984 revival, it was only his fifth time on Broadway in a brilliant career that has now spanned six decades.

It took the California-born-and-raised Hoffman only a few years to make the transition from the Pasadena Playhouse to Broadway in an original 1961 comedy called *Cook for the General*. The play ran for only 28 performances, but it was an inauspicious start to a career that would take off with the 1968 Mike Nichols film *The Graduate*. Once considered too short to succeed as an actor, Dustin Hoffman would proceed to land leading roles in films such as *Midnight Cowboy, Lenny, Papillion, All the President's Men, Kramer vs. Kramer, Tootsie, Rain Man,* and *Meet the Fockers.*

Meanwhile, Hoffman was able to find occasional moments to step away from the film sets and onto the New York stages. Not long after his breakthrough in *The Graduate*, he landed his first starring role on Broadway as Jimmy Shine, in the play of the same name. Six years later, he tried his hand as a director for the comedy farce *All Over Town*. In the late 1980s, Hoffman returned to Broadway one last time, taking on the role of the Jewish moneylender Shylock in *The Merchant of Venice*, a role first brought to Broadway in 1903 by the legendary Yiddish theater actor Jacob Adler.

As for Arthur Miller, despite the enormous fame and monetary success from *Death of a Salesman*, Miller would soon find himself shocked and saddened by the actions of one of his closest associates. Just three years after the debut of the play, Elia Kazan, who had directed the classic drama, and with whom Miller had been close friends for many years, went before the HUAC and provided the names of others whom he believed to be Communist sympathizers, including Hellman, Odets and Edward G. Robinson. Miller, who in good conscience could never risk destroying the careers of those around him, could not forgive Kazan, and they did not speak for many years.

The episode with Kazan, and the activities of Senator Joseph McCarthy, however, set Miller on the path to writing his next play, which, like *Salesman*, would emerge as a literary classic, and also a must read for American students, even today. As mentioned earlier, Miller likened the Communist witch hunts of the 1950s with the Salem witch hunts of the late 1600s, and the result was *The Crucible*, which opened in 1953 and won a Tony Award for best play.

Also, as noted earlier, *The Crucible* infuriated those on the anti–Communist crusades and eventually brought Miller before the Committee under the agreement that he would answer questions pertaining only to his own activities. Nonetheless, the Committee still asked Miller to name names of other Communist sympathizers, but unlike Kazan, he refused. For this, Miller was denied a passport, fined and sentenced to 30 days in prison. The ruling, however, was overturned because it was determined that the Committee had misled Miller, essentially telling him that there would be no repercussions for his appearance at the hearing.

Throughout the '60s, Miller would continue to bring plays to Broadway, including *After the Fall, Incident at Vichy* and *The Price*. He would then open plays in other parts of the country while also writing for television, as well as screenplays. Until his death in 2005, at the age of 89, Miller was still writing. While he never again could achieve the acclaim and success of *Death of a Salesman* or *The Crucible*, Miller was a master of modern tragedy, bringing intense dramas, often based on true stories, to the stage through characters wrestling with social and personal conflicts. Miller was very aware of social injustice, as evidenced in his works and in his life. He was adept at articulating his social, moral and political convictions. He even denounced anti–Semitism in a 1945 novel called *Focus,* which he did not turn into a play.

Miller also generated attention for his marriage to film legend Marilyn Monroe in 1956. The two had met some six years earlier and reportedly had an affair while Miller was married to his first wife, Mary Slattery, to whom he was married for 16 years. Of course as Stephen J. Whitfield noted in his article titled "The Cultural Cold War as History," those in disfavor of Miller wrote headlines such as "Pinko Playwright Weds Sex Goddess." Nonetheless, Monroe, who converted to Judaism shortly before marrying Miller, stood by him, risking her own career, through the congressional hearings and subsequent sentencing. Their marriage lasted only five years. He would subsequently marry Inge Morath just a year after he and Monroe separated. Miller and Morath would remain married until her death some 40 years later.

Not only was Miller the most important playwright of the 1950s, but arguably the most significant American playwright of the 20th century. Miller's works earned him the Pulitzer Prize and seven Tony Awards. He holds honorary doctorate degrees from Oxford University and Harvard University. Above and beyond this, his works continue to have significant influence. They have been (and still are) discussed, debated, translated and interpreted by students worldwide.

In fact, just as modern-day witch hunts continue in societies around the world, reminding us of Miller's *Crucible,* one of his earliest Broadway productions from 1947, *All My Sons* ties in closely with recent stories of General Motors. Miller's play focuses on Joe Keller, a businessman who lied to his sons and others about faulty airplane cylinder heads used during World War II, which were made by his company. As a result of the faulty parts, which Keller knew about, 21 American pilots were killed and Keller's business partner ended up taking the rap and going to prison. The play, which was revived on Broadway in 2008, starring John Lithgow, Dianne Wiest, and Katie Holmes, was typical of Miller's work, which brought moral, ethical, and controversial dilemmas to the forefront that are still relevant today, as evidenced when real-life stories mirror theater, such as the General Motors headlines. It was widely reported that flawed automobile ignition switches, which General

I was able to grab this shot with one of the greatest American playwrights, Arthur Miller, left (photograph by Anita Shevette).

Motors knew about for years, caused the deaths of over 120 people. Recalls were finally made in 2014.

Zero Mostel

Along with Hellman and Miller, another of the many blacklisted celebrities was one of the most talented and respected performers ever to grace the stages of Broadway.

The son of Jewish immigrant parents, Samuel Joel Mostel was born in Brooklyn in 1915. However, like many stars of Yiddish theater, vaudeville and Broadway, he and his seven brothers and sisters would grow up on the Lower East Side of Manhattan. Mostel's father, a rabbi, wanted his son to follow in his footsteps. Mostel, however, was interested in art and began painting and drawing at an early age. His love of art would continue for years, and after college he would be accepted to NYU's challenging Master's art program. Mostel, however, also had a gift for comedy and began performing at private parties and various functions in New York, which soon led to nightclub performances and radio shows. In the early 1940s, Mostel even landed in a couple of Broadway revues in small roles before heading overseas during the war to perform for the U.S. troops.

By the 1950s, Mostel's comic genius was generating attention, not only from audiences, but from the House Committee on Un-American Activities. It seemed that Mostel mocked the red scare and the seriousness of the anti–Communist investigations. Of course this only angered those chasing down Communists. But it was one of his own, show business colleague Jerome Robbins, who actually went so far as to name Mostel as a Communist. The result was that Mostel was brought before the Committee. Like Miller, he refused to name names while also denying that he was a Communist Party member. While no charges were ever leveled at Mostel, he was blacklisted in the industry and denied work for several years. As a result, to make ends meet, he sold paintings and found work in smaller Off Broadway productions where "blacklisting" was irrelevant.

Mostel would finally find his way off the blacklist when he was asked to perform in the play *Rhinoceros*, written by absurdist playwright Eugene Ionesco, in which almost everyone in the cast is transformed into a rhinoceros. There have been various interpretations of this thought-provoking work which to some portrayed the universe as being ultimately meaningless, irrational, and absurd. Others saw it as an allegory for the spread of Nazism in Germany in the 1930s. While the play sparked much philosophical debate, it brought Mostel a Tony Award and drew the attention of producer Harold Prince, who asked Mostel to be in his upcoming musical, *A Funny Thing Happened on the Way to the Forum*. There was one problem with casting of Mostel in the show. George Abbott was directing along with Jerome Robbins. Mostel and Robbins had not been in contact since Robbins had named him as a Communist. Mostel, however agreed to work on the show even though it meant working with Robbins. Rumor has it that at the first rehearsal, the tension was thick as the two entered the same room. "Robbins made the rounds of the cast, shaking hands. When he got to Mostel, there was silence. Then Mostel boomed, 'Hiya, Loose Lips!'"[2] This evoked laughter from those on the set and served to minimize the tension.

Forum opened in May of 1962 and played nearly 1,000 performances. The tremendous team of Stephen Sondheim, Burt Shevelove and Larry Gelbart, plus Harold Prince, along with Abbott and Robbins produced this comedy, inspired by the works of Titus Maccius Plautus who wrote humorous plays in ancient Rome back around 200 B.C. The lead role of the slave Pseudolus went to Mostel, who supposedly wasn't the first choice. Apparently both Phil Silvers and Milton Berle were ahead of Mostel in line for the role. Mostel would not only shine in the role, but won his second Tony Award.

Of course Mostel would go on to greater heights, and another Tony Award in *Fiddler on the Roof*, which will be discussed in greater length in the next chapter. Zero Mostel, who died in 1977 of a heart attack while working on a musical called *The Merchant*, based on the famed Shakespearian character Shylock from *The Merchant of Venice*, was one of the most extraordinary performers in Broadway history. His command of the stage, ability to handle a dramatic or comedic role with the same exuberance and his resounding singing voice won him consistently high acclaim from critics, applause from audiences and respect from his peers, three goals of any actor.

Jack and Madeline Lee Gilford

Both Jack and Madeline Lee Gilford also saw their careers derailed by the anti–Communist express. Born Jacob Aaron Gellman to Jewish immigrant parents in 1908 on the Lower East side of Manhattan, Jack Gilford had a knack for impressions from an early age, especially odd ones like pea soup coming to a boil. In time, he would develop his own night club act and soon became the emcee at a café in Greenwich Village where Zero Mostel (with whom he became good friends) and jazz great Billie Holiday performed.

Gilford went on to make his Broadway debut in the musical revue *Meet the People* in 1940 and followed it with *They Should Have Stood in Bed* in 1943. It was also in the '40s that he met his wife to be, Madeline Lee Lederman. Both were married at the time, and they divorced their respective spouses to be together. Madeline Lee, some 15 years younger than Gilford, was also an up and coming performer, born to Polish-Jewish immigrants living in the Bronx.

It was, however, just as Jack was making headway on Broadway and Madeline Lee was building her own following in radio and on stage that the brakes were put on their respective careers. Jerome Robbins named the Gilfords as Communists, based on their passion for social change and their strong support for labor unions. For most of the decade, Madeline Lee and Jack struggled to get work. Gilford did make the best of his Off Broadway status, drawing attention for his roles in *The World of Sholem Aleichem* and *Once Upon a Mattress*, in which he teamed with Carol Burnett. While Gilford, like his buddy Mostel, found low-paying work in Off Broadway shows, he did manage to land a Broadway role in *The Diary of Anne Frank*. But such roles were hard to come by. It took Gilford nearly a decade to re-emerge from his blacklisting and finally hit his stride on the Broadway stage in *A Funny Thing Happened on the Way to the Forum,* with Mostel. That success was followed by *Cabaret.* While Gilford went on to film and television roles for years to come, Madeline Lee was essentially out of the business for years, in part because of the blacklisting and later to raise their three children. She returned in the 1990s as a producer.

Who Were They Really After?

As it was, many Jewish-American artists were, and still are, to the left on political matters. While the hunt for Communists was not aimed at any one cultural or religious group, the liberal-minded Jews were among those most clearly targeted.

From the early years of film, first in Astoria, Queens and New Jersey, and later in Hollywood, California, it was evident that the Jewish people played a significant role in the entertainment industry. It was a new industry in the United States and as such, not controlled by a particular ethnic group. So, when the anti–Communist crusades began after the Second World War, with a major focus on the entertainment industry, the question was raised as to whether the House Un-American Activities Committee was really after the Communists or after the influential Jews in show business. It was evident that many Jewish writers and performers were then, and still are, outspoken about social issues, but were they Communists? And if so, were they actually dangerous?

The question was, "Are you now, or have you ever been, a Communist?" Some, like author Michael Freedland, whose book *Witch Hunt in Hollywood* (JR Books, 2009) explores the subject in detail, believe the question could have been "Are you now or have you ever been a Jew?" Freedland is among those who point to the attack on Hollywood celebrities as an opportunity to get the Jews who were so prominent in the entertainment world. And while non–Jews were certainly called to testify, the number of Jews was disproportionately high considering the overall Jewish population in the nation at that time. The first ten Hollywood writers, known as the Hollywood Ten, were jailed for not providing the names of their alleged Communist peers. Six of the ten were Jewish.

Freedland also points out, in his book, that Congressman John Rankin made a speech denouncing Communism and consisting almost entirely of Jewish names. He read many of the real names of those changed by Jewish performers, as if to implicate some secret agenda, as opposed to not wanting to appear too ethnic for fear of not getting work. Freedland mentioned Larry Adler, a blacklisted musician who recalled a letter from Rankin that started with the words "Dear Kike," a derogatory term for Jews, which emanated from the Jewish immigrants who used to sign their name by drawing a circle, rather than an "x" which was too much like a cross. The Yiddish word for circle was keikl, so they became known as Kikes, much as other minorities were given other names, most of which were later considered derogatory.

While Broadway was not a direct target, being much smaller than the Hollywood studios, the effect was felt by the absence of performers and playwrights. However, unlike the studio system, where the Jewish executives were being scrutinized and feared for their own businesses, Broadway producers had greater freedom to hire as they chose. As a result, blacklisting, while having an effect, did not have the same impact as it did in Hollywood.

Nonetheless, the question still persists: were the anti–Communists going after the Jews? While stories of anti–Semitism were less prevalent in the 1950s than they were in the 1930s, there are several valid statements and numbers to support such arguments that the Hollywood Jews were indeed very much a target of the witch hunt and that blacklisting was a means of getting prominent Jews out of the industry, even if only temporarily.

Mega Hit Musicals

Despite McCarthyism and the Cold War, the 1950s featured some of the most triumphant musicals in Broadway history, and the Jewish influence upon these shows was quite significant.

The decade was ushered in with the smash hit, *Gentlemen Prefer Blondes*, which opened in December of 1949 at the Ziegfeld Theatre. It ran for over 700 performances and featured Carol Channing. Jule Styne, born in London to Ukrainian-Jewish immigrants, wrote the music for the show. Styne took to the stage at the age of three and learned piano on a rental. By the time he was ten, his family had moved to Chicago, and Styne had become quite accomplished on the piano and was performing with major symphony orchestras. After attending Music College in Chicago, he would embark on a music-writing career. Styne, despite being an early protégé, had his first Broadway hit while he was in his 40s, teaming with Sammy Cahn on a show called *High Button Shoes* starring Phil Silvers.

Two years later, he would collaborate with Leo Robin on *Gentlemen Prefer Blondes*, from the 1926 Anita Loos novel about the roaring 20s, with Robin providing lyrics. Styne would write music for *Peter Pan, My Sister Eileen* and *Bells Are Ringing* in the '50s, and continue a long career writing for Broadway and leaving a legacy of more than 1,500 songs including "Don't Rain on My

Parade," "Diamonds Are a Girl's Best Friend," "Everything's Coming Up Roses," "Let It Snow! Let It Snow! Let It Snow!" and the Streisand hit from the early 1960s, "People."

Less than a year after *Gentle Prefer Blondes*, in November 1950, *Guys and Dolls* opened its run of over 1,200 performances with George S. Kaufman directing. While the show did enjoy great success, it did not hit Broadway as originally planned. *Guys and Dolls* was originally supposed to be a serious romantic musical based on a short story. However, after Frank Loesser wrote the music, and 11 librettists tried unsuccessfully to pen the lyrics, producers Cy Feuer and Earnest Martin brought in a radio/television comedy writer named Abe Burrows. The result was a musical that evolved into the comedic classic. Burrows went on to win a Tony Award. He also went on to direct Cole Porter's classic *Can Can* in 1953 and write the book for *How to Succeed in Business Without Really Trying*, again winning both a Tony and a Pulitzer Prize. A prolific writer, with a knack for comedy, Burrows was also called in as a script doctor on a number of other Broadway shows.

The mega-hit musical of 1951 was Rodgers and Hammerstein's *The King and I*, with Jerome Robbins as choreographer. The show ran for 1,246 performances. While *Can Can* trumped all musicals from the class of '53, Weill's *Threepenny Opera* opened in '54 and posted more than 2,600 performances, featuring over 200 actors in the show's 22 roles during its long run. Another major musical of the era emerged in 1955 as an adaptation of the Douglass Wallop novel, *The Year the Yankees Lost the Pennant*. The story of a middle-aged Washington Senator's fan who sells his soul to the devil to beat the New York Yankees ran for over 1,000 performances under the name *Damn Yankees* and defied the long-standing theory that a show about baseball would never last. The Jewish team of Richard Adler and Jerry Ross supplied the music and lyrics for the show, which featured a book by George Abbott. Learning from their mentor Frank Loesser, the young writing team went from obscurity to success with the song ironically called "Rags to Riches," a chart-topping hit for Tony Bennett in 1953. They would move on to Broadway in the same year, first with a revue and then with the hit musical *The Pajama Game* which opened in 1954, featuring the proactive show-stopper "Steam Heat." The team moved right to *Damn Yankees,* which debuted on Broadway a year later. Sadly, their collaboration would come to an abrupt end with the sudden death of Jerry Ross at just 29 years of age. Adler continued a long successful musical career, but never quite enjoyed the notoriety of the two Broadway musicals he had written with Ross.

In 1956, Weill's *Threepenny Opera* would be topped by a record-setting 2,717 performances of *My Fair Lady*, directed by Moss Hart and produced by

The
PLAYBILL
for the St. James Theatre

• THE KING AND I •

Rodgers and Hammerstein's *The King and I* opened in March of 1951 with Yul Brenner, Gertrude Lawrence (above) and five-year-old Baayork Lee, in the first of her thirteen Broadway appearances. To date, there have been four Broadway revivals, the latest of which opened in the spring of 2015. Also, to date, the musical still remains banned in Thailand due to its representation of the King, which is considered to be inaccurate (courtesy Playbill Inc.).

Herman Levin, a Jewish Philadelphia-born attorney who turned to theater in his 40s.

The musical, based on George Bernard Shaw's *Pygmalion,* was first attempted by Rodgers and Hammerstein, who were unable to get the necessary rights. It would later go to the musical team of Lerner and Loewe. The classic story was that of a professor, Henry Higgins, teaching a poor flower girl, Eliza Doolittle, how to speak proper English, while making a lady out of her, only to see the student excel beyond the hopes of the teacher. That, however, was only part of the tale. The romance that ensues was the last piece of the puzzle added to Shaw's original work, and the rest was history. After nine years on Broadway, six years on tour, plus a London production, a blockbuster film and several revivals, *My Fair Lady* would clearly be enshrined as one of the legendary shows of all time.

For Alan Jay Lerner and Frederick "Fritz" Loewe it was the crowning achievement in a stunning career. Lerner, born in New York in 1918, and brother of the founder of the Lerner Stores, Alexander Lerner, was the grandson of Ukrainian-Jewish immigrants. He had an interest in music from an early age, starting to play piano, and taking lessons, at the age five. After his parents divorced, he went to plays frequently with his father, which was something he enjoyed very much. By his teens, Lerner was quite proficient at music and an excellent student. He attended The Juilliard School of Music and Harvard University, from which he graduated in 1940. Lerner went on to write radio advertising but always wanted to try his hand at theater. Just two years later, the opportunity would present itself when he met Frederick "Fritz" Loewe in New York City in the Lambs Club, a theater club established in the 1870s. Loewe, some 14 years older, had already achieved some minimal success on Broadway with a show called *Great Lady,* which ran for a few weeks in 1938.

The son of a well-known Austrian operetta tenor, Loewe came to America at the age of 20 with his father, and, like Lerner, he had started playing piano by the age of five. He had already enjoyed a huge hit song in Europe, called *Katrina,* by the time he arrived in the United States. His initial attempts to make it as a performer in the U.S. were unsuccessful, so he took on a series of odd jobs while still writing songs in hopes of making a splash on Broadway.

It was the chance meeting of Lerner and Loewe that would set the wheels in motion for this significant writing team that would follow the likes of the great musical teams of the '30s and '40s. After two less-than-stellar shows with short runs on Broadway, they hit their stride with *Brigadoon* in 1947, which opened at the Ziegfeld Theatre and ran for 581 performances. The unusual story about a couple of tourists who stumble upon a Scottish town that reawakens once every hundred years was a hit largely because of the fabulous Lerner and Loewe score.

After some Hollywood screenwriting success, the duo returned to Broadway with the musical *Paint Your Wagon*, which opened in late 1951 and ran at the Shubert Theater for 289 performances. Then came *My Fair Lady*, which ran for more than nine years. *Gigi* and *Camelot* followed, the latter having a run of 873 performances, cementing Lerner and Loewe as Broadway legends. Interestingly, *Camelot* did not receive favorable reviews by the critics. In an age long before the Internet or viral marketing, there was one recourse to take following such negative reviews. Moss Hart, who co-produced the show with Lerner and Loewe, managed to book the stars—Richard Burton, Julie Andrews, and Robert Goulet—on *The Ed Sullivan Show*, television's most important place to be seen. Lerner and Loewe also went on the show and as a result ticket sales soared and *Camelot* was a hit. It was, however, *My Fair Lady* that immortalized the team of Lerner and Loewe forever.

The second half of this amazing decade for musicals continued with a show called *Bells Are Ringing* which began a run of over 900 performances with Jule Styne, Comden and Green and Jerome Robbins among those credited with creating this hit musical about a friendly phone operator who falls for an unknown caller and ends up romping around New York with him. The star of the hit musical, Judy Holliday, born Judith Turvin, was a Jewish actress and favorite of Comden and Green. Holliday was born to Zionist/socialist parents and grew up with left wing political views that would also lead to her being questioned by the Senate Subcommittee as part of the anti–Communist crusade, resulting in her being blacklisted for several years. Holliday had come to prominence in 1946 in a show called *Born Yesterday* written by Garson Kanin, who had collaborated on several screenplays with his wife, Ruth Gordon. Kanin would later direct *The Diary of Anne Frank* and co-direct *Funny Girl* with Jerome Robbins. Holliday had tried making a name for herself in Hollywood before the 1952 blacklisting. The Theater Guild, producers of *Bells Are Ringing*, was more sympathetic to the plight of such blacklisted performers than many of the Hollywood producers, who were fearing for their own jobs. As a result, the Theater Guild, along with Robbins, who served as director and knew the power of the anti–Communists, was more than happy to cast Holliday in the leading role. She went on to win a Tony Award for her efforts and was later cast in the film version of the musical as well.

While one blockbuster musical typically abounded each year in the '50s, 1957 saw two shows that would become classics open within two months of each other in the fall. *West Side Story* opened at the Winter Garden in September, and *The Music Man* followed in December at the Majestic. A modern day *Romeo and Juliet*, *West Side Story* was originally supposed to be *East Side Story*, about an Irish Catholic girl and a Jewish boy. The four Jewish boys at the helm

My Fair Lady

Lerner and Loewe's triumphant *My Fair Lady* debuted on Broadway in March 1956 and ran for a record-setting six and a half years. While Rex Harrison went on to win a Tony Award and Julie Andrews, in her second Broadway show, was a Tony nominee, the original choices to play the leading roles were supposedly Noel Coward and Mary Martin, both of whom were said to have turned down the roles (courtesy Playbill Inc.).

of this production—Leonard Bernstein, Jerome Robbins, Stephen Sondheim and Arthur Laurents—however, could not find enough time in their busy schedules to work together in the early 1950s and get the project off the ground. By the time they all cleared their respective schedules, they thought the story about a Polish boy and Puerto Rican girl would be timelier, and so the classic musical began to take shape.

For Stephen Sondheim, *West Side Story* was the huge break he had been hoping would come along. Born in New York City, Sondheim would later move to a farm in Pennsylvania, where he would grow up with his mom after his parents' divorce. Estranged from his father and wanting nothing to do with his allegedly psychologically abusive mother, Stephen was essentially on his own as he headed into his career as a lyricist. Sondheim's first work for Broadway, *West Side Story* launched a career that would continue with two more major hit shows, *Gypsy* and *A Funny Thing Happened on the Way to the Forum*. Despite a disastrous flop called *Anyone Can Whistle*, Sondheim went on to team with Harold Prince on several musicals in the 1970s and then continued on his own with hit shows such as *Sweeney Todd*.

Meanwhile, Arthur Laurents, who first teamed with Sondheim and Robbins on *West Side Story*, was a Brooklyn native whose mother kept a kosher home and whose paternal grandparents were orthodox Jews. After graduating from Cornell University, Laurents became a writer of radio scripts before serving time in the military. Actually he didn't see much action, as he was stationed in Astoria in Queens, where he served his time writing scripts. His first Broadway show, *Home of the Brave*, was not a major success, but once he turned his attention to being a librettist, his luck changed. Along with *West Side Story*, he would go on to write the lyrics for *Gypsy* and several shows throughout the 1960s. He would also go on to direct a number of hit musicals including *La Cage aux Folles*, discussed later.

While *The Music Man* was another significant hit musical of the era, it was one of only a few musicals of the decade without much influence from the Jewish Broadway contingent. The sons and daughters of the Jewish immigrants had a foothold of sorts as they established themselves as the forces behind a litany of blockbuster musicals. In fact, two more shows would wrap up this amazing decade, both from Jewish composers, librettists, producers and/or directors. They were *Gypsy* and *The Sound of Music*, both of which opened in 1959.

Gypsy brought most of the team from *West Side Story* back together, linking Robbins, Sondheim and Laurents with the music of Jule Styne, who had ushered in the decade with *Gentlemen Prefer Blondes*. This time the show was about the life of the famous Minsky's Burlesque stripper, Gypsy Rose Lee. While

Gypsy ran for a successful 702 performances, it was a far cry from some of the other blockbuster hits of the era. Nonetheless, *Gypsy* would emerge as a classic, first moving to London for another 120 performances, upon closing in New York, and then returning for several Broadway revivals. It was also one of Ethel Merman's triumphant roles, playing the part of Momma Rose, Gypsy's domineering mom, and belting out "Everything's Coming Up Roses."

Rodgers and Hammerstein's *The Sound of Music*, with a run of over 1,400 performances, ended a remarkable decade for musicals. It was a show adapted from Maria Von Trapp's autobiography, *The Trapp Family Singers*, which was also a German film. While the music and lyrics for *The Sound of Music* are uplifting and joyful in spirit, the undercurrent of a family escaping Nazi Germany took on a different, more somber tone than most of the musicals of the decade. Nonetheless, with a happy ending, it emerged as one of the most heartwarming musicals ever to grace the Broadway stage. It was a stage hit through the early '60s, a classic film, and an often-seen Broadway revival.

Although Jewish culture was not a theme of any of these 1950s blockbusters, the music and stories of most of these significant shows came from Jewish theater legends, the majority of whom retained their Jewish identities while assimilating into mainstream America. As was the case with the children of the early immigrants who opted for vaudeville over Yiddish theater, this generation also chose not to follow the wishes of their parents, which now typically included graduating college and finding more stable careers in law or business. The passion and desire to reach out and touch an audience through music, lyrics and dialogue, as was the case in Yiddish theater, was still seductive and the primary focus for this generation of Jewish talent.

Most of the musicals of the 1950s took on optimistic, life-affirming themes. These were not the revue-style musicals of the pre-war era, nor did they focus on the patriotic and social issues that were more prominent in many of the productions during the war years. Broadway musicals were now telling a wide range of stories about everything from the King of Siam to a love story infused with rival gangs to an abridged biography of the most famous stripper of the century, and they were doing so through the strength of collaborative efforts. While this was not group theater, the talented teams behind most of these hit shows were very much in sync with one another, and each knew his or her role in a production very well. In some cases, they would even take on dual roles, such as Jerome Robbins, who was both a choreographer and director.

Along with writers, composers, lyricists and actors, the Jewish knack for comedic expression was also reflected in the words of Abe Burrows, George S. Kaufman and the performances of Milton Berle, Zero Mostel and others. In fact, a Jewish training ground of sorts, for such comedy, had emerged in the area known as the Catskill Mountains in upstate New York.

The Borscht Belt

In the early part of the 20th century, the Catskill Mountains began to emerge as a vacation destination. The rural area residents saw the potential to lure city dwellers into their serene neck of the woods with plenty of ground food and excellent entertainment. It would be a place where vacationers, mostly Jewish, could get away from the city. As a result, hotels, inns and bungalow colonies sprang up. The response was favorable, so more were built, and those that were already packing in visitors began expanding, which they continued to do as the demand for accommodations grew. To create the full-vacation experience, many of the hotels included meals (mostly kosher), planned activities, golf courses and entertainment in the form of both singers and comedians. Yes, from humble beginnings, resorts were formed and they kept on expanding and expanding. In fact, for years, comedy routines were based on the fact that the hotels had become so large and sprawling that it could be a half-day's activity or more just locating your room.

Among the first entertainment venues in the area were those of Boris Thomashefsky, the Yiddish theater star, who built both an indoor and outdoor theater in the nearby Hunter Resort. From these theaters and the many newly built hotel ballrooms, which could accommodate hundreds of people, and in some cases over a thousand, the training ground for numerous comedians emerged. It was nicknamed the Borscht Belt. The name Borscht Belt was derived from the Eastern European vegetable soup (borscht), which was well known to the Jewish immigrants and served on the traditional menu of Jewish cuisine at the resort hotels.

Over the years, these Catskill resorts, including Grossinger's, the Concord and Brown's, would become the training ground for many of the most significant comedians of the century. The comics would work out their material and establish their on-stage personas in front of adoring fans. It was a unique place in which they could be funny and be Jewish. Catskills comics had an ongoing inside joke with the audiences who enjoyed the mainstream material, but identified more closely with, and laughed harder at, the routines about Jewish families, Jewish customs and Jewish life. Like Yiddish theater, the performers shared so much with their audience, which was typically 90 percent Jewish. For the comics, it was the ideal place to fuse their Jewish identity with their comedy. From jokes about their immigrant parents to Jewish delicatessens to planning their son's Bar Mitzvah (Bat Mitzvah's were not yet as popular as they are today), there was plenty of familiar fodder for humor, not to mention the typical wife and mother-in-law jokes.

By the late 1940s and through the heyday of the '50s and '60s, the Catskills resorts were packing in more than a million visitors a year. The summer months, especially on weekends, were prime spots for comics, and headlining on the holiday weekends, such as July 4 or Labor Day, meant you were at the top of your game.

Many of the comedians from the Borscht Belt went on to become stars of television, film and yes, even Broadway. Among those Catskills comics who also had an impact on the Great White Way were Woody Allen, Milton Berle, Mel Brooks, Sid Caesar, Danny Kaye, Robert Klein, Jackie Mason, Zero Mostel and Carl Reiner. Other comics on the legendary circuit included Buddy Hackett, Jerry Lewis, Don Rickles and Totie Fields.

In the early days of what would become a legendary film career, New York–born and raised Allen Stewart Konigsberg, better known as Woody Allen, started performing stand-up comedy in the early '60s, after being expelled from NYU. From appearances at The Duplex (a nightclub in Greenwich Village) to other nightclubs in and around Manhattan and then in the Catskills, Allen's nervous, neurotic humor emerged and was very well received. Meanwhile, Woody Allen was also part of the legendary writing team on Sid Caesar's *Your Show of Shows*, which included Mel Brooks, Larry Gelbart and Neil Simon.

By the mid–1960s, Allen was already established, with a few films under his belt, and his stand-up career intact. He took his chances at writing for Broadway with two comedies, *Don't Drink the Water* in 1966, and *Play It Again, Sam*, in 1968. Both shows were successful and were also two of the nearly 50 screenplays written by Allen, who not only starred in most of his films but also took the lead role on Broadway in *Play It Again, Sam*. The role suited Allen perfectly, as he played a socially awkward film critic, Alan Felix, who hoped his bad luck with women could be remedied through confidential talks with the ghost of Humphrey Bogart. The show ran for 453 performances.

Woody Allen also brought the Catskills to life in his 1984 film, *Broadway Danny Rose*. Playing a former Catskills comic who now managed several absurd novelty acts, Allen tells the tales of his Borscht Belt days to a table of comics including Sandy Baron, Jackie Gale, Corbett Monica, Howie Storm, Will Jordan, and Morty Gunty, all of whom played the Catskills.

Not unlike Woody Allen, another Jewish New Yorker, Sid Caesar, also wore several hats, as a writer, performer and musician (Allen plays clarinet and Caesar played saxophone). In fact, Caesar got his start in the Catskills, as a teenager, playing in one of the hotel bands before becoming a comedian. He would go on to work on his comedy material to the delight of Catskills audiences. The new medium of the late 1940s, television, proved to be the breakthrough for Caesar. His second television series, in 1950, *Your Show of Shows*, topped the ratings and brought numerous top celebrities into the homes of a nationwide audience dazzled by what was thought by some to be a passing fad.

It was in the early 1960s that Neil Simon, along with composer Cy Coleman, lyricist Carolyn Leigh and choreographer Bob Fosse, would put together the musical comedy *Little Me*. It was perfect for Caesar who got to utilize many of the dialects he used in his comedy act while playing multiple characters and making 34 costume changes. The show ran for 257 performances (or over 8,000 costume changes) before moving to London in 1964 for another successful run, without Caesar. *Little Me* would return twice to Broadway, also without Caesar, who moved on to films, plus occasional television and nightclub appearances.

If anyone truly exemplified the Catskills humor, it was Jackie Mason. The son of a rabbi, Mason was born Yacov (Jacob) Moshe Maza in 1934 in Sheboygan, Wisconsin. He later moved to the Lower East Side of Manhattan where a litany of show business greats had already honed their talents. Mason, however, followed in the footsteps of his father and three older brothers, all of whom became rabbis. He soon found himself working at a synagogue in Pennsylvania. In time, however, he would begin to interject humor into his weekly sermons while also sprinkling in jokes while talking to members of the congregation. This was the beginning of the end of his career as a rabbi and the start of a long, rocky, but ultimately highly successful comedy career.

Working as a social director in the Catskills, Mason learned from the comics he watched on stage and soon became part of the hotel circuit, getting regular bookings, while also making his way to nightclubs and on to television. While working to lose the heavy Jewish accent in an attempt to be more easily understood, he was also honing the Jewish stage persona that suited him well. And yet, he drew his share of criticism for playing the Jewish stereotype, somewhat like those in the vaudeville days before him. Nonetheless, Mason appeared often on the most popular entertainment program of the 1960s, *The Ed Sullivan Show*, until one fateful event derailed his career for a number of years. It didn't take a senate subcommittee to blackball Mason; it took one inappropriate hand gesture on *The Ed Sullivan Show* to ban him from television for years to come. Mason claims the entire thing was an accident, but Sullivan disagreed. The outspoken Mason, always on top of politics, added fuel to the fire with a number of controversial actions and comments over the years.

Nonetheless, he was able to take his act from the stages of the Borscht Belt in its heyday and end up with a very successful Broadway show called *The*

World According to Me. With his usual focus on the differences between Jews and Gentiles, plus plenty of political observations, Mason's show took off in 1987 for a two-year run. Following that show, Mason would land on Broadway with seven more original one-man shows over the next 20 years, making him the most successful comic crossovers to the Broadway stage.

Another comic to make his mark in the Catskills was Gerald Issac Stiller, who grew up on the Lower East Side, although he was actually born in Brooklyn. Jerry Stiller, as he came to be known, would team with his Irish-born wife, Ann Meara, to become one of the most celebrated husband-and-wife comedy teams of the twentieth century. Regulars on *The Ed Sullivan Show*, with 36 appearances, they were also featured on a number of popular variety shows of the '60s and '70s while continuously touring to appreciative audiences.

Stiller would later gain significant notoriety as part of the cast of *Seinfeld,* playing George Costanza's bad-tempered dad. Following the conclusion of the series in 1998, he would make a smooth transition to Carrie Heffernan's bad-tempered dad in the series *King of Queens,* which ran until 2008, giving him a significant prime-time run. Stiller also appeared in a number of movies, from *The Taking of Pelham One Two Three, The Ritz,* and *Airport 1975* to the more recent *Zoolander, Hairspray,* and a remake of *The Heartbreak Kid* with his son Ben.

Yet there was always time for theater, for which the former drama major at Syracuse University had a passion. Back in 1954, the year he and Meara were married, Stiller made his Broadway debut in a show called *The Golden Apple.* He later returned in the hit *Threepenny Opera,* followed by several short-lived shows, before appearing in *The Ritz* with F. Murray Abraham, Rita Moreno, and Jack Weston, and later reprising the role in the film. Perhaps the most notable role for Stiller was as Artie, an old-school Hollywood scriptwriter still chasing development deals in David Rabe's comedy *Hurlyburly,* produced by Mike Nichols in 1984. Stiller's 1997 role in *The Three Sisters* marked sixteen trips to Broadway in a span more than forty years.

Like father, like son, the versatile Ben Stiller also moved from television— *The Ben Stiller Show, Burning Love, Arrested Development,* plus many guest appearances—to a string of hit films, including *There's Something about Mary, Along Came Polly, Zoolander, Night at the Museum, Meet the Parents, Meet the Fockers,* and *Zoolander 2.* While never having the opportunity to make a splash in the Catskills, like his dad, Ben would also make it to Broadway, twice in the same role, first appearing in *The House of the Blue Leaves* in 1986 and then 25 years later in the revival with Jennifer Jason Leigh, also a Jewish performer from a show biz family. Leigh's father was Vic Morrow, who made a career in westerns, such as *Bonanza* and *The Rifleman,* while her mom, Barbara Turner, was in television shows, such as *Ben Casey* and *The Virginian,* before becoming a screenwriter. Prior to teaming with Ben Stiller, Leigh made her Broadway debut in the Kit Kat Club, featured in *Cabaret* in the summer of 1998. She would later take over the role of Catherine in the original drama *Proof* in 2000.

Whether it was Robert Klein moving from the Catskills to the hit show *They're Playing Our Song,* or Mel Brooks bringing *The Producers* to Broadway many years later, a number of the funnymen who would write, produce and/or perform on the Broadway stages started in the Catskills. Some started by literally working at the hotels, as busboys or in similar jobs. But, no matter how they began, they worked hard to meet the challenges of audiences that became tougher to please. As their expectations for excellence increased, Catskills audiences, much like Broadway audiences, became more discerning as one comic raised the bar for the following night's performer.

Unfortunately, over time, destination resorts emerged and cost-effective air travel made long-distance locations more easily accessible, and the casinos in nearby Atlantic City became the lure for New York City vacationers. As a result, the resorts in the Catskills began a decline that, by the end of the century, left them almost completely obliterated.

In late 1991, however, one of the remaining Catskills funnymen, Freddie Roman, would bring a show to Broadway celebrating the humor of the Borscht Belt. In essence it was nothing more than four comics doing what they did best in the mountains: stand-up comedy. The show, *Catskills on Broadway,* featured Mal Z. Lawrence, Marilyn Michaels, Dick Capri and of course Roman, all of whom spent years making audiences laugh on the stages of Catskills resorts. It ran for 452 performances and at one point even brought long-time legendary funnyman Henny Youngman to the Broadway stage for a stint in the show.

It's also worth noting that while she was never a "Catskills comic," comedic actress/writer Gertrude Berg, born Tillie Edelstein in East Harlem, produced comedy skits for one of the Catskills resorts owned by her father. One of Berg's many skits, about a Jewish family living in the New York tenements, would turn into one of the most famous radio programs of all time, called *The Goldbergs,* starring Berg as Molly Goldberg. The radio hit would run from 1929 to 1946 and later move to television, with Berg still writing and starring in the series. She would also take the famous fictional Goldbergs to Broadway, writing and staring in the original comedy *Me and Molly* in 1948. Ironically, she would later win a Tony award, not for her portrayal as Molly Goldberg, but for her role as Mrs. Jacoby in *A Majority of One* in 1959.

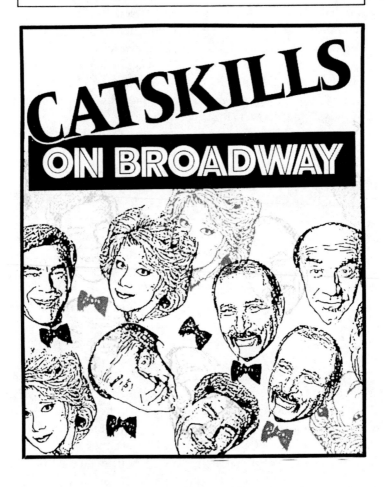

Catskills on Broadway brought a marvelous era of great Jewish comedy to life in the fall of 1991, led by veteran funnyman Freddie Roman and a few of his Catskills cohorts. Mel Gussow summed it up in his *New York Times* review (December 6, 1991): "The title of the show, *Catskills on Broadway,* deserves a truth-in-advertising award … you pay your money and you get the jokes, unless you happen to miss the punch lines because of the laughter" (courtesy Playbill Inc.).

On a Serious Note

While the blockbuster musicals of the '50s drew a lot of attention and the comedians of Broadway's future were honing their skills in the Catskill mountain resorts, there were also several key dramatic works. Along with Arthur Miller's *The Crucible*, one of the most significant dramatic works of the time was *The Diary of Anne Frank*. The epic dramatization by Frances Goodrich and Albert Hackett was based upon the actual published diary of a young woman who hid seven Jewish children from the Nazis during World War II

The Tony Award–winning play of 1956, which opened at the Cort Theater and later moved to the Ambassador, ran for 717 performances. It featured Susan Strasberg, who was nominated for a Tony Award, and was produced by Kermit Bloomgarden, who received his third Tony Award for his work (he had also received Tony Awards for *Death of a Salesman* and *The Crucible*.) He would later go on to win a fourth Tony Award for *The Music Man*.

Unlike many of the Jewish writers and performers who disappointed their parents by venturing into the unstable world of theater, Susan Strasberg, daughter of acting teacher Lee Strasberg and former actress Paula Strasberg, was encouraged to go against her dreams of becoming a scientist and venture into acting. Born in 1938, Susan did not attend classes at her father's Actors Studio, but instead ventured into acting as a teenager, first in an Off Broadway production called *Maya*, then on television before moving to Broadway as the star of the Pulitzer Prize–winning drama, *The Diary of Anne Frank*. At just 17, Susan Strasberg's career had instantly taken off. From this auspicious beginning, she went to Hollywood where she made several movies, returning in 1957 to appear in the Broadway show *Time Remembered*, with Richard Burton, with whom she had a well-publicized affair. Unfortunately, her career may have taken off too soon, as she never again enjoyed her early success on screen or on stage, although she did generate some acclaim during a few years she spent acting in Italy.

Another of the most significant dramas of the 1950s was *Inherit the Wind*, written by Jerome Lawrence with Robert E. Lee, and starring Paul Muni. Another Jewish performer to emanate from the Lower East Side of Manhattan, Muni had appeared on Broadway in *This One Man*, *Counselor-at-Law* and *A Flag Is Born*, among other shows. However, he would win a Tony Award for *Inherit the Wind*, the 1955 drama about the Scopes Monkey Trial, which took place in the 1920s. The trial brought national attention to the conflict between those teaching Darwin's theory of evolution, which included a schoolteacher who was arrested in Tennessee, and those who believed in the fundamental teaching of the Bible. Not unlike Miller's hit *The Crucible*, the play was brought to the stage largely to focus on the threat against intellectual freedom as posed by the Communist investigations by McCarthy and the Senate subcommittee. Lawrence commented in an interview that, "It's not about science versus religion. It's about the right to think."[3]

Along with Robert E. Lee, Jerome Lawrence wrote 39 plays in 15 years, a dozen of which made it to Broadway. Born Jerome Lawrence Schwartz, like many other celebrities, he changed his name, or in this case simply dropped the Jewish sounding "Schwartz" in order to appear less ethnic. After working as a reporter for small newspapers, he began writing for radio, including Armed Forces radio during World War II. Lawrence and Lee both entered the military in 1942 and served their country together. They followed *Inherit the Wind* with *Auntie Mame*, which became the musical hit *Mame*, and in the mid–'60s, *The Night Thoreau Spent in Jail*, about Thoreau's imprisonment for tax evasion based on moral reasons, and *First Monday in October*.

And Through It All

The Cold War prevailed throughout the 1950s and into the '60s, but the intensity of the anti–Communism fervor began to erode. For years, however, the debate went on regarding those who spoke out and named names of Communist sympathizers. Were they being patriotic or were they ratting out their peers? It seemed that those who took a side were all quite adamant about their position. Yet today, the blacklisting of the era is little more than a footnote in history. At the time, however, it affected (and in some cases ruined) the careers of many people in show business, including a significant number of Jewish playwrights and performers.

And through it all, the indomitable spirit and positive attitude of the Jews in theater prevailed. Zero Mostel, among others, stepped back into the spotlight and worked hard to prove that he belonged onstage and not on a blacklist. In fact, Mostel teamed with Woody Allen and Herschel Bernardi (another Jewish performer who was blacklisted) to appear in the 1976 film, *The Front*, about the anti–Communism crusades and subsequent blacklisting.

While off-stage news regarding who was being grilled by a subcommittee made newspaper headlines, the theater world was making headlines of its own. The Broadway musicals of the 1950s were among the most extraordinary ever produced, and even before they became major motion pictures, these shows were generating attention, not only around the theater district but also well beyond the city borders. While New York is always a major tourist destination, these soon-to-be- classic musicals brought people from all over the country to Broadway, which was part of the reason for extended record-breaking runs.

In the meantime, while tourists were flocking to Broadway, the hotels of the Catskills were the vacation Mecca to which New York and Connecticut Jews could escape. They were also the only comedy training ground of their kind.

I can attest to the popularity of the area from my own visits. But I can also attest to the genius of one of the many comedic geniuses who emerged, Sid Caesar, whom I saw on stage in *Little Me* on my first-ever trip to see a Broadway musical. Like the many young future performers who sat watching Yiddish theater, or Fanny Brice during the days of vaudeville, I sat watching Caesar in awe.

As I described it in my book *Let's Put On a Show:*

> My love affair with the theater started when I was invited to see my first Broadway show. I was eleven at the time, and the father of my best friend, Ricky, was an actor. I had never heard of him so I never thought much about it (except it was kind of cool that he worked at night, when it was fun, and not like everyone else who worked during the day). We drove from Long Island into the City, which alone was an exciting event in itself, and everything kept snowballing from there. Seeing my first beautiful Broadway theatre, getting a ticket with the name of the show printed on it (not just "Admit One" that you'd get at the movie houses), being handed a Playbill (two souvenirs and the curtain wasn't even up yet!) and quickly being ushered into the first row in front of a huge, plush crimson curtain. The Overture began and my mouth dropped open. The curtain rose and my eyes popped at what they saw. Indeed, Ricky's father, Sid Caesar was starring in the musical *Little Me*, with music by Cy Coleman, lyrics by Carolyn Leigh and book by Neil Simon. The audience roared with laughter and, because we were in the front row, I could see some behind the scenes preparation by the actors in the wings. I was now an insider (and after only five minutes). Afterwards we went backstage where Sid was holding court. There were so many well-wishers and plenty of backslapping, and hugging going on. So much laughter on stage and off, I thought. With a refrigerator, bed, T.V., and hot plate, this place was like a home away from home. My heavens, why would anyone want to do anything else?[4]

While I went on to see many more plays during the 1960s, Broadway would begin to change. New and innovative shows were produced, some for better and some for worse. But there was also a coming of age, of sorts, for the presentation of Jewish family life, culture, and history on the Broadway stage. *Fiddler on the Roof* was the most notable of several shows that touched on Jewish life and extended the culture to a new generation of young theatergoers. It was a show that I saw in my youth and produced many years later, realizing that my own daughters had not seen it. Like so many Jewish people, I felt connected to the show and wanted to pass on its great tradition.

The next chapter looks at the Jewish-themed shows, as well as the new breed of performers, writer and directors who continued the tradition, and the influence of the Jewish people on Broadway throughout the 1960s and '70s.

6

Jewish Themes, Legends and Life in the 1960s and 1970s

With *The Sound of Music* soaring high on theatergoers' must-see list, the 1960s began. It was a decade that would have a tremendous impact upon American culture and politics. From the Bay of Pigs to the assassination of John F. Kennedy to the rise of the Beatles, the civil rights movement, the war in Vietnam and man finally walking on the moon, the '60s was a decade unlike any in America's short history.

Theater, of course, would follow suit with a wide range of subject matter presented in new and innovative manners, many of which were experimental in nature, echoing the changes taking place in American society. African American performers, who were not even cast in Broadway shows just a few decades earlier, were finally getting their long-overdue opportunity to star in major productions. It was also a welcome change from a Jewish cultural perspective. Not only were there Jewish playwrights, composers, lyricists and performers, but audiences were also enjoying full-blown musicals about the Jewish people. The fears of anti–Semitism and Communism had dissipated, giving way to new shows that brought the Jewish people to the forefront, not as stereotypes as in the days of vaudeville, but as prominent individuals and as families with their own joys, concerns and struggles.

Fiddler on the Roof

It's hard to argue that the most defining, and certainly most successful, musical about the Jewish family was *Fiddler on the Roof*, rich in Jewish tradition and customs. Considered by some to be the last great musical of the golden era that extended from the early 1950s into the mid–'60s, it was a monumental show that broke box office records, as it became the first musical to surpass 3,000 Broadway performances.

Imperial Theatre | **PLAYBILL**
the magazine for theatregoers

Fiddler on the Roof

No production has ever brought the Jewish experience to Broadway as *Fiddler on the Roof* did in the fall of 1964. Running for eight years, the show set box-office records and has returned to Broadway five times. During the initial Broadway run, the musical opened in London and Australia (both in 1967) and the film debuted in the United States in 1971 (courtesy Playbill Inc.).

However, *Fiddler* was more than just a mega hit musical. It became a part of American Jewish culture, quoted by religious leaders and discussed in Jewish households. While the show focused on Jewish life, the idea that progress intrudes upon tradition also resounded with mainstream audiences. In fact, *Fiddler* was later presented in Japan where it was once again a hit, largely because of the theme … tradition! The songs from *Fiddler* were ingrained in the minds of those who saw it and even many of those who did not. *Fiddler* also provided a history lesson of sorts about life in Russia for the Jewish people at the beginning of the 20th century.

Jerry Bock and Sheldon Harnick provided the music and lyrics for *Fiddler*. Bock was born in New Haven, Connecticut, in 1928 but grew up in Flushing, Queens. He cultivated an interest in music as a youngster, writing his first musical comedies in high school and college. A college musical that Bock co-wrote with a school friend, Larry Holofcener, called *Big as Life*, was awarded the top prize in a show competition between colleges sponsored by BMI, one of the major music licensing houses.

After graduating, Bock and Holofcener would make their way into television, becoming the musical writers for *Your Show of Shows* before moving on to Broadway with contributions to a show called *Catch a Star!* Their songs drew attention and they were hired to write the music and lyrics for the show *Mr. Wonderful* and for the 1956 version of *Ziegfeld Follies*.

By the end of the '50s, Bock and Holofcener had gone their separate ways. Bock began teaming up with another Jewish lyricist, Sidney Harnick, who was looking for his first big break. A native of Chicago, Harnick took to the violin as a youngster. After a stint in the army, he earned a bachelor of music degree in 1949 from the Northwestern University School of Music. Wanting to take a shot at writing lyrics for the theater, he headed to New York City where he landed a witty song in Broadway's *New Faces of 1952*. For the next several years, Harnick contributed lyrics to other people's shows before connecting with Bock.

Following an unsuccessful first show, *The Body Beautiful*, they had their first collaborative hit, celebrating the life of New York City Mayor, Fiorello La Guardia. The show, *Fiorello!*, ushered in the 1960s at the Broadhurst Theater with a run of 795 performances and earned them a Tony Award and a Pulitzer Prize. A few more collaborations followed over the next several years, none matching the success of *Fiorello!* And then came *Fiddler*.

Based on stories written in Yiddish by Jewish writer Sholem Aleichem, including one entitled *Tevye and His Daughters,* the book evolved through the hard work of librettist Joseph Stein, who had started his career as a television writer before moving to theater. Stein had previously teamed with Carl Reiner on the hit comedy *Enter Laughing*, which had an all-star cast including José Ferrer, Shelley Winters, Elaine May, Jack Gilford and even legendary comedian Don Rickles. For *Fiddler*, Stein would win two Tony Awards. He would also win Tony's for collaborating on the book *Take Me Along*, as well as for *Zorba* and for *Rags*.

While Bock and Harnick were handling the music and lyrics for *Fiddler*, and Stein was writing the book, Harold Prince served as producer and brought in Jerome Robbins, whom he felt was the only director who could give the material the universal quality necessary to play successfully for the mass audience.

When *Fiddler* finally hit the stage, it rang true to the concerns of the broad audience, while having a special significance for Jewish theatergoers. The show focused on a dairyman living with his wife in Russia just after the turn of the 20th century and how he tried to cling to the old-world religious and family customs and traditions while raising five daughters in a world that was rapidly changing around them. The show ran, appropriately, through the 1960s, in which, as mentioned at the opening of the chapter, social and political changes were challenging long-standing family and cultural traditions in America. The roles of women were changing, a sexual revolution was emerging and typically rebellious youths were now uniting as part of the anti-culture that was widely protesting the war in Vietnam. Traditions were indeed hard to cling to. Jewish families were also dealing with a growing trend of interfaith marriages and changes in traditional home life. As the suburbs grew quickly, TV dinners, television, and other diversions were slowly replacing the Sabbath family meal, and fewer Jews were attending Friday night or Saturday morning temple services. Even Jewish traditions themselves were being questioned by the new generation of young Jews. As a result, *Fiddler* hit home, touching the hearts of theatergoers.

As is the case with many blockbuster musicals, *Fiddler* went through a number of changes en route to Broadway. The name changed several times until *Fiddler on the Roof* was pulled from a Chagall painting called *The Green Violinist*, which depicted a violinist hovering over the roofs of a village. The stars of *Fiddler* included Zero Mostel, who reportedly was not the first choice of Robbins. Initially Robbins wanted Danny Kaye. In the end, however, Mostel would take ownership of the role and walk away with a Tony Award for his work. Luther Adler, Herschel Bernardi and Fyvush Finkel were among several others to take over the starring role of Tevye during the long run. Bea Arthur, Bette Midler, Adrienne Barbeau, and Pia Zadora were among a number of actresses to take on some of the many significant female roles.

Along with Bock and Harnick winning Tony Awards for best composer and lyricist, *Fiddler* won for best musical of 1965. The show was such a box office success that it is estimated that if someone had invested $1,000 at the onset of the original Broadway production, they would have walked away with over $1.5 million.

In 1967, the play opened in London, lasting for over 2,000 performances starring Chaim Topol, who would then star in the 1971 film version, which also included Yiddish theater star Molly Picon as the village matchmaker. Broadway revivals brought the show back in 1976 and 1990. Then, in 2004, knowing my own daughters had never seen *Fiddler*, I decided it was time to once again bring *Fiddler on the Roof* to Broadway, for the fourth time. It had been 13 years since the previous production and was now time for a new generation to see this classic musical on stage. It took some time to get the rights and bring everyone together, but with new and innovative sets and Alfred Molina starring as Tevye (later replaced by Harvey Fierstein), we were able to bring the show back again for two years and 781 performances. We even replaced Yente's song "The Rumour" with a new song called "Topsy-Turvy." Sure enough, my daughters laughed and cried and took in this marvelous show, much as I had done many years before.

Fiddler was not only an important vehicle for numerous Broadway notables, but it was also a stepping stone for many young Jewish performers. One such performer was Judy Kaye, who appeared in four theater companies as Hodel before making her way to Broadway, in a very different role as Rizzo in the original version of *Grease*, a role she took over from Adrienne Barbeau. A theater major at UCLA, she would later step into the role of Lili Garland as a replacement in *On the Twentieth Century*.

A road warrior, Kaye was always found somewhere in a major musical between stints on Broadway, whether it was Los Angeles, St. Louis, Miami, or Dallas. In fact, it was during a five-month, 63-city tour of *On the Twentieth Century*, which she called "the bus and truck tour from hell," that she met her future husband, David Green. He made his 1988 Broadway debut in *Teddy & Alice.*

Kaye would return to Broadway in 1988 and begin a run of appearing in some of the biggest musicals of the last thirty years, making her debut as Carlotta in *Phantom of the Opera*, before spending two years in *Mama Mia*, a stretch in *Wicked*, and a brief stint in the revival of *Sweeny Todd*. Most recently, she played the Fairy Godmother in Rodgers and Hammerstein's *Cinderella*. And it all started by honing her craft in many versions of *Fiddler*.

More Than Fiddler

It took more than *Fiddler* to infuse Jewish culture and characters into the fabric of Broadway. Three years prior to *Fiddler*, a musical opened featuring music and lyrics by Broadway newcomer Jerry Herman. The 1961 show, *Milk and Honey*, was the first Broadway musical set in Israel. A romantic tale of a man traveling without his wife, who meets a widow also visiting Israel, provided the impetus to introduce Jewish characters to a mainstream audience. The show also featured an older widow seeking a husband, played comically by Molly Picon. *Milk and Honey*, originally titled *Shalom*, opened at the Martin Beck Theater and ran for 543 performances.

In 1965, six months before *Fiddler* opened, two legends became one onstage as Barbra Streisand stepped into her first (and only) starring role as Fanny Brice in *Funny Girl*, also directed by Jerome Robbins, with music by Jule Styne and lyrics by Bob Merrill. Streisand's only previous Broadway appearance was in *I Can Get It for You Wholesale*, in which she had a much smaller role, but generated immediate attention from both critics and audiences.

The musical, *I Can Get It for You Wholesale*, featured words and music by Harold Rome, another Jewish contributor to Broadway who gave up a more stable career in architecture to venture into theater in the 1930s. Rome hit Broadway with music and lyrics for the revue *Pins and Needles* in 1937, but later became well known for the shows *Call Me Mister, Wish You Were Here* and *Fanny*, all prior to *I Can Get It for You Wholesale*.

The *Funny Girl* writing team of Styne and Merrill had not teamed on a Broadway musical before. Styne, however, had been writing for Broadway for some two decades. Merrill, meanwhile, had debuted in 1957, writing both music and lyrics for a musical called *New Girl in Town*, based on Eugene O'Neill's 1921 play *Anna Christie*, followed by *Carnival* in 1960. Merrill had grown up on the East Coast, first in Atlantic City and later in Philadelphia. After fighting in World War II, he returned to the United States and settled in Hollywood. He had a talent for writing upbeat songs, even novelty tunes, such as "If I Knew You Were Coming I'd've Baked a Cake" and "(How Much Is) That Doggie in the Window?" Merrill would proceed from *Funny Girl* to a number of other Broadway hits including *Breakfast at Tiffany's* in 1966 and *Sugar* in 1972, once again with Jule Styne. Like many others, Merrill shifted his attention to Hollywood and enjoyed a successful career writing film scores including one for the Academy Award–winning *American Beauty*.

Meanwhile, *Funny Girl* depicted the life and comic mastery of Brice, whose career extended from vaudeville and the Ziegfeld Follies to radio and film success, to the stage. The show served to introduce a largely forgotten Jewish icon

The Jerry Herman musical comedy *Milk and Honey* was more than just a love story set in Jerusalem featuring Israeli folk songs and dances. The musical also illustrated the pride and strength of the new nation of Israel. It was only thirteen years earlier that David Ben-Gurion proclaimed the creation of the state of Israel and became its first prime minister. Pictured from left are Mimi Benzell, Robert Weede and Molly Picon (courtesy Playbill Inc.).

to an entirely new generation. It was also an important work for Isobel Lennart, the Jewish screenwriter and playwright who wrote the book for *Funny Girl*. Lennart, after writing several films, had been blacklisted for several years by the House Un-American Activities Committee for having joined the Communist Party. She had managed to resume her career, but this was her first, last and only Broadway show. Ironically, it would also be the last Broadway show (to date) for Streisand, whose musical career had taken off in 1962 and had already enjoyed a major hit with the song "People." The song, written for the production, was released and became a major hit before the show actually opened.

The story behind the story, or the making of *Funny Girl*, might have made a show in itself. There were numerous delays and a significant number of rewrites while trying to get *Funny Girl* to Broadway, with disgruntled creative team members coming and going … and in some cases, such as that of Jerome Robbins, being coaxed into returning again. In fact, even the young Streisand was not the first choice for the role. Supposedly Mary Martin, Anne Bancroft and Carol Burnett had all turned down the lead role before it was given to Barbra.

There were also various names for the musical being penciled in, such as *A Very Special Person*, and the *Luckiest People* before *Funny Girl* was suggested by David Merrick, who wasn't even working on the show, but he was David Merrick. Opening night was also up in the air and postponed several times.

When *Funny Girl* finally opened, on March 26, 1964, at the Winter Garden Theater, it was met with terrific reviews and continued with a run of over 1,300 performances. Not only would Streisand go on to shine in the role, but she would enjoy success with the soundtrack and star in the movie version of the musical, as well as the sequel, *Funny Lady*. A Tony Award, however, was not to come for Streisand, who was nominated, but lost to Carol Channing who starred in *Hello, Dolly!*

For the Brooklyn-born Streisand, whose unprecedented singing career has resulted in roughly 150 million records sold worldwide, Broadway has always been near and dear to her heart. Her first several hit albums included Broadway favorites, something she would return to a number of times throughout her career. *Funny Girl* was a major step in launching her acting career that would result in numerous hit films.

Another show with a Jewish theme was *The Rothschilds*, a musical that would open six years after *Fiddler*, featuring the same musical team of Bock and Harnick. This was also a story about a poor European family, with five sons rather than five daughters. *The Rothschilds*, however, was the story of a family that not only escaped poverty but rose to great wealth in Germany in

Funny Girl opened in March of 1964 and was roughly based on the life of Fanny Brice. It was the Broadway breakthrough for Barbra Streisand (with Sydney Chaplin, the son of Charles Chaplin, right) in a cast that also included Jean Stapleton and Lainie Kazan. The musical was produced by Ray Stark, son-in-law of the legendary vaudeville performer, who wanted to be very careful to present Brice in the best light. *Funny Girl* was also the last time Streisand performed in a Broadway show (courtesy Playbill Inc.).

the banking industry between the 1770s and early 1800s. In fact, they became one of the most influential families in all of Europe. Adapted from the Frederic Morton book chronicling the family's history, the show drew comparisons to *Fiddler*. However, it fell short in such assessments. Nonetheless, *The Rothschilds* was successful, starring Hal Linden and running for 507 performances.

One more show of significance made it to Broadway a little later on, in 1975, and was based on the noted Polish American Jewish short story writer Isaac Bashevis Singer's work *Yentl the Yeshiva Boy*. The story centered around a girl who was disguised as a boy in order to study the Torah, which was forbidden, in the late 19th Century, for females. This short story would evolve into the 1975 drama *Yentl*, which opened at the Eugene O'Neill Theater where it ran for over 200 performances. While there was some difficulty in building a full-fledged show from a story of less than 25 pages, *Yentl* enlightened audiences to male and female roles in the Jewish religion while bringing back the question of tradition, as presented a decade earlier in *Fiddler*. Led by Barbra Streisand's steadfast determination to bring *Yentl* to the screen, the movie would follow several years later, based on a film treatment written by Streisand herself.

Considering that great composers, lyricists and playwrights led the Jewish influence on Broadway for decades, such Jewish-themed shows were long overdue. The anti–Semitism of the '30s, the war years of the '40s and the anti–Communism witch hunts of the '50s delayed such stories and Jewish characters from making a definitive statement and enjoying mass audience acceptance. But with directors like Jerome Robbins and the determination of people like Jerry Bock and Sheldon Harnick, Joseph Stein and Jerry Herman, the Jewish influence on Broadway had finally made its way into the spotlight.

Doc Simon Takes Over the Great White Way

Born on the 4th of July in 1927, Marvin Neil Simon grew up in the Bronx and after the divorce of his parents, moved to Forest Hills, Queens with his mother. One story is told that his penchant for playing doctor as a child and carrying around a toy stethoscope earned him the nickname of "Doc" which he still holds today. The more commonly known reason for the nickname is that Simon was often called in during his early years as a writer to serve as a script doctor to mend shows in need of wittier dialogue.

Simon's knack for taking the stories of real people, with relatable, dramatic situations, and adding the appropriate humor made him one of the most successful and best known playwrights in Broadway history. Not unlike Woody

Tovah Feldshuh took the lead role as a Jewish girl disguising herself as a boy to read
the Torah in a play that took audiences back to Poland circa 1873. *Yentl* was just one
of many plays co-produced by Cheryl Crawford, who rose to prominence with the
Group Theatre and The Actors Studio (courtesy Playbill Inc.).

Allen as a screenwriter, Simon would emerge from the 1960s as one of the most prolific playwrights of the 20th century. Also like Woody Allen, much of the inspiration for his commercially successful storylines came from his own life experiences. And while his plays rarely touched upon Jewish themes, his Jewish family, friends and culture were evident in his works. And finally, like Allen, Neil Simon would start out writing for early television comedies of the 1950s. Together with his brother Danny, Neil Simon would write for *The Jackie Gleason Show, Sgt. Bilko,* starring Phil Silvers, and *Your Show of Shows* featuring Sid Caesar. Although they enjoyed great success together in the 1950s, by the '60s, Neil and Danny Simon would go their separate ways. Danny wanted to remain in television as a director, while Neil preferred to try his hand at writing for Broadway.

Simon's run of over 30 Broadway shows began with a comedy called *Come Blow Your Horn* pairing a 30-ish swinging playboy with his younger, far less sophisticated brother. Many years before the popular sitcom *Two and a Half Men,* the show was a hit, running for 675 performances. Being quite familiar with Sid Caesar's comedic genius from writing for *Your Show of Shows,* Simon would then pen the musical *Little Me,* a vehicle in which Caesar got to portray his many characters on Broadway. With two hit shows under his belt, Simon felt more confident about bringing aspects of his own life to the stage and did so with *Barefoot in the Park,* in which he turned the trials and tribulations of his early years of marriage, such as struggling to make ends meet in a small apartment, into a delightful comedic romance. While the leads in the original version were Robert Redford and Elizabeth Ashley, neither of whom were Jewish, one of the stars of Simon's 2006 revival, Amanda Peet (in her Broadway debut), not only has Jewish roots from her mother's side, but also has some interesting theatrical family history. Peet, whose screen credits include the *Whole Nine Yards,* the HBO hit *Togetherness,* and a recurring role on the television series *The Good Wife,* is the granddaughter of Beta Rothafel, who made it to Broadway in 1932 in the play *Chrysalis* with Humphrey Bogart. Beta's father (Peet's great-grandfather), Roxy Rothafel, opened the famous Roxy Theater in Times Square and would later open Radio City Music Hall featuring a dance troupe known as the Roxyettes. Rothafel is also credited as the producer of the Radio City Music Hall inaugural program in 1932.

As for Neil Simon, his characters always remained genuine. Even if the stories were not about his own life, they were based largely on the narratives of people he knew, whom he portrayed complete with their foibles and insecurities. The 1965 comedy classic *The Odd Couple* puts a beer-drinking, cigar-smoking slob and an obsessively neurotic neat-freak under one roof. The original comedy was not only a hit on Broadway for nearly 1,000 performances,

That's me with Doc Simon, right. In 1983, I co-produced Simon's *The Goodbye Girl* with music by Marvin Hamlisch and lyrics by David Zippel (photograph by Anita Shevette).

but it was also unique in that it spawned a major movie and a long-running television series. It also gained Simon his first Tony Award. But *The Odd Couple* was more than a stage and screen hit. The show introduced Oscar Madison and Felix Unger to the American public, and they would go on to symbolize sloppy and neat in American culture. It also marked the final Broadway appearance of Walter Matthau, who after nineteen roles on Broadway, would focus his attention on making movies, which would include reprising the role of Oscar Madison on the big screen, opposite Jack Lemmon as Felix Unger in *The Odd Couple.* Matthau and Lemmon proceeded to work together a number of times in their film careers.

Another protégé from the Lower East side to immigrant Jewish parents, Matthau discovered his love of acting at sleep-away camps and later studied at New York acting schools. His Broadway debut came in the 1948 play *Anne of the Thousand Days,* starring Rex Harrison and Joyce Redman. He also performed in the 1955 revival of *Guys and Dolls* and the 1961 farce *A Shot in the Dark* with Julie Harris, William Shatner, and Gene Saks. The show landed Matthau his first Tony Award; his second would come from Simon's *The Odd Couple.*

Following *Sweet Charity, The Star-Spangled Girl* and *Plaza Suite,* Neil Simon would collaborate on a musical with one of the hottest songwriting teams of the era, Burt Bacharach and Hal David. The show, *Promises, Promises,* based on the 1960 film *The Apartment,* opened in late 1968 and ran for 1,281 performances. The cast album went on to win a Grammy Award for best cast recording, and the musical returned to Broadway for a 2010 revival.

Simon moved from the 1960s into the '70s with one hit after another, introducing a variety of leading characters in which audience members often saw a glimpse of themselves. *Last of the Red Hot Lovers* was about a mid-life crisis, and *The Prisoner of Second Avenue* wove humor into the realities of a couple losing their jobs and grips with their sanity. Among the other Neil Simon hit shows of the '70s was *The Sunshine Boys* about a once-famous vaudeville team whose bitter breakup years earlier was now interfering with an attempted reunion for a television special honoring them, some 40 years later. Trying to get the unreasonable pair in the same room, much less on the same page, became the challenge from which humor ensued. Inspired by a couple of actual vaudeville teams, *The Sunshine Boys* ran for 538 performances and, as was usually the case with Simon's works, became a popular film.

Veteran actor Sam Levene, who was initially Sam Levine until he changed his name to make it slightly less ethnic, costarred with Jack Albertson in Doc Simon's *The Sunshine Boys.* He played the role of Al Lewis, which would later be played by George Burns in the film.

Levene's Broadway career began with a mere five lines in the 1927 original melodrama *Wall Street.* The show lasted only three weeks, but his Broadway career would last for over 50 years. It was his fourteenth Broadway show, the hit comedy *Three Men on a Horse,* which ran for over 800 performances, that would prompt Levene to take off for Hollywood to star in the movie version of the show. Part of the lure of Hollywood was also the fact that he would get

$1,000 to do the film, which was significantly more than the $40 a week he was making on Broadway in 1936. The bi-coastal Levene would continue his screen career with the *Thin Man* films and over 40 other movies before his final feature *And Justice for All.*

Levene would also land roles in 38 Broadway shows, mostly original productions in which he would become known for bringing new characters to life, perhaps none more significant than Nathan Detroit in the classic musical *Guys and Dolls.* Ironically, it was only one of a couple of musicals in Levene's career, primarily because he couldn't sing. In fact, his only solo number in *Guys and Dolls,* "Sue Me," was specifically written in one octave for Levene's limited vocal range. Among Levene's other Broadway credits were *Room Service, The Impossible Years,* and *The Royal Family.* Although Levene did not generate the fan base of some of his contemporaries, he was one of the hardest-working actors in the business and highly respected by his peers.

While Simon's shows were drawing high-profile cast members and excellent box-office numbers, the 1970s would become an introspective time for Simon as he coped with the death of his first wife. The play *Chapter Two* focused on a man starting the second chapter of his life after losing his spouse. The highly acclaimed show was touching, funny, poignant and successful, moving from the Imperial to the Eugene O'Neill Theater, and playing a total of 857 performances. *Chapter Two* won a Tony Award for best play of 1978.

Always looking to diversify, Simon would follow with a musical. Not unlike working with Bacharach and David in the '60s, he joined forces with one of the most significant songwriting teams of the '70s, Marvin Hamlisch and Carole Bayer Sager. The show, *They're Playing Our Song,* was based on the musical team's relationship which starts out rocky and ends with them falling in love. Essentially a two-person show, with no major musical production numbers, it gave Simon the opportunity to do what he does best: move a story along with sharp, witty dialogue. Comedian Robert Klein and actress Lucie Arnaz opened in the leading roles, and the show was an instant hit, playing for nearly 1,100 performances. The Jewish-born Klein was not entirely new to Broadway having been in the Bock and Harnick musical *The Apple Tree,* while Arnaz made her Broadway debut.

Small casts, moderate set design and linear story lines that related easily to the human experience helped facilitate Simon's worldwide presence. In fact, *They're Playing Our Song* was seen not only on the stages of London, but also in Argentina, Australia, Belgium, Budapest, the Philippines, Singapore and in other parts of the globe.

By the 1980s, with more than 20 years of success, Neil Simon earned the unprecedented opportunity to write, and stage, a trilogy about his own life, using the character Eugene to portray himself. *Brighton Beach Memoirs, Biloxi Blues* and *Broadway Bound* took Simon from his youth through his military service to his start on Broadway. All three parts of the Eugene trilogy were very well received. They brought events from Simon's own life, including friends and family members, to the stage and showcased his ability to siphon out humor and make challenging life events, such as military training in Biloxi, Mississippi, more bearable.

But what good is a trilogy if you don't add to it? Following hits such as the Tony and Pulitzer Prize Award–winning *Lost in Yonkers* in 1991 and the stage adaptation of his own movie, *The Goodbye Girl* in 1993, Simon took on one more autobiographical story with *Laughter on the 23rd Floor*, also in 1993. The comedy brought Simon full circle, returning him to his days as a television writer by recreating the atmosphere of the famous 1950s writing team behind *Your Show of Shows*, featuring actors playing Woody Allen, Carl Reiner, Mel Brooks, Selma Diamond and Larry Gelbart. The show saw only marginal success.

Through his many works, Simon always maintained the ability to create or recreate characters experiencing familiar life events, whether it's in a small walk-up first apartment (*Barefoot in the Park*), military training (*Biloxi Blues*) or trying to cope with deeply embedded stubborn behavior among elderly relatives (*The Sunshine Boys*). Some characters had a Jewishness about them, while others specifically did not, allowing his work to be both reflective and mainstream.

One such Neil Simon character, the Jewish mother Kate in *Broadway Bound*, was played by Linda Lavin, who won a Tony Award for the role. Lavin, a Jewish actress originally from Portland, Maine, made a name for herself in the 1960s, first Off Broadway and then on Broadway in the show *It's a Bird, It's a Plane, It's Superman*. She was later featured in the comedy *Last of the Red Hot Lovers* before taking the starring role in the popular television sitcom *Alice*. By the time Lavin took on the role of Eugene's mom in *Broadway Bound*, she had firmly established herself as an accomplished stage performer. Now in her sixth decade on Broadway, Lavin has appeared in revivals of *Gypsy* and *The Diary of Anne Frank* as well as original hits such as Wendy Wasserstein's *The Sisters Rosensweig*, and *The Tale of the Allergist's Wife*. In early 2016, she had the leading role in an original play called *Our Mother's Brief Affair*.

Another Jewish star of stage and television who also made his Broadway debut thanks to Neil Simon is Judd Hirsch, who played the telephone repairman in *Barefoot in the Park*. It was a small role but a big step for the Bronx-born Hirsch, the son of a Russian-born Jewish mother and a father whose Jewish roots were from Germany. After graduating from City University in New York, Hirsch served a stint in the military and then worked at Westinghouse before landing the role in Neil Simon's hit musical. He would later return in 1977 to a starring role in Simon's *Chapter Two*. It was also in the late '70s that Hirsch became a household name for his Emmy-winning role as Alex Reiger in the classic sitcom *Taxi*.

A dedicated professional, Hirsch received extremely favorable reviews in nearly everything he did, from television, which also included his own series *Dear John* and in the CBS drama *Numb3rs*, to films, including *Independence Day* and *A Beautiful Mind*. Clearly Broadway theater critics and Tony voters were also won over by his roles in the original comedy *I'm Not Rappaport* and the dramatic *Conversations with My Father*, winning him a pair of Tony awards. After appearing in the revival of *A Thousand Clowns*, Hirsch reprised the role of Nat in the 2002 revival of *Rappaport*. Now over 80, Hirsch has joined the ranks of those who have seamlessly, and effectively, made the transition between television, film, and the Broadway stage.

Directing for Neil Simon … and Many Others: Mike Nichols

Michael Igor Peschkowsky was born in 1931, in Berlin, Germany, to German/Russian Jews. His father, a known anarchist, would flee Nazi Germany to settle in the United States and then send for his two sons, Michael (age seven) and his younger brother Robert (age three) in 1938. Their mother would soon follow.

The young Nichols grew up in New York City but went to college in Chicago, where he took up improvisation. It was while doing improv that he would meet Elaine May, another aspiring actress/comic who had first set foot on stage as a young child with her father, a Yiddish theater actor. Before long, Mike Nichols and Elaine May had formed a comedy team that would gain notoriety in the late 1950s at nightclubs and from television appearances. They would finally make their way to Broadway with a show simply entitled *An Evening with Mike Nichols and Elaine May*, which opened in late 1960 and ran for over 300 performances.

Unfortunately, disagreements would cause a split not long after their initial Broadway success. Both, however, would go on to successful careers, and they would reunite years later. Nichols would emerge as a Broadway director working with Neil Simon, directing *Barefoot in the Park*, *The Odd Couple*, *Plaza Suite* and *The Prisoner of Second Avenue*. He also took on a comedy called *Luv*, written by Elliott Baker and Murray Schisgal. *Luv* ran for over 900 performances on Broadway, and the movie version would include Elaine May.

From his improvisational days and his years on stage touring with Elaine May, Nichols simply knew comedy. He knew the timing, the pacing and the nuances that made a comedy work on stage, and an audience laugh. He also knew how to direct for the silver screen, and starting with *Who's Afraid of Virginia Woolf?* in 1966, he would go on to direct numerous films including *The Graduate, Working Girl* and *The Birdcage* among others.

But for Nichols, there was always a love of theater, and he never strayed far from the Broadway stage. In fact, it was a few years after directing *Annie* that Nichols would take a chance and bring young comic/actress Caryn Johnson, better known as Whoopi Goldberg, to Broadway in 1984 and essentially introduce her to the world in her own one-woman show, which drew critical acclaim and launched Goldberg's career.

Nichols would continue directing through five decades with the comedy *Spamalot* in 2005, receiving a Tony Award for his efforts. In fact, Nichols holds the rare distinction of winning an Oscar, Emmy, Grammy and Tony. If you consider that Nichols is a comedic genius, it may be because genius runs in the family. Supposedly, Albert Einstein was a cousin on his mother's side.

One of the many stars Nichols brought to Broadway was film legend Richard Dreyfuss, who in 1992 was cast alongside Gene Hackman and Glenn Close in the three-person drama *Death and the Maiden*. Technically, it wasn't the first time on Broadway for Dreyfuss, but it was the first time audiences truly had a chance to see him, since his previous two appearances in *But Seriously* and *Total Abandon* ran for a combined five performances. Like many other significant screen actors who never had a "career on Broadway," Dreyfuss was glad to have the opportunity to be a part of theater, and the reviews showed that he rose to the occasion.

Born to Jewish parents in Brooklyn, Dreyfuss would later move with his family to Bayside, Queens. It was shortly thereafter that he began racking up frequent flier miles as his family moved to Europe and then settled in Los Angeles, where he would hone his acting skills at a temple arts center and the local Jewish community center.

At 20, Dreyfuss landed two uncredited roles in *Valley of the Dolls* and *The Graduate*. But his big break came from his outstanding role in the film *American Graffiti* in 1973. He followed with a string of major films, including *Jaws, Close Encounters of the Third Kind*, Neil Simon's *The Goodbye Girl, Whose Life Is It Anyway?*, and, more recently, the television movie *Madoff*, where he played the legendary swindler Bernie Madoff.

Dreyfuss enjoyed the stage and did Off Broadway work and repertory theater along the way before returning to Broadway in *Death and the Maiden*. He later returned once more in 2004 in a revival of Larry Gelbart's comedy

Sly Fox, which ran for 173 performances. Through a long and illustrious career, Dreyfuss has also maintained his political and ethnic ties and speaks proudly about his Jewish heritage. In a *Jerusalem Post* article from 2015, he was quoted as saying, "Jews are the ones who, in any real terms, invented the open mind, negotiation, compromise, and learning how to live among those who dislike you, and still prevail."

David Merrick's Broadway Magic

While Neil Simon was the most prolific playwright of the 1960s and '70s, David Merrick was the producer with the most Broadway credits. Yet, Simon and Merrick only teamed up on one Broadway hit. Unlike Simon, who took a low-key, understated approach with smaller shows, Merrick was a producer with a flair for the dramatic. In fact, along with more than 80 productions, he often garnered media attention for his off-stage activities in the form of publicity stunts. For example, when his show *Fanny* met with unfavorable reviews, he drew attention to the production by erecting a statue of the show's belly dancer in Central Park. For another show that generated negative reviews, *Subways Are for Sleeping*, Merrick hired seven namesakes of major New York critics to provide quotes in newspaper ads praising the show. It was a trick that would only work once, since the legitimate critics were not pleased. And then there was the time he had a woman run onstage during *Look Back in Anger* and slap one of the actors. While Merrick's many hit shows drew their share of press, he also had writers, reporters and theatergoers wondering what stunt he would do next in an attempt to salvage a sinking show.

Merrick was born in 1912 to Jewish parents living in St. Louis, Missouri. His birth name was David Lee Margulois, but like many Jewish celebrities he would change his name to something less ethnic. After graduating from Washington University, he went on to law school and actually began a legal career. However, after only a few years in the profession, he grew tired of law and pursued a career in theater production. It took several years until he had his first play produced, and a few more years until he had his first of 27 Broadway shows, entitled *Fanny*, which he co-produced with Joshua Logan, who also co-wrote the book and directed the musical. Based on a French film trilogy, *Fanny* was about one woman and two men who love her, one with whom she has a child and the other whom she marries. The show opened at the Majestic Theater and ran for 888 performances.

Just four shows and three years later, Merrick would bring the sights, the sounds and the ambiance of *Jamaica* to Broadway for 558 performances starring

Lena Horne and Ricardo Montalban. Merrick always had a knack for bringing major name stars, as well as soon-to-be stars, to the Broadway stage.

Never one to be predictable, Merrick veered from the usual musical fare to bring Joan Osbourne's 1956 hit London drama *Look Back in Anger* to Broadway, where it won a Tony Award for Best Play, and ran for over 400 performances, while infusing the term "angry young men" into American culture. Merrick would do comedy as well, bringing Woody Allen's *Don't Drink the Water* to Broadway in 1961. It was also in '61 that Merrick introduced a teenaged Barbra Streisand to Broadway in the musical *I Can Get It for You Wholesale,* perhaps Merrick's most "Jewish" show, based on a novel by Jerome Weidman. Merrick was constantly on the move seeking out new shows, while bringing in top performers. He was also seeking out new wives as he was married six times.

Being that Merrick was producing numerous shows, it was not unusual for him to have several running at the same time and to compete against himself for Tony Awards. For example, in 1959 he was co-producing *Gypsy*, starring Ethel Merman and Jack Klugman at the Broadway Theatre. Then, within five months, he had Jackie Gleason, Walter Pidgeon and a young Valerie Harper on Broadway in *Take Me Along* at the Shubert Theater. Both *Gypsy* and *Take Me Along* went up for Best Musical in 1960, but neither was able to grab the award from *The Sound of Music*. In 1963, he had *Tchin-Tchin* up for Best Play, as well as *Stop the World—I Want to Get Off* and *Oliver!*, both up for Best Musical. Again, he did not win in either category. In 1964, however, he won for Best Play, with Joan Osbourne's *Luther* and for Best Musical with a show called *Hello, Dolly!*

Yes, it was in 1964, when Merrick brought *Hello, Dolly!* to Broadway, with music by Jerry Herman. Prior to *Dolly*, Jerry Herman had written both the music and lyrics for *Milk and Honey* in 1961. Like most of Broadway's Jewish musical legends, Herman grew up in a house with a piano. As Stella Adler's daughter, Ellen, noted earlier, "Jewish families had pianos. Music was part of Jewish family life."[1]

Jerry Herman's mom sang and played piano in Catskills hotels, and his parents owned and ran a summer camp in the Berkshire Mountains in Massachusetts. It was at the camp that they regularly staged theatrical productions. Clearly, music was a major part of Jerry Herman's early years.

After graduating from the University of Miami, Herman settled in New York City where he produced an Off Broadway revue called *I Feel Wonderful*. Despite a limited run, it was the starting point of Herman's theatrical career, which would bring him to Broadway in 1960 with a revue called *From A to Z*. However, it was his work on *Milk and Honey* that generated attention, and from there it was on to *Hello, Dolly!*, which featured Herman's immensely popular title track, written in just one afternoon. Much to the surprise and delight of Herman and Merrick, Louis Armstrong's recording of *Hello Dolly!* became a huge chart-topping single. Petula Clark's cover version in French resulted in a hit overseas.

Adapted from Thornton Wilder's story *The Matchmaker* (which was adapted from Johann Nestroy's comedy *The Merchant of Yonkers*), *Hello, Dolly!* featured Dolly Gallagher Levi as the Yonkers-based matchmaker. Like many major musicals, *Dolly* was the result of many transformations in the long, arduous process of bringing a musical to Broadway. Ethel Merman, whom Merrick had worked with in *Gypsy*, was asked to play Dolly, but turned the role down. Her lost opportunity gave Carol Channing the biggest break in her long career. It didn't come easily, however, as director Gower Champion, and Merrick, asked Channing to audition for the role. She agreed to do an audition since she very much wanted the part. Channing had not been in a Broadway hit since *Gentlemen Prefer Blondes*, more than a decade earlier. A year after her audition, she would walk away clutching a Tony Award for her performance as Dolly.

Hello, Dolly! would play for what was then a record 2,844 performances, broken less than a year later by *Fiddler*. The musical would win ten Tony Awards in 1964, a record that would stand for 37 years until *The Producers* topped it with 12. During the long run of the show, there were even more Dollys than Merrick had wives. Following Channing, the list included Ginger Rogers, Martha Raye, Betty Grable, Pearl Bailey, Bibi Osterwald, Phyllis Diller and finally Ethel Merman. It seemed that no matter who donned the magical Dolly headdress, she would enjoy the notoriety that came with being part of a show that epitomized the Broadway musical on a grand scale.

Following *Hello, Dolly!*, Jerry Herman would help bring to Broadway another matchmaking widow with an infectious theme song when he introduced the musical *Mame* in 1966, based on the novel *Auntie Mame*, which had been a play in 1954.

Meanwhile, Merrick's next significant hit was a very small two-person musical spanning the life of a married couple called *I Do! I Do!*, starring Mary Martin and Robert Preston. The show ran for over 550 performances and proved, as Neil Simon had done with *They're Playing Our Song*, that musicals need not have large ensembles to be successful.

After bringing Robert Goulet to Broadway in the 1968 musical *The Happy Time*, based on a novel by Robert Fontaine, Merrick and Simon had their one Broadway moment together with *Promises, Promises*, which after a long Broadway run spent 14 months on tour.

By the 1970s, Broadway was indeed changing, with *Two by Two*, *Godspell*, *Jesus Christ Superstar* and *Joseph and the Amazing Technicolor Dreamcoat* bringing the Bible and Christianity to the stage, albeit with the help of some Jewish writers, performers and producers. Merrick however, turned his attention to the 1959 film classic, *Some Like It Hot* for his latest venture, and by 1972, despite tremendous friction between almost everyone associated with the stage production, the musical *Sugar* was born. With Jule Styne writing the music and Merrick's usual director/choreographer Gower Champion on board, plus a cast that included Robert Morse and Tony Roberts, one would have expected *Sugar* to be a runaway hit. It was not. While it ran for over 500 performances, *Sugar* was not as sweet as expected at the box office.

There would be one more mega hit in the long, impressive career of David Merrick. It was a musical that would pay tribute to the street from which the theater district grew to the north. The show, *42nd Street*, with Gower Champion once again as director/choreographer, was based on the 1933 film about life behind the scenes in show business. A simple story about a chorus girl who gets her big break, literally, when the star breaks an ankle, and then goes on to stardom, was enough to carry the show with plenty of songs and excellent dance numbers. Sadly, director/choreographer Champion never saw the success of his significant efforts in making this show a hit as he died on opening night. Merrick announced the news to a stunned cast and audience after the opening performance. The musical went on to run for 3,486 performances.

In his long career, Merrick was able to take dramas, small musicals and major extravaganzas and make them work with star power, dynamic staging and even promotional gimmicks when necessary. He was indeed one of the most significant producers of the century.

And the Music Played On: Strouse, Schwartz and Marvin

Berlin, the Gershwins, Bernstein, Rodgers and Hammerstein ... the lineage of Jewish composers and lyricists continued. Along with Jerry Herman, Stephen Sondheim and the team of Bock and Harnick, Charles Strouse would come into prominence in the 1960s, and Stephen Schwartz would follow in the '70s, along with Marvin Hamlisch.

Strouse was born to Jewish parents, Ira and Ethel Strouse, in New York City in 1928. His mom played a straddling piano in their home and had a feel for swing and jazz. His dad was in the tobacco industry. Strouse recalls some of the anti–Semitism while growing up during the 1930s. "We were living on a street with a Parochial School and they bullied us, threw things at us and stomped us," says Strouse. "We were never really hurt but it was very real," he

I was honored to receive a doctor of humane letters award from Five Towns College, along with Ervin Drake, left, and Charles Strouse, right, who were also receiving honorary awards (photograph by Rob Rich).

adds. "I also remember anti–Semitism when working on a farm in Massachusetts. The locals were not happy about having Jews in their town, so they beat up my brother and tied me to a tree and lit a fire under me. Fortunately, I was rescued," recalls Strouse of the horrifying experience that resulted from the fact that he was Jewish.[2]

Strouse went on to attend the Eastman Conservatory in Rochester. He would become an accomplished piano player by his early teens and study with Aaron Copland. Later he would write music for newsreels and early television programs before heading to Paris to study music abroad. Strouse recalls, while abroad, seeing the grand opera houses existing within a world of royalty, which was not open to Jews. The Jews as he saw it, in parts of Europe, had to make their own theater, which they did.

Upon returning to the United States, he began writing music for Movietone News, which played before films at the movie theaters. "It was canned music that they could use in films, but I didn't care, I just wanted to make beautiful music," he adds.[3]

In 1949, Strouse met a Jewish lyricist from Mansfield, Ohio, named Lee Adams, who had earned a master's degree from Columbia University. Together they would team up on some major musicals, starting with *Bye Bye Birdie* in 1960.

Birdie was the breakthrough hit Strouse and Adams were seeking. The musical, which was similar to the story of Elvis Presley, focused attention on a young fictional pop icon, Conrad Birdie who, much like Elvis, was being drafted into the military. In this case, the news wreaked havoc on a small town in Ohio where teenage girls were overwhelmed at the thought of their hero going off to the army. It might be noted that Conrad Birdie was supposed to be called Conrad Twitty until the real Conrad Twitty (who later went on to become a popular country singer), stepped out of the woodwork and threatened to sue the producers.

The uplifting score by Strouse and Adams, coupled with the book by Michael Bennett and direction and choreography from Gower Champion, created a pop-culture classic that would open the door for other teen-based musicals such as *Grease* and *Hairspray* years later. *Birdie* ran for 607 performances and became a major hit film in 1963. The show won a Tony Award for Best Musical, while charming audiences young and old. Dick Van Dyke, Michael Bennett and Gower Champion also won Tony Awards (Champion actually won two for both directing and choreography).

Following the success of *Birdie*, Strouse and Adams worked with Broadway newcomer Mel Brooks on the unsuccessful football-themed show *All American*, which came and went in a couple of months. From football, Strouse and Adams turned their attention to boxing and created a musical version of Clifford Odets' 1937 drama, *Golden Boy*. Changing the theme from the struggles of an Italian American to those of an African American boxer, played by a Jewish actor, Sammy Davis, Jr., *Golden Boy* was well-timed, at the onset of the growing civil rights movement. As a result, it ran for more than 500 performances. Davis had appeared a few years earlier, making his Broadway debut in *Mr. Wonderful*. Then, in a complete turnabout, Strouse and Adams brought the comic strip hero *Superman* to life with *It's a Bird, It's a Plane, It's Superman*. Unfortunately, theatergoers were not taken in by the man of steel on stage, and the play had a short run.

It was the 1970 show *Applause*, at the Palace Theater, that brought Strouse and Adams back to prominence. With a book by Comden and Green, *Applause* brought a musical version of the 1950 film classic *All About Eve* to the Broadway stage and ran for nearly 900 performances, making it the biggest hit for Strouse and Adams to date. It was also the breakthrough for actress Lauren Bacall (discussed later) who starred as fictional theater star Margo Channing. In the story, Channing falls prey to a ruthless newcomer named Eve who plots to steal her career and her man. *Applause* brought Strouse his second Tony Award.

While the popular theme song for the classic sitcom *All in the Family* was also attributed to Strouse and Adams, the next major Broadway musical for

Strouse was based on the comic strip *Little Orphan Annie*. This time, Strouse teamed with director/lyricist Martin Charnin. Another New Yorker, Charnin was one of the gang members in the original *West Side Story*. He also collaborated on musicals with Richard Rodgers.

Annie was set in a New York City orphanage in the depression era, and it promoted courage and optimism in the face of hard times. Unlike Superman, *Annie* was successful at bringing a comic strip character to Broadway as the young orphan girl won the hearts of theatergoers and the song "Tomorrow" became a modern standard.

Following Annie, which ran for a whopping 2,377 performances, Strouse wrote music for a number of major motion pictures plus several other Broadway shows. One particular show, *Rags*, was about an immigrant Jewish mother who escapes Europe with her children, settles on the Lower East Side of Manhattan and falls in love with a Jewish labor union leader. Despite being a box office bust, *Rags* drew high critical acclaim and was nominated for a Tony Award for best musical in 1987.

Rags was probably the most "Jewish" show Strouse ever wrote. Yet, Strouse feels that his religion was reflected in much of his work, as was the case with most of the Jewish composers, especially "Lenny" (Bernstein), as Strouse calls him. "I feel the Jewish heritage in me, but I am an Atheist," explains Strouse. "There's a cynicism among Jews that enables them to appreciate the vulgarity of the world. It seems to me that there's a kind of worldliness and acceptance of the 'crap' that's in the world and that's where musical theater grew, not out of the royalty of the opera but out of being oppressed," says Strouse, claiming that musicals are the bastard of the arts.[4]

Rags was later revised and revived in 1991 by the Jewish American Theater, and then again in Florida in 1999. *Rags* also brought Strouse together with lyricist Stephen Lawrence Schwartz, whose career, like that of Strouse, also took off in the 1960s, although for Schwartz it was the late '60s. The son of Sheila and Stanley Schwartz, a teacher and businessman, respectively, Stephen was born in 1948 and grew up in the Jewish community of Minneola on Long Island. His musical prowess, which began at an early age, landed him in the prestigious The Juilliard School of Music while he was still in high school. After college, Schwartz had a short career as a record producer before trying his hand at writing lyrics for musicals. His first success came at the age of 21, with the 1969 hit musical *Butterflies Are Free*, which opened at the Booth Theater and ran for over 1,100 performances before becoming a film in 1972.

Meanwhile, the 1970s saw a number of experimental and nontraditional musicals make their way to Broadway. This was, in part, due to the late '60s box office success of the counter-culture hit *Hair*, which did not follow linear story lines and threw many of the conventions of theater out the window. In addition to the changing style and face of Broadway, the names and faces of the cast and creative teams were also changing. A down economy meant that fewer new shows were opening on Broadway, and as a result many of the established performers picked up and moved to California to focus their attention on film and television.

Nonetheless, there were still hit musicals, and two of the most significant brought the music of Schwartz back to the Broadway stage. *Godspell* was actually a college project that emerged as one of the longest running Off Broadway shows in history, opening in Greenwich Village and moving to the Promenade Theater, which is technically on Broadway at 76th Street, but is not considered a "Broadway theater." The musical, featuring parables presenting Bible stories, drew criticism for the hippie-esque clothing and pop-culture manner in which Christ was portrayed. The music, however, by Schwartz, infused gospel, rock and other styles into the score along with Episcopal hymns, which won over audiences night after night. Along with a very successful cast album, the song "Day by Day" became a major hit. While *Godspell* ran for just over 500 performances on Broadway, it saw some 2,600 overall staged performances in New York City before going on tour and becoming a very frequently staged musical by local theater troupes. It was also made into a successful film.

Pippin, meanwhile was also initially a college project, this one by Schwartz himself. It is the story of the son of Charlemagne (Charles the Great), King of the Franks in the A.D. 700s. Like *Godspell, Pippin* tells the stories through a series of events, this time using a commedia dell'arte performance style originally developed in Italy in the 16th and 17th centuries. The style of performance features an improvisational comedic approach incorporating masks and costumes, often clown like. The success of *Godspell,* and the conviction of Bob Fosse to take a chance, helped bring *Pippin* directly to Broadway where it ran for 1,944 performances. A 2013 revival brought *Pippin* back to Broadway for over 700 more performances, and, once again, great reviews.

Schwartz would go on to write the music for a number of other Broadway musicals over what is now a career that has spanned six decades. One of his biggest hits is *Wicked,* the current box-office smash, discussed later in the book. Schwartz is also one of a few elite lyricists who have had the honor of topping 1,500 performances with three musicals, the first of which being *Pippin* and the most recent being *Wicked.* In between would be the more difficult one to recall, even for those with Broadway trivia expertise. It just happened to be Doug Henning's *The Magic Show,* which topped 1,900 performances in the mid–1970s. Schwartz wrote ten songs for what was primarily a vehicle for Henning's talent with a thin plot line built around his amazing sleight of hand.

Schwartz would also pen the lyrics for a number of films including the Disney hits *Pocahontas, The Hunchback of Notre Dame* and *The Prince of Egypt.*

And then there was Marvin Hamlisch. While Hamlisch was far better known for more than 50 film scores, his claim to Broadway fame was being part of one of the most successful shows in musical history, *A Chorus Line.*

Born in New York City to a Viennese-Jewish couple, Lilly and Max Hamlisch, young Marvin was playing piano by the age of five and accepted into The Juilliard School Pre-College Division at the age of seven. After graduating from Queens College, he started writing film scores, including some for early Woody Allen movies including *Take the Money and Run* and *Bananas.* It was, however, in 1974, at the age of 30, that Hamlisch would be asked to write the music, with lyricist Edward Kleban, for a show about 19 dancers auditioning to be part of a chorus line. The auditioners would become the show and the audience would get to know them intimately as they bared their souls on stage. This inside look at the trials and tribulations of Broadway dancers resulted in *A Chorus Line,* which was initially produced by Joseph Papp Off Broadway at New York's Public Theater. The demand for tickets was so great that the show moved to the Shubert Theater on Broadway where it held fort for over 6,100 perform-

I had the pleasure of working with Marvin Hamlisch, right, on *The Goodbye Girl.* He was a very talented and genuinely nice gentleman (photograph by Anita Shevette).

ances, shattering all previous Broadway records as 6.5 million attendees took in the groundbreaking production.

While Hamlisch would go on to write the music for the autobiographical *They're Playing Our Song, The Goodbye Girl* and a handful of other Broadway shows, nothing could match the magnitude of *A Chorus Line*. The musical earned Hamlisch a Tony Award and a Pulitzer Prize, to go along with Emmys, Grammys and Oscars, a feat which only Richard Rodgers had previously accomplished.

The Definitive Musical Team of the '60s (and Beyond)

The music of composer John Kander and the lyrics of Fred Ebb were also prominently featured in the theaters in the 1960s as the duo joined forces on the first three Broadway musicals in their long and prosperous partnership.

Kander hailed from Kansas City, Missouri, where he began studying music at an early age. After college the young Jewish musician moved to New York City and attended Columbia University where he received his master's degree. It was also in New York that Kander would get his first taste of Broadway as a rehearsal piano player for *West Side Story*.

Ebb, meanwhile, was a New York Jew, born and raised in the Big Apple. He too earned a master's degree from Columbia University. However, despite their shared alma mater, Kander and Ebb did not meet until several years later. Ebb, while working odd jobs, such as bronzing baby shoes, began writing lyrics for nightclub acts and theater revues as well as for the musical *From A to Z*, which had a short run on Broadway in 1960.

It was in 1962 that Kander and Ebb first met. Together they would forge a career that would last five decades. Prior to their Broadway success, the two sat down and wrote songs together, two of which were recorded by an up and coming vocalist named Barbra Streisand. One of the two Streisand recordings, "My Coloring Book," became her second single.

In 1965, the duo had their first Broadway show entitled *Flora the Red Menace*, based on the novel *Love Is Just Around the Corner* by Lester Atwell. *Flora* focused on a young fashion designer seeking work during the Great Depression. She finds herself drawn into the Communist Party, in part because of the man with whom she has fallen in love. While the show lasted only 87 performances on Broadway, at a loss of some $400,000 (which was very significant for 1965), it also featured another up and coming female star, 19-year-old Liza Minnelli, in a Tony Award–winning performance.

From that point on, it was onward and upward for Kander and Ebb as they took on the score for *Cabaret,* which opened in 1965, ran for over 1,165 performances and won the Tony Award for Best Musical Score. In 1968 they teamed with David Merrick and Gower Champion to compose words and music for *The Happy Time.* Also in '68 they would provide the music and lyrics for *Zorba,* adapted from the novel *Zorba the Greek* by Nikos Kazantzakis. *Zorba* played for over 300 performances in 1968 and again for over 300 more performances in 1983.

Once established, the team of Kander and Ebb stepped up again for the musical version of a 1926 play about the gangsters of the era in the city of Chicago. The musical simply titled *Chicago* opened on Broadway in 1975 with Bob Fosse serving as director and choreographer. Much like the sleazy atmosphere that was the backdrop for the Berlin nightclub in *Cabaret, Chicago* was a musical about the underworld and Roxy Hart's journey to vaudeville stardom despite killing her ex-lover. Once again there was also a master of ceremony, this time with a vaudeville flair. The show ran for just shy of 900 performances starting in 1975 ... but it wasn't finished. *Chicago* would return in 1996 as *Chicago: The Musical* and win the Tony Award for Best Revival of a Musical. It would proceed to run for more than 8,000 performances and is still going strong as of the second edition of the book, putting it in the top ten all-time longest running Broadway musicals.

As for Kander and Ebb, following Liza Minnelli's *The Act* in 1977, I would be fortunate to work with them on *Woman of the Year* in 1981. They would later usher in the new decade, the 1990s, with *Kiss of the Spider Woman* in 1991. They continued to work together for years to come, until Fred Ebb died of a heart attack in 2004.

Along with Broadway musicals, Kander and Ebb penned the music and lyrics for films and television specials, including those for Liza and for Frank Sinatra. They also have the distinction of writing the most notable song for the city they called home, recorded separately by both Sinatra and Minnelli, "New York, New York." They were called by some the Rodgers and Hammerstein of the second half of the 20th century.

Under the Spotlights

The 1960s and '70s were also a time when Jewish performers were once again prominently featured under the spotlights, as they had been back in the days of vaudeville. Along with Zero Mostel, Jack Gilford, Phil Silvers, Bea Arthur and other established Jewish stage performers, there were newcomers such as Streisand, mentioned earlier, who made their mark on Broadway.

One such newcomer to the Broadway stage was Lauren Bacall, whose film career had begun over 25 years earlier and included *The Big Sleep, Dark Passage, Key Largo* and *How to Marry a Millionaire.* Bacall first hit Broadway in the early '60s in *Goodbye, Charlie* and the Abe Burrows comedy *Cactus Flower.* But her triumph of the Broadway stage was yet to come.

Born in 1924 in New York City to Polish-Jewish immigrants, Bacall took her mother's name since she had little contact with her father after her parents' divorce. Working as a theater usher, she was discovered by a modeling agent and became a fashion model in the early 1940s. While modeling, she studied at the American Academy of Dramatic Arts. By the age of 20 she would begin a long and celebrated film career. But Broadway was always a passion of Bacall. Then in 1970, she would enjoy her most celebrated stage performance in the Charles Strouse, Lee Adams, Comden and Green hit musical *Applause.* Bacall brought with her to Broadway the Hollywood elegance and grace that had established her as a film star. Rave reviews and a Tony Award clearly indicated that Bacall had indeed made a major impact. Ten years later I would have the pleasure of working with her when she took on the leading role in *Woman of the Year,* for which she once again walked away with a Tony Award. The show, meanwhile, ran for 770 performances.

It was also during the 1970s that Joel Katz followed in the footsteps of his father, nightclub and Catskills performer Mickey Katz. As it would turn out, the younger Katz would eclipse his father's show business success under the name Joel Grey. Born in Cleveland, Ohio, in 1932, Grey started performing when he was ten. After landing understudy roles in *Come Blow Your Horn* and *Stop the World—I Want to Get Off,* Grey would win over audiences and critics in his mid–30s as the emcee at the sordid Kit Kat Club in pre–Hitler Berlin in the musical *Cabaret.* In fact, Grey won a Tony Award for his supporting and very memorable role. He would later be called upon to reprise the role for the film version. For his efforts he won an Oscar. Grey then returned to Broadway in his signature role once more when the musical was revived.

The next significant role for Grey had him starring as the legendary George M. Cohan in 1968. The show, simply entitled *George M!* ran for only 427 performances, but it established Grey as a serious triple threat, singing, dancing and acting his way to critical acclaim and a Tony Award nomination (he lost to Jerry Orbach in *Promises, Promises*).

After another Tony nomination for his role in *Goodtime Charley* in 1975, Grey would be cast in the Jerry Herman musical *The Grand Tour.* Although the show was not a box office hit, it was an ambitious effort set just prior to World

War II, about a Jewish man who finds himself having to team up with an anti–Semite in order to stay one step ahead of the approaching Nazis.

Following the 1987 revival of *Cabaret*, as well as his appearance in a revival of the hit musical *Chicago*, Grey would land in the hugely successful hit *Wicked*. While Grey also made his share of feature films and television appearances, he is best known as one of the elite stars of Broadway. A true song and dance man in the style of many greats who came before him, Grey has been recognized by both theatergoers and by his peers for his on-stage prowess. He is also known for his charitable work for organizations such as the Children's Defense Fund. In keeping with the family's show business lineage, Grey's daughter Jennifer became a screen actress, best known for her role in the 1997 film *Dirty Dancing*.

Kevin Kline, Goldie Hawn, Bebe Neuwirth and other Jewish performers were also seen on Broadway during this era, while establishing their television

and film careers. One stage actress who was always considered for Jewish roles was Terri Sue Feldshuh (pronounced Feld-shoo), better known as Tovah. Unlike the early Yiddish theater performers, Tovah, also born in New York City, did not know about poverty during her youth, growing up in an affluent community.

Also unlike many of those who preceded her, she would first change her stage name to the less ethnic-sounding Terri Fairchild before deciding to go instead with her Hebrew name, Tovah, and return to her real last name, Feldshuh.

For someone who loves theater as much as I do, it's always an honor to be around someone as multitalented as Joel Grey, right (photograph by Anita Shevette).

Tovah Feldshuh has lit up the stages of Broadway for four decades, while also winning the Eleanor Roosevelt Humanities Award and the Israel Peace Medal (photograph by Rob Rich).

Her first Broadway experience was seeing Gwen Verdon in the original run of *Damn Yankees* in 1955 as a very young child. She knew at that time that this was something she definitely wanted to pursue. Years later, she would make her own Broadway debut in the show *Cyrano*, in 1973, which had a shorter run than *Cyrano's* nose. Nonetheless, it was a starting point for the young performer. "I was in a little more than the chorus, with fourteen lines," says Feldshuh.[5]

It was in *Yentl*, however, first Off Broadway and then on Broadway, that Tovah made her mark, generating critical acclaim, audience attention and a Tony Award nomination. Feldshuh appeared in other Broadway shows and expanded her career to films and television. She would then establish herself in the record books for bringing the life of Israeli Prime Minister Golda Meir to the stage in *Golda's Balcony*, the longest-running one-woman show in the history of Broadway, lasting nearly 500 performances. It is a role for which she became forever associated.

In contrast to the many Jewish performers who changed their names to be "less Jewish," Tovah benefitted to some degree by keeping her Jewish name. "When you see the name Tovah Feldshuh, assumptions would go along with that name. I would work hard and master these roles, but people assumed I had a foot in the door," explains Feldshuh.[6] However, she did later acknowledge that when it came to Jewish roles in plays such as *Kissing Jessica Stein* and *Golda's Balcony*, among other shows, she was thought of immediately. Conversely, when Neil Simon or a director was looking for a non–Jewish, or "less Jewish," actor to play a Jewish character for more mainstream appeal, she had a much harder time landing such roles. Nonetheless, she did land her share of non–Jewish roles in several shows including *Lend Me a Tenor* and *She Stoops to Conquer*, where she performed Off Broadway with Nathan Lane.

Feldshuh, whose Jewish identity has always remained a significant part of who she is, also weighed in on why the Jewish people gravitated to the entertainment industry and theater in particular. From her perspective, the Jewish immigrant population in America wanted to participate and have a voice in their new world. "For centuries, the Irish were mauled by the British, so when they emigrated to the United States, they became cops and elected officials. They wanted to have some control over their environment. Similarly, the Jews in Europe were denied entry into so many aspects of society that when we arrived here, we took the opportunity to participate in the media, not only entertainment, but the newspaper industry as well,"[7] explains Feldshuh about the Jews making sure to have a voice, fair representation and some control over the message. "We didn't want the message to be about the country clubs that denied access to Jewish people. We wanted it to be about opportunities for everyone to reach the American Dream and we wanted to be champions of that dream,"[8] she adds. The media and the stage (and later the screen) provided the opportunity to be part of the message. In fact, Feldshuh also explains that theater allowed the Jewish people to present the message using two things the Jewish people are very good at: storytelling and humor. "We were always great storytellers, and we could be self-deprecating before others could deprecate us,"[9] says Feldshuh.

Tovah also notes that as a child she was taught to ride a horse at a young age. As she points out, the Cossacks and military leaders in Eastern Europe rode horses and wielded great power, especially over the Jewish people. "It was important to get up on a horse not just as a means of assimilation, but as a way of showing that the Jews had arrived in a place of power from which we were once murdered in the old days,"[10] explains Feldshuh.

Tovah Feldshuh continues to have a tremendous commitment to both the theater and to her Jewish heritage, to which she remained dedicated through her tireless involvement in numerous Jewish organizations and causes.

From Streisand playing Fanny Brice to Mostel in *Fiddler* to Tovah Feldshuh as Golda Meir, the Jewish presence was indeed felt through the performers on the stages of Broadway in the 1960s and '70s.

JOSEPH PAPP

One key contributor to Broadway in the 1960s and '70s was Joseph Papp. The sheer determination to bring quality theater to the people of New York City epitomized Papp's long career. Often very critical of Broadway, claiming those who were involved were in it for the money, Papp nonetheless had a major influence on Broadway and helped save it when box office numbers dropped in the '0s.

"I feel better when I lose Tony's than when I win them. When I win, I become part of that Broad-

Joseph Papp revolutionized American theater with rainbow casting, controversial topics and affordable ticket prices to attract a wider, more diverse, audience (photograph by Joe Marzullo).

way thing. When I lose, it makes me feel clean," Papp was quoted as saying in a *New York Daily News* article.[11]

Born Joseph Papirofsky in Brooklyn in 1921, to Jewish immigrant parents from Russia, Papp spent his youth helping his family make ends meet with a series of jobs ranging from telegraph messenger to chicken plucker. It was in the Navy, during World War II, that he discovered his knack for staging shows with limited resources. After the war, while working as a stage manager at CBS television, Papp fell victim to the anti–Communist scourge, being labeled as a Communist sympathizer. Despite having just served in the United States Navy, his work with a radical acting group in California and his left wing views were enough circumstantial evidence to cause Papp to lose his job. But his loss was New York City's gain. Papp had always wanted to bring affordable theater to the people of the city by presenting free Shakespearian plays in the city's parks. In the late 1950s, his dream became a reality when he would stage the first Shakespeare plays in Central Park. Of course, Papp and the newly named Shakespeare Festival in the Park would be challenged by politicians, such as the mayor of New York City at that time, Robert Moses, who tried to shut down the free shows for fear of ruining the park. Papp would go head to head with the mayor and win public support. With many prominent New Yorkers backing his efforts, he would proceed to win the battle and dazzle New Yorkers, which is not an easy feat.

In the many years of the Shakespeare in the Park Festival, stars including James Earl Jones, George C. Scott, Richard Dreyfuss, Martin Sheen, Meryl Streep, Sam Waterson, Kevin Kline and Linda Ronstadt have participated. And when the festival needed money, the public was generous and donated what they could so that the shows would continue.

Once the Shakespeare in the Park Festival found a permanent home in Central Park's open air Delacorte Theater, Papp turned his attention to his other goal of presenting public theater. He wanted to find a venue in which new, innovative and alternative plays and musicals could be introduced to the public. Such a people's theater would be a place where plays could be developed and where theatergoers could enjoy a performance for a reasonable price. In 1967, following a new law in New York City which stated that buildings deemed as landmarks could not be torn down, Papp found an ideal venue in the old Astor Library in New York's East Village. The price was right as the city charged just $1 per year in rent.

Following a massive renovation, the new Public Theater would present many original plays, generating attention from a diverse audience that was not the typical "Broadway theater crowd" by Papp's assessment. These shows took on major issues of the time, much as the Group Theater had done in the 1930s.

Little did Papp know that some of the shows in the Public Theater would have a major effect on Broadway. One of the first productions was the countercultural hippie tribal rock musical *Hair*. Of course the musical would eventually move to Broadway in 1968 and become a triumphant success, revived in recent years. Other Papp productions would follow the path to Broadway, the most famous of which being *A Chorus Line*, followed by *I'm Getting My Act Together and Taking It on the Road*, *The Pirates of Penzance* and *The Mystery of Edwin Drood*, among others. The difference was that following the success of *Hair*, Papp remained attached to the other shows as producer once the shows made their transition to the Great White Way. While still not a fan of Broadway's commercialism, Papp was no fool, and he knew he could use the money earned by one Broadway smash hit to maintain the Public Theater and the New York Shakespeare Festival as well as support other ventures such as the Theater for a New Audience and the Riverside Shakespeare Company. In addition to presenting new shows, Papp supported nontraditional, rainbow casting and, in part spurred on by his son being gay, responded to the growing AIDS crisis in New York City by presenting Larry Kramer's controversial play on the subject, called *The Normal Heart*, which generated critical acclaim and brought the issue to greater public awareness.

Sure, Papp criticized Broadway, but his influence was, and still is, significant. Public Theater provided a starting point for shows, some of which clearly impacted Broadway, while others left their mark on audiences in Off Broadway productions. A true visionary, Papp actually saved Broadway in the '70s with *A Chorus Line*, and in the process also saved the struggling Shubert Organization that brought the show to one of its theaters. For young performers he was a godsend. Whether he was doing Shakespeare in the Park or *The Basic Training of Pavlo Hummel*, part of David Rabe's Vietnam War trilogy (*Sticks and Bones*, which went to Broadway and won a Tony Award), Papp gave young performers of all races, colors and religions an opportunity to be part of meaningful theater. He truly believed in opening the doors for new talent including up-and-coming playwrights, producers and directors.

Nine years after his death in 2000, the Joseph Papp Children's Humanitarian Fund was formed to help Jewish children in the Ukraine receive the food, shelter and medical care they so badly need.

A Jewish Supporter in Washington

Clearly, one of the most notable figures of the 1960s was Lyndon Baines Johnson, the 36th president of the United States. During one of the most turbulent decades in American history, Johnson, or LBJ as he was called, had his hands full with an unpopular war in Vietnam and growing civil unrest during the civil rights movement. And yet, with all of that on his plate, LBJ, as it would come to be known many years later, was a major supporter of Israel and the Jewish people.

A 2015 Associated Press report revealed LBJ's "personal and often emotional connection to Israel." Recently released tapes revealed that during Johnson's presidency the United States became Israel's primary arms supplier, during (and after) the 1967 Six Day War with the United Arab Republic.

Tracing Johnson's history back further, long before his support of Israel, or even the State of Israel, he was active in rescuing many Polish Jews during the Holocaust by supplying them with visas during his years as a Texas congressman in the late 1930s. Aware of the increasing threats to European Jews, he provided signed immigration papers that were used to get more than forty Jews out of Warsaw. Historians also point out that he was able to bring many Jewish immigrants into the United States through Galveston, some legally and some illegally, saving possibly more than 500 European Jews. It is also believed that during World War II, Johnson was reportedly shipping arms to Jewish underground freedom fighters in crates marked Texas Grapefruit.

There is much more now being reported by historians on LBJ's tremendous support of the Jewish people and the State of Israel. As for his personal connection, historians note that both of Johnson's great-grandparents on the maternal side were Jewish. Therefore, when Bryan Cranston, who also had a Jewish grandmother, went on to win a Tony award for his portrayal of Johnson in the 2014 play *All the Way*, he might have been portraying the first Jewish president. Either way, the latest documentation of the former president from Texas shows that he was a major supporter of the Jewish people in the 1960s and for years before that.

Jewish Life in the '60s and '70s

Many of the half-million Jewish soldiers in World War II took advantage of the GI Bill and went to college. The result was that by the 1960s, there was an increase in Jewish professionals living the good life in the vastly growing suburbs, especially around New York City.

While assimilation, money and stability also planted the seeds for a new conservatism among some Jews, many others followed the lineage that leaned to the political left. Members of the Jewish community, now more firmly entrenched in the greater community at large, became active in the growing feminist movement, the gay and lesbian community, the anti-war protests and other social and cultural issues that epitomized the '60s and spilled over into the '70s. From rabbis to social, community and political leaders, to playwrights, producers, directors and performers, the Jewish people took part in addressing the issues that came to the forefront during these eye-opening decades. From the Public Theater of Joseph Papp, to Off Broadway to Broadway itself, theater remained one place in which to shed light on many of the important issues and concerns of the day ... while also providing marvelous entertainment.

In addition, American Jews brought attention to the struggles of their fellow Jews abroad. For example, there was growing awareness and support for Soviet Jews who were still seeking a better life. There was also a growing commitment to the young state of Israel, support that has remained a common bond throughout the Jewish community.

As was once the case with the Yiddish theater, the Jewish community continued to embrace Broadway, especially as they saw more of themselves and their culture on stage. The regular, typically more affluent, Manhattan-based "theater crowd" now extended off the island and into the boroughs, onto Long Island, up north into Westchester and Connecticut, and across the river into New Jersey. Jewish families were among the most frequent supporters and visitors of Broadway.

And yet, despite enjoying numerous shows from their seats in the orchestra or the balconies, and recognizing the significance of the many hugely successful Jewish stars behind the scenes or under the stage lights, many Jewish parents, including my own, still had great skepticism about their sons and daughters embarking on a career in theater. I guess some things never change.

7

Young Playwrights
with a Message,
Inflation, Disney and Me

The 1980s and 1990s brought a new breed of Jewish playwrights to Broadway. Not unlike the writers of the 1930s Group Theater, these young writers were politically astute and were also hoping to raise awareness to significant social issues and political oversights through their work. For them, issues such as the anti–Semitism of the 1930s were no longer among the prominent concerns. The impact upon Broadway by Jewish writers, composers and performers was now quite well accepted, and being a Jewish playwright or composer may have even proven to be advantageous considering the track record.

Many of the new generation of Jewish playwrights were gay, and they had very serious concerns about social acceptance and about the growing AIDS epidemic. One of the best known of these playwrights was Larry Kramer.

Born in 1935, Kramer grew up in a Jewish family in Maryland. Although he dated women in high school, he was exploring his sexuality, and by the time he was in Yale, in the mid–1950s, he realized that he was gay. By the late 1970s, Kramer had already enjoyed screen success with *Women in Love*, by D.H. Lawrence, and had written a satirical novel entitled *Faggots*. Along with his involvement in gay causes, Kramer gained a lot of attention for his views on the gay lifestyle. He frequently spoke out against gay promiscuity and promoted lasting monogamous relationships. As the AIDS epidemic grew, Kramer's voice became more prominent as he sought to increase public awareness, political action and funding for the medical community to conduct research in an effort to find an effective cure. He was highly critical of the society's blind eye toward the growing crisis.

Kramer's success and status as a playwright was based largely on one epic drama, *The Normal Heart*, which ran through the 1980s at the Public Theater. While the illness is unnamed in the play, it is the central theme of a show that came in part from the deaths of many of Kramer's friends and tugged at the hearts of both gay and straight audiences. It was a landmark play that has since been produced hundreds of times throughout the United States and in countries around the globe. *The Normal Heart* became synonymous with promoting awareness of the AIDS crisis. In 2000, the Royal National Theater in London included *The Normal Heart* among the one hundred greatest plays of the 20th century.

Another prominent, gay, Jewish playwright, Tony Kushner also made a major impact in the struggle to generate greater awareness about the AIDS crisis. Born in 1956, Kushner grew up in Louisiana, where he developed an interest in writing. He would come to New York City in the 1970s to attend Columbia University. After several attempts to get his work staged, Kushner's play *The Age of Assassins* was produced Off Broadway at the Newfoundland

Playwright and social activist Tony Kushner was quoted as saying, "If you have value as an artist, it's probably going to be in your capacity to let things inside you get past things that are placed there to keep you from telling the truth." And Kushner did just that (photograph by Joe Marzullo).

Theatre. From there, Kushner began having other plays produced Off Broadway and outside of New York City. He wrote both original works and adaptations of successful other playwrights' works ranging from Bertolt Brecht's *Mother Courage and Her Children* to Shakespeare's *A Midsummer Night's Dream* and *The Tempest.*

It was his 1992 seven-hour epic, *Angels in America* (a play in two parts: *Millennium Approaches* and *Perestroika*), about the HIV epidemic and the political climate of the time, that brought Kushner to national attention. *Angels* won Kushner a Pulitzer Prize and was later turned into a movie. It drew attention to the epidemic and was considered one of the most significant works of the decade.

Kushner would later generate attention once again for the musical *Caroline, or Change* which followed a successful Off Broadway run with several

PLAYBILL®

WALTER KERR THEATRE

Tony Kushner's *Angels in America: Millennium Approaches* was the first of a play in two parts. Both installments won Tony Awards for best play, while examining the most significant issues facing the gay population. Ron Leibman and Marcia Gay Harden were among the eight performers taking on multiple roles in the two productions (courtesy Playbill Inc.).

months on Broadway in 2004. Kushner wrote the book and lyrics while Jeanine Tesori, a noted Jewish arranger and composer, supplied the music. Kushner would also team up with a successful Jewish film producer, Steven Spielberg, on a couple of major films, *Munich* and *Lincoln*.

Tesori, a Barnard College graduate, first made it to Broadway in 1995 while working on the revival of *How to Succeed in Business Without Really Trying*. In 2000, she worked with Dick Scanlon composing original songs for *Thoroughly Modern Millie*. Tesori also worked with Kushner on his revival of *Mother Courage and Her Children* as part of the Shakespeare in the Park Festival in 2004.

Her work on *Caroline, or Change* was particularly interesting in that it combined numerous musical styles including Jewish klezmer and folk music that was originally brought to America by the Eastern European immigrants. Klezmer music influenced many composers, including Leonard Bernstein. The versatile Tesori would later provide music and arrangements for the family comedy *Shrek the Musical* and then add original music to the dramatic *A Free Man of Color*. Her music has most recently been featured at Circle in the Square's production of the introspective *Fun Home*.

Jonathan Larson was another of the young Jewish forces in theater in the 1990s, in this case with his music and lyrics as well as his playwriting. Born in 1960 and raised in White Plains, New York, Larson not only learned piano as a youngster, but also learned the trumpet and tuba. His music was accompanied by his passion for acting. In college, he performed in, and composed music for, several productions at Adelphi University.

Settling in the West Village, Larson wrote plays about social issues including homophobia and acceptance. His somewhat autobiographical production of *Tick … Tick … BOOM!* ran Off Off Broadway and generated attention in the early 1990s. During this time, Larson would begin work on a show called *Rent*, a rock opera about struggling artists on New York's Lower East Side. Sadly, Larson would never see the huge success of *Rent* on Broadway. Larson died of a rare disorder known as Marfan's syndrome. *Rent*, nonetheless, took on a life of its own, running on Broadway for an incredible 5,124 performances over 12 years and winning the Tony Award for Best Musical. Larson received a Pulitzer Prize posthumously for his work on *Rent*.

While young playwrights and activists from the gay community and the theater community worked hard to spread the word about the growing epidemic in hopes of generating support, the number of victims was rapidly growing. One of those to succumb to AIDS was choreographer/director Michael Bennett.

Born in 1943, Bennett's mother was Jewish, his father Roman Catholic.

A dancer from a young age, Bennett dropped out of high school at the age of 16 to join a touring company of Jerome Robbins' *West Side Story*. Although Bennett danced his way to Broadway in the musical *Subways Are for Sleeping* in 1961, he opted instead to set his sights on choreography.

His career as a choreographer included *Promises, Promises*; *Coco*; Stephen Sondheim's *Company*; and *Seesaw*, a show on which he also served as librettist and director. Bennett brought openly gay characters to Broadway in this 1973 show, a rarity at the time. It was, however, in 1975 that Bennett's innovative concept of creating a show won him both critical acclaim and Tony Awards. Using numerous hours of interviews with actual performers, Bennett created *A Chorus Line*, which earned over $37 million for the Public Theater. Bennett would have another huge hit in 1981 with *Dreamgirls*, producing and directing his way to Tony nominations. Sadly, Bennett was only 44 when he died in 1987, three years before *A Chorus Line* closed. Much like Robbins before him, Bennett made an impact as a choreographer and a director, bringing new energy to the dance and movement of an entire production. He was part of the gay Jewish theater community that lost too many members to a modern day plague.

Another Jewish-born spokesperson for gay civil rights who emerged in the 1980s was playwright and actor Harvey Fierstein. A raspy-voiced Brooklyn native, Fierstein launched his career as an openly gay comic, actor and female impersonator at New York clubs. He catapulted to fame with his play *Torch Song Trilogy*, starring in his own work, which had rarely been done on Broadway since Woody Allen in *Play It Again, Sam*. Originally an Off Broadway show staged in Greenwich Village, *Torch Song Trilogy* moved to Broadway in 1982. Fierstein won Tony Awards for both the play and for his acting. The show broke conventional norms, using three one-act plays to create one four-hour, three-part trilogy about a Jewish drag queen living in New York City and searching for love and acceptance. While *Torch Song Trilogy* continued for over 1,200 performances, Fierstein took on the job of writing the book for *La Cage aux Folles*, which would open on Broadway in 1983.

Following *La Cage*, Fierstein would move on to other projects, writing or performing. His role as Tracy Turnblad's stage mother Edna, in *Hairspray*, won him another Tony Award in 2003. I also brought him in to play Tevye in *Fiddler on the Roof* in 2004, a role he enjoyed so much that he returned to play it again when the production went on tour. Most recently, Fierstein wrote the book for *Newsies the Musical* and for the Broadway rendition of the 2005 film *Kinky Boots* which, as of the writing of this book, has passed the 1,300 performance mark.

Not unlike Zero Mostel on Broadway, or Boris Thomashefsky in Yiddish theater, Harvey Fierstein established himself as a consummate stage performer,

That's my wife and often coproducer Bonnie Comley and me with Harvey Fierstein, right, whom I have worked with on *La Cage aux Folles* (with Fierstein as the writer) and *Fiddler on the Roof* (with Harvey as an actor). He is always a joy to work with (photograph by Rob Rich).

able to take on a wide variety of roles, some serious, others comical, and always put his signature on the show. Along with Nathan Lane and a few other select performers, Fierstein has a drawing power on Broadway that does not come from another medium, but from his Tony Award–winning body of stage work and his reputation as a performer.

And finally, there is David Mamet, a Jewish-born playwright and director who grew up in the Chicago area but settled in New York City where he helped form an Off Broadway theater company from which many of his early plays emerged. Throughout the 1970s, Mamet became known for tackling a wide range of subject matter in his work, often with dark humor and profanity laced within his tightly crafted dialogue. Shows such as *Sexual Perversity in Chicago*, *Duck Variations* and *American Buffalo* all generated significant attention Off Broadway.

It was in the 1980s that Mamet made it to Broadway with *Glengarry Glen Ross*. The show, which depicted unethical and amoral business practices, became a highly acclaimed hit. In fact, the Pulitzer Prize–winning drama was widely considered Mamet's most significant work. Mamet would follow with *Speed the Plow* in 1988, which took a satirical look at the film business.

Mamet continued turning out plays that were rich in dialogue and prompted many critical discussions, such as his 1992 two-person show, *Oleana*. Not unlike Lillian Hellman's *The Children's Hour*, *Oleana* skillfully explored how one person's accusations could destroy someone else's life. Mamet's knack for exploring the human condition clearly made him one of the most heralded playwrights of the late 1980s and 1990s. He remains a respected writer and spokesperson on the American theater today.

Wendy Wasserstein

While the successful Broadway playwrights of the 1980s and '90s were primarily male, and gay, there was also room for a Jewish woman with a comedic flare. From Fanny Brice, Molly Picon and Sophie Tucker to Joan Rivers, Gilda Radner, Rita Rudner, and Sarah Silverman, Jewish women have always had a knack for making audiences laugh. Despite the wealth of Jewish comediennes, there have been few females to tickle the funny bones of Broadway audiences with original plays. Wendy Wasserstein not only brought comedy to Broadway through her work, but not unlike her male counterparts, brought forward her own social concerns. Wasserstein presented the voices of women on stage, particularly in her breakthrough hit, *The Heidi Chronicles*, in 1988.

One of five sisters, Wendy Wasserstein grew up in Brooklyn. Her father was very successful as a textile executive, and her mother was an amateur dancer who immigrated to the United States from Poland. Her grandfather, on her mother's side, was a playwright, and an influence on Wasserstein, who would go on to earn a master's degree in creative writing from the City College of New York and an M.F.A. from the Yale School of Drama.

In *The Heidi Chronicles*, Wasserstein used her knack for sharp comedic dialogue to shed light on the social issues faced by women including liberation in the 1960s, feminism in the 1970s and betrayal in the 1980s. She made audiences laugh while also drawing their attention to the changing issues that women faced. The show, which opened Off Broadway, later moved to Broadway for over 600 performances and won not only the Tony Award for best play but also a Pulitzer Prize for Wasserstein.

While there were few plays with Jewish themes in the 1990s, one that garnered attention Off Broadway and later on Broadway in 1993, running for 556 performances, was Wasserstein's follow-up to *The Heidi Chronicles*, entitled *The Sisters Rosensweig*. The comedy about three middle-aged Jewish-American sisters in London to celebrate one of their birthdays was described by Wasserstein in the Huntington Theater program as: "A practicing Jew, a wandering Jew and a self-loathing Jew [who] are sitting around a living room in London."[1] But the show proved to be much more than that, as it epitomized the strong bond between these three very different women. From personal revelations to their ongoing sibling rivalry, they draw in an audience by way of Wasserstein's richly humorous dialogue that drives the show forward.

Wasserstein would continue to write plays through the 1990s and into the new century, including *Isn't It Romantic, The American Daughter* and *Old Money*. Sadly, she died in 2006 at the age of 55. In her plays, Wasserstein utilized her Jewish sense of humor to bring the female voice to Broadway in a manner that had not been done before. As a result, stars such as Jane Alexander, Madeline Kahn, Linda Lavin, Joan Allen and other notables appeared in her plays. One such notable, the daughter of an Eastern European Jewish dad and a German/English mom, was Sarah Jessica Parker, who, after several television and film roles, landed in Wasserstein's play *The Heidi Chronicles* in 1990, where she stepped into a role played by Cynthia Nixon.

Parker, who started out doing ballet and children's theater while growing up in Ohio, had actually been on Broadway before. An audition for the role of Flora in the play *The Innocents* brought her to New York, where she landed her first Broadway show at the age of eleven. Unfortunately, the show lasted for just over a week. Nonetheless, convinced their daughter had a future on stage, her family moved to New Jersey.

Within a couple of years, Parker was back on Broadway in the far more successful run of *Annie*. She would soon find herself stepping into a role in the 1995 hit revival of *How to Succeed in Business Without Really Trying*, alongside Matthew Broderick, whom she married a year after the closing of the show. She then followed with a starring role in the revival of *Once Upon a Mattress*. It would be later, in 1998, that the former child actress would truly reach maturity in the steamy/romantic HBO hit series *Sex and the City*, alongside Cynthia Nixon.

As for the Jewish playwrights, now that they were no longer accused of being Communists for standing up for social issues, writers such as Kramer, Kushner and Wasserstein, were able to make their voices heard without having to look over their shoulders. They followed Odets, Kaufman and others in their belief that the theater was, and still is, a forum for expression and a means of making an impact.

"More Traditional" Newcomers

Among the other new Broadway talents to emerge in the 1980s and '90s were Maury Yeston and Jerry Zaks. Unlike the new breed of playwrights, both were closely associated with the more "traditional" style of Broadway musicals. Yeston surfaced as a composer and lyricist, while Zaks had a brilliant sense for directing, preferably comedy.

Yeston, who grew up in Jersey City in the 1950s, was, like many Jewish composers, the grandson of a cantor. Both of his parents also had musical talent. So, like many of his musical predecessors, Yeston was weaned on music and took to the piano at a very young age. An early trip to New York City to see *My Fair Lady*, not unlike my own trip to Manhattan to see *Little Me*, turned out to be an eye-opening experience for Yeston who, like myself, was immediately drawn to the theater.

Yeston possessed great musical talent that would become quite evident as he grew up. By the time he attended Yale University to study music composition and theory, he had studied all sorts of musical styles and was proficient on several instruments. He would not only go on to receive his Ph.D. from Yale, but would teach music for nearly a decade at the Ivy League institution.

In the early 1980s Yeston would emerge as a Broadway lyricist and become known for his contributions to three successful musicals. Based on Fellini's film *8½*, Yeston provided music and lyrics for the musical *Nine*, a show fueled by director Tommy Tune whose persistence brought it to Broadway. Also based, in part, on Fellini's own mid-life crisis, as he dealt with turning forty while coping with writer's block, along with having trouble with his wife and his mistress, *Nine* opened on Broadway in 1982, and later returned in 2003 for a revival. The original production ran for 729 performances and garnered a Tony Award for Best Musical.

The second significant musical for Yeston was the 1989 hit *Grand Hotel* for which he wrote some of the music and lyrics. Based on a 1929 novel, and 1932 film, the musical focused on the stories of several distinctive guests at a German hotel in 1928. *Grand Hotel* saw 1,077 performances on Broadway before closing its doors.

The third of Yeston's triumphs was the musical *Titanic* in 1997, with Peter Stone, of *1776* notoriety, writing the book. An unusual subject for a Broadway musical, the show, unlike the ship, stayed afloat for two years, despite soaring costs that precluded it from seeing a profit. Nonetheless, it sailed away with the 1997 Tony Award for Best Musical.

Yeston also wrote Off Broadway shows, an album about the life of Francisco de Goya and classical compositions. His flair for "old-school" composition was welcomed in an ever-changing progressive theater environment and has made him a highly respected composer by his peers and by the theater audience.

One of the premiere directors to emerge during the late 1980s was Jerry

Zaks. Born in Germany to Holocaust survivors of Russian and Polish descent, Zaks' family immigrated to the United States in 1948, when Jerry was two years of age. Zaks grew up in New Jersey where his father owned a kosher butcher shop. He later recalled in interviews that while his parents did not talk much about the horrors of their Holocaust experiences, he was led to believe that the world was a very hostile place and that being Jewish meant you had to be especially careful and even fearful.

While Zaks enjoyed music during his childhood in the 1950s, he was not a musician nor did he have any particular interest in theater. It was, however, when he attended Dartmouth College that he not only discovered theater but fell in love. Wanting to be popular, Zaks took to acting. He appeared in everything he could at Dartmouth and then went on to Smith College where he received a master of fine arts degree in theater. Upon moving to New York City, he became one of the founders of the Broadway Theater Ensemble from which he honed his acting skills in Off Broadway productions and commercials. But by the time he made it to Broadway as Kenickie in the musical *Grease,* he had become more fascinated by directing than performing.

Zaks began directing Off Broadway shows at the start of the 1980s, with a focus on comedy. It was an offbeat Larry Shue comedy, *The Foreigner,* that first drew significant attention in 1984. The show went on the win the Outer Critics Circle Awards for Best New American Play and Best Off Broadway Production. Zaks would then go on to win his first Tony Award in 1986 for John Guare's tragic comedy *The House of Blue Leaves,* which was staged at Lincoln Center Theater. But it was a revival of Cole Porter's *Anything Goes* in 1987 starring Patti LuPone that confirmed Zaks' rightful place on Broadway. The musical revival received excellent reviews and ran for over 800 performances.

Zaks would move into the 1990s with *Lend Me a Tenor* and the John Guare play *Six Degrees of Separation,* which explored the premise that everyone is connected to everyone else in the world by a chain of no more than six connections, long before LinkedIn or other social media tried to prove that point. The concept has obviously continued to intrigue people long beyond the successful run of the show, which opened Off Broadway, and then ran for nearly 500 performances on Broadway.

Having enjoyed success with the revival of *Anything Goes,* Zaks then decided to bring back *Guys and Dolls* starring Nathan Lane. The result was 1,143 performances and four Tony Awards including Best Revival of a Musical. Zaks was clearly on a roll. After teaming with Neil Simon on *Laughter on the 23rd Floor* and bringing the music of the 1950s to life for over 2,000 performances of *Smokey Joe's Café,* Zaks would pull off another successful revival with the comedy classic of the early '60s, *A Funny Thing Happened on the Way to the Forum*, this time starring Nathan Lane, and later Whoopi Goldberg.

Along with television credits for directing episodes of popular sitcoms such as *Frasier* and *Everybody Loves Raymond*, and film credits that include *Outrageous Fortune* and *Crimes and Misdemeanors*, Zaks continues to be the consummate director of comedy, bringing *Little Shop of Horrors* and *The Addams Family* to Broadway in a directing career that is now in its fourth decade.

Inflation and Broadway

By the late 1980s, inflation had kicked in and Broadway was feeling the effects. While *Cats*, *Les Misérables* and *Phantom of the Opera*, three of the longest-running Broadway musicals ever (as of the writing of this book) all emerged in the 1980s, many producers and theater owners opted for revivals of tried and true hits rather than take on new shows. *Zorba*, *Sweet Charity*, *Anything Goes*, *On Your Toes*, and *Carousel* were among the many classic Broadway musicals that saw revivals in the 1980s and '90s. The cost of putting on a musical was becoming prohibitive, and as a result taking the chance on a new show was a greater risk. In some cases, revivals took a creative approach, such as the musical *Crazy for You*, which was an adaptation of *Girl Crazy*, bringing back the music of the Gershwins not only from the original show but including other Gershwin songs as well. *Crazy for You* won a Tony Award in 1992 for Best Musical. Despite over 1,600 performances, the musical hit did not see a profit until it went out on tour.

The problem of inflation was indeed making it harder to make money for those backing Broadway shows. The costs of production continued to rise rapidly, and star performers were seeking enough money to make it worth their while to commit to a Broadway engagement rather than take on a film or television role. From the $700,000 that it took to stage *Annie* in 1977 to the $3.75 million to bring *Woman of the Year* to Broadway in 1981 to the $5 million it took to stage *La Cage aux Folles* in 1983, the costs were indeed rising quickly, and ticket prices lagged behind. Even hugely successful musical talents, such as Paul Simon and Peter Allen, were unable to buck the odds and land hit shows during this risky era for Broadway. Simon's show *Capeman* lasted only 68 performances on Broadway, after a ten-year gestation period and a cost of $11 million. Allen's *Legs Diamond* actually lasted longer in previews (72) than with actual performances (64). Even with Harvey Fierstein writing the book, the doomed show closed in 1989, epitomizing the high risk of bringing a new musical to Broadway.

One avenue that proved fruitful, and took some of the gamble out of staging a brand new production, was to import an established hit show from Great Britain. While this was not an entirely new concept, it became more common to seek out shows that had an English pedigree, so to speak. Such British hits typically had already enjoyed box-office success when brought to America, not unlike many shows that took the reverse route from Broadway to London. *Evita, Joseph and the Amazing Technicolor Dreamcoat, Cats, Starlight Express* and *Me and My Gal* were just a few of the influx of shows that came over in a London invasion of Broadway musicals, largely with Andrew Lloyd Webber and Tim Rice leading the charge. While not all of the British imports were hits, their overseas success gave producers a greater level of comfort, having seen audience support for these shows in London. Two such shows were the work of an international Jewish writing team. *Les Misérables* made its way from Paris to London's West End, where it became the longest-running musical in history. The American version would land on Broadway in 1987 for an amazing run of more than 6,000 performances. The other significant musical of the era from the same writing team was *Miss Saigon*. Similar in story to that of *Madama Butterfly*, only set during the Vietnam War, *Miss Saigon* opened in 1991 and dazzled theatergoers for over 4,400 performances.

The team behind the two blockbusters was Claude-Michel Schönberg, a French songwriter, actor and composer, who wrote the music for both shows, and Alain Boublil, a librettist born in Tunisia who met Schönberg in France. On *Les Misérables*, the talented duo were joined by Herbert Kretzmer, an older Jewish writer with credits that ranged from British television to screen documentaries to newspaper columns. Kretzmer, originally from South Africa, provided English lyrics. All three walked away with Tony Awards for their work on *Les Misérables*.

Of course there's no sure thing in the theater business, as proven by Schönberg and Boublil several years later. Following two of the most successful box-office and critically acclaimed musicals in Broadway history, the duo worked diligently on the story of 17th century Irish pirate Grace O'Malley. The resulting show, *Pirate Queen*, ran for only two months on Broadway, at a loss of roughly $16 million.

Along with revivals and British imports in the '80s and '90s was the growing practice of moving shows that had enjoyed prolonged success Off Broadway onto Broadway. This was also not a new concept, but had become more common largely thanks to the efforts of Joseph Papp whose shows, such as *Hair* and *A Chorus Line*, had grown to prominence Off Broadway before their lengthy Broadway runs. Many shows such as *Secret Garden* and those of the new breed of Jewish playwrights mentioned earlier were sustained Off Broadway by students and niche audiences who were not always able to afford the spiraling cost of Broadway tickets. The shows gained notoriety through word of mouth and favorable reviews, making them more likely to succeed at the higher ticket prices of Broadway.

Despite some major musical hits, by the start of the 1990s Broadway attendance was off, and the number of new shows was down. Higher ticket prices, the new popularity of home theater and video entertainment and the increasingly unsafe area around Times Square and the theater district all factored into the attendance woes. Something had to change ... and it did.

The Decade of Disney

The 1990s marked the cleanup of 42nd Street which had steadily declined after the depression years, especially after World War II, forcing some of the older theaters on the street to close or show movies. The actual Broadway theater district now started a block or two north of the famed street that had been the impetus for a major film and smash Broadway musical. The area around Times Square, with a rising crime rate and an increase in drug traffic and prostitution, had been deemed unsafe for what was now becoming four decades.

Redevelopment of the area was a must. So, along with New York City mayor Rudy Giuliani, the charge for change was led by a mouse named Mickey. Yes, The Walt Disney Company announced in 1994 that they were going to bring their own family brand of theater to, of all places, crime-ridden 42nd Street. Naturally, the optimism of Disney's executives was met by cynicism from those who doubted that their efforts would have a positive impact. After all, the area declined steadily for many years and was anything but Disney-esque. In fact, David Letterman epitomized the cynics with his Top Ten List of upcoming Disney Productions that included *Hookers of the Caribbean* and *Beauty and the Bobbitt.*

Nonetheless, Disney, led by Chairman Michael Eisner, pressed on. Eisner, born to a Jewish family in Mount Kisco, New York, spent much of his youth growing up in Manhattan. He was still a New Yorker at heart, despite spending a number of years in Los Angeles where he worked briefly at all three major networks before becoming the Chairman of Paramount Pictures in Burbank. It was from there that he established himself as a major player in the entertainment industry. Films including *Saturday Night Fever*, *Grease* and *Raiders of the Lost Ark* were made during his tenure, along with major hit television sitcoms such as *Cheers* and *Happy Days.*

In 1984, Eisner was brought into Disney where he began expanding the already successful Disney name, starting with the film *The Little Mermaid* in 1989 and continuing with some of the most significant animated movies of all time. Eisner called the 1990s the Disney Decade, and was it ever. The company grew, buying up movie studios, expanding their theme parks and adding their own cable network plus ESPN and other television properties.

Broadway, however, was uncharted territory for Disney, and 42nd Street was uncharted territory for anyone since the days of Ziegfeld. Developers had come and gone, throwing up their hands in dismay at the challenge that stood in front of them. Commercial office buildings might provide jobs by day, but at night lurked a seedy crowd that frequented the peep shows and porn theaters. The key for Disney was not simply to add structures, but to transform the ambiance and infuse entertainment that could jump-start the neighborhood in a positive uplifting Disney manner.

Ironically, despite the decline of the area, much like the lost city of Pompeii, classic, elegant art nouveau theaters sat unscathed in the midst of the chaos. One of those theaters, built in 1900 by Oscar Hammerstein, called the Theatre Republic, featured a Venetian-styled façade with a grand exterior staircase leading to the first of two balconies, all of which sat beneath an elegant domed ceiling. The theater had opened shortly after the turn of the century with the show *Sag Harbor* featuring Lionel Barrymore. In a short time, the Republic would become home to vaudeville shows and to *Abie's Irish Rose*, one of Broadway's longest-running productions of the 1920s. But in the '30s the depression made it difficult to stage major productions, so it was taken over by Billy Minsky and turned into Minsky's Burlesque featuring Gypsy Rose Lee. In 1942, Minsky's, however, would close, and by the 1970s the theater would sink to a new low, emerging as the city's first XXX theater.

Nonetheless, the classic venue would return in the 1990s as the New Victory Theater, a full-time performing theater for children and their families created by a non-profit organization dedicated to cleaning up 42nd Street. While this major renovation and reopening of the classic theater had no connection with Disney, it certainly indicated that changes to the area could be achieved.

Another classic old 42nd Street theater, the New Amsterdam, sat right across from the old Republic, and it would serve as the anchor for Disney's redevelopment plan. Much like the senior Oscar Hammerstein had built up the theater district at the turn of the 20th century, Eisner and his associates were determined to transform the theater district on the verge of the 21st century.

The New Amsterdam Theater was built in 1903 with a seating capacity topping 1,700. The lavish theater was opened with Shakespeare's *A Midsummer Night's Dream*, which played for a couple of weeks before giving way to the theater's first original play called *Her Own Way*, by Clyde Fitch. From *Mother Goose* to *Ivan the Terrible*, musicals, revues and serious plays called the New Amsterdam Theater home over the coming years. Then, starting in 1913 and continuing through the late 1920s, the numerous renditions of *Ziegfeld's Follies* became the most notable tenants of the New Amsterdam. However, the depression years took their toll, and in 1937, following the Sigmund Romberg and Otto Harbach musical comedy *Forbidden Melody*, the theater would close, just as it had opened, with a Shakespearian classic. This time it was *Othello*.

Of course, a transformation of the theater district by Disney meant more than just rebuilding and renovating a theater and cleaning up the area. Along with a signature Disney Store, it meant staging productions that would draw an audience and bring family entertainment to the street which had gone from Follies and frenzied revues to down and dirty. During this same time, Disney was enjoying a rebirth of their animation excellence. *Cinderella*, *Sleeping Beauty* and *Snow White* had given way to *Beauty and the Beast*, *The Lion King* and *Aladdin*. The new generation of baby-boomer children was delighted by these animated films. The question was: Would these movie mega hits work on stage with real actors? Would they generate the same excitement from a young audience? Only time would tell. But the brass at Disney was not taking any chances. They opened *Beauty and the Beast* out of town, in Houston, and followed the results closely before moving it to the Palace Theater in 1994, which I had co-purchased years earlier. They were very pleased with what they saw as the show played for over 5,000 performances, making it into the all-time top-ten for performances by a Broadway musical. Needless to say, I was very pleased as well. Yes, Disney's second wave of classic children's favorites would indeed provide the new entertainment on 42nd Street.

After the major three-year, multi-million-dollar renovation project, the New Amsterdam would open once again some 60 years after the *Ziegfeld's Follies* with *The Lion King*, in 1997 (and still running as of this printing). Disney had signed a 99-year lease and now had their own Broadway theater and, along with *Beauty and the Beast*, their second smash-hit Broadway musical, with others lined up to follow.

Since 1994, Thomas Schumacher has led Disney Theatrical Productions to the record breaking shows *The Lion King*, *Beauty and the Beast*, *The Little Mermaid*, *Mary Poppins*, *Tarzan*, *Aladdin*, *Newsies* and *Frozen*.

Meanwhile, one of the foremost creators of the era, and part of the reason for Disney's unprecedented success, was Alan Menken, who joined the long line of successful Jewish Broadway composers after establishing himself as the musical force behind several of Disney's major animated classics.

ALAN MENKEN

Menken, like many Jewish composers before him, hailed from New York City. He was born in 1949 in Manhattan, but as was the case with many families of the era, his parents opted to move to the burgeoning suburbs, New Rochelle to be exact. He took to piano and violin at an early age and was weaned on Broadway musicals as his family frequented the theater often, enjoying classics, such as *My Fair Lady* and *The Sound of Music* among other favorites of the '50s and early '60s.

While Menken enjoyed playing piano, he also enjoyed making up his own versions of the songs he was told to practice, and hence his composing career began. After graduating from New York University, Menken took to writing jingles, while performing his own material in small clubs, in hopes of becoming the next major singer-songwriter. While that did not happen, he did soon discover that he had a knack for writing musical theater.

His first official theater writing job came when he was asked by Harold

The Broadway debut of Alan Menken, right, was at my Palace Theater with Disney's *Beauty and the Beast,* the first of his many hit musicals (photograph by Bonnie Comley).

Ashman to write music for an adaptation of Kurt Vonnegut's 1965 play *God Bless You, Mr. Rosewater*. He was then asked by Ashman to write the music for what would become an Off Broadway cult favorite, *Little Shop of Horrors*. The quirky comedy featuring Audrey II, a very large, outspoken Venus flytrap, would later become a film and eventually land on Broadway in 2003 for 372 performances.

But once Disney got hold of Menken, they would not let go. It was indeed a match made in heaven. Menken would proceed to write the family-friendly, light and spirited music for one animated Disney hit after another, including *Beauty and the Beast, Aladdin, Pocahontas* and *The Little Mermaid*.

When Disney decided to make 42nd Street their new theatrical version of Main Street USA, it was Menken's music that was played in *Beauty and the Beast*. And when *The Little Mermaid* moved to Broadway, once again Menken's music was featured. The show ran for 685 performances. While several of his Disney animated favorites would make their way to Broadway, such as *Aladdin*, which opened in 2014, Menken moved on to other endeavors which have included writing the music for the stage presentation of the classic *A Christmas Carol* now performed at Madison Square Garden each holiday season.

I recall my own interaction with Alan Menken in 1987, during his pre–Disney days. We were working on the musical adaptation of *The Apprenticeship of Duddy Kravitz*, which I was going to produce at the American Theater Festival in Philadelphia. Alan was great, an amazing talent, and we had a terrific relationship. We were working on the book for the show and trying to get other producers interested as backers. I wanted Jimmy Nederlander, with whom I had worked on productions for many years, to hear the score because I thought it was going to be a big hit. In those days you would sit down and play the music for potential producers or backers during an audition; this was before using CD cuts or anything like that. Songs were literally played in the offices of the producers. It was a throwback to the days of Tin Pan Alley. So, we decided to play half a dozen songs from the show for Jimmy. The problem was that there was one song that could be considered a little anti–Semitic, so I asked if we could change the lyric. David Spencer was the lyricist and the song included the line, "that's the way we feed Jews." I suggested changing it to "that's the way we amuse Jews" or something that was not so offensive. But they came back and told me that David did not want to change it. While I was not in a position to rewrite a lyric, I was in the position to decide that we should skip that song in the upcoming Tuesday meeting.

It was Mother's Day weekend and upon returning to work on Monday, after visiting my own mom, I received a phone call from Alan Menken. "Hi, Stewart, we're going to change the lyric," was Alan's opening remark. So I asked him what happened. "Well, I was at my mother's house and I played the song for her. She looked at me and said 'Alan, that's so anti–Semitic, you can't use that song,'" explained Menken. I told him to please thank his mom for me.

Much of Menken's success was with Howard Ashman, a lyricist whose words complemented the music of Menken perfectly. The two were a marvelous team; from *God Bless You, Mr. Rosewater* through many of the Disney favorites. Sadly, Ashman would become another of Broadway's list of casualties to HIV. He died at age 40 in 1991.

Prior to Menken and Ashman, who were to come to writing music for Disney films, there were the Sherman Brothers. Born to Russian-Jewish immigrants in the 1920s, Robert and Richard Sherman began their long and esteemed songwriting careers in the early 1950s, following in the musical footsteps of their father, Tin Pan Alley songwriter Al Sherman. Their lineage reportedly dates back to Franz Joseph, the emperor of Austria in the late 19th century, and King of Hungary.

It was in the late 1950s that the Sherman Brothers would team up as staff writers for Disney, where they were kept very busy, writing everything from music for Annette Funicello of *The Mickey Mouse Club* to "It's a Small World After All," which first appeared at the 1964 World's Fair in New York, before becoming a staple at both U.S. Disney theme parks. They also wrote the songs for the Disney movies *Mary Poppins*, *The Jungle Book* and *The Aristocats*. They would later take time off from Disney to pen music and lyrics for the 1968 kid-favorite film, *Chitty Chitty Bang Bang*, which made it to Broadway many years later, without great success. They also wrote the Andrews Sisters' Broadway tribute, *Over There*. It was, however, when Disney brought *Mary Poppins* to Broadway that the Sherman Brothers would enjoy their greatest theatrical success with music they had written more than 40 years earlier.

Another of the Disney "alumni" to enjoy great success on Broadway is David Zippel, an Easton, Pennsylvania, native who graduated from Harvard Law School but opted to be a lyricist rather than a lawyer. In a career that has now spanned more than 25 years, Zippel had been teamed with a wide range of musical talents on Broadway and in Disney films.

His Broadway debut came in 1989, when he teamed with Cy Coleman and Larry Gelbart on the musical comedy *City of Angels*. Zippel received a Tony Award for his work on the show, which ran just over two years (879 performances). In 1993, Zippel worked with Marvin Hamlisch to create the musical comedy *The Goodbye Girl*, based on the 1977 Neil Simon film. *The Woman in White* paired Zippel with Andrew Lloyd Webber in 2005. Unfortunately, the musical only lasted for 109 performances.

Zippel's Disney credits include lyrics for the animated film *Hercules* on which he teamed with Alan Menken, for *Mulan* with Matthew Wilder providing the music and then for *Tarzan* with music by Phil Collins. With songs recorded by a wide range of talents from Ricky Martin to Mel Tormé to Stevie Wonder, Zippel has established himself as a premiere lyricist for both stage and screen.

It was also thanks to the Decade of Disney that Jewish director Julie Taymor made her Broadway breakthrough as director of *The Lion King*. In fact, thanks to *The Lion King*, she became the first woman to win a Tony Award for directing. However, Taymor was not at all a newcomer to theater, only to Broadway.

Born and raised in a suburb of Boston, Taymor began her theatrical journey in children's theater at the age of ten. But it was years later, after her travels to the Far East and years spent living in Indonesia, that she would discover and develop her passion for puppetry. Upon returning to the United States in the early 1980s and on into the 1990s, Taymor would utilize puppets along with masked and unmasked actors as well as film and stage devices to create unique imagery in her own works. Meanwhile, she would also continue directing plays for the New York Shakespeare Festival, the American Repertory Theatre in Cambridge, Massachusetts, and elsewhere. But it was in 1997, after some 25 years of creating and directing internationally, that Taymor's amazing talents were recognized. She brought together the magnificent fusion of people and puppets in Disney's spectacular stage version of *The Lion King*, by leaving the puppet handler's faces visible so that the theater audience could see the performances of both the actors and the puppets. This also served to diffuse any fear younger children might have when seeing these larger-than-life puppets in the theatrical performance. Still running, *The Lion King* is now among the all-time top-five longest running musicals of all-time. It is also now being staged in more than a dozen countries.

Following her work on *The Lion King*, Taymor ventured into films and directing opera, including *The Magic Flute* for the 2005/2006 season of the Metropolitan Opera. Taymor then took on the arduous, somewhat monumental task of co-writing the book and directing *Spider-Man: Turn Off the Dark*, which, despite just over 1,000 performances, reportedly lost upwards of $60 million by its closing at the start of 2014.

Broadway Veterans Thrive

Neither Cy Coleman nor Stephen Sondheim were newcomers to Broadway in the '80s or '90s, yet both would see resurgence and enjoy some of their greatest successes during these decades. Coleman, born Seymour Kaufman to

Eastern European–Jewish immigrants in 1929, grew up in the Bronx, where he took to music as a child. He was, in fact, so proficient that he appeared in piano recitals at New York's Town Hall and the famous Carnegie Hall before the age of ten.

By age 17, Coleman was playing jazz at New York City nightspots and by 19 he had formed the Cy Coleman Trio, while attending the New York College of Music. The trio enjoyed some success with their recordings in the early 1950s. Coleman also wrote a couple of songs that became hits for Frank Sinatra, "Why Try to Change Me Now?" and "Witchcraft" as well as the hit "Firefly" for Tony Bennett.

His first Broadway show, *Wildcat*, was in 1960 and starred Lucille Ball making her Broadway debut. Unfortunately, Ball took ill during the run of the show, and since she was the reason people were coming to see it, the show was closed until she recovered. The musicians union insisted that the show's musicians be paid during the nine weeks the show would be closed. Since this was not feasible, the show was ultimately doomed after only 171 performances. Coleman, however, would go on to success with *Little Me*, *Sweet Charity* and other hit musicals throughout the '60s and '70s.

In 1980, at the age of 51, Coleman would enjoy one of his biggest hits, the musical focusing on the life of circus impresario P.T. Barnum, simply called *Barnum*. The circus-themed musical would run for over 850 performances, bringing the magic and excitement of the big top to the Broadway stage. Then in 1989, Coleman would compose the music for *City of Angels*, which brought cinema and Broadway together in a comedic detective musical, which topped *Barnum*, running for 879 performances. Coleman would continue into his fourth decade of writing for Broadway when he collaborated with Comden and Greene on *Will Rogers Follies* in 1991. This time Coleman enjoyed 981 performances of his latest musical hit. Coleman won Tony Awards for best score for both *City of Angels* and *Will Rogers Follies*.

Like Coleman, Stephen Sondheim had certainly enjoyed his share of Broadway credits by the start of the 1980s with shows including *A Funny Thing Happened on the Way to the Forum* and *Gypsy*. Nonetheless, Sondheim had a resurgence of sorts in the 1980s and '90s. Actually, the resurgence began in 1979 with the grisly musical hit *Sweeney Todd*, about the fictional demon barber of Fleet Street, who slit the throats of his customers then had them turned into meat pies. The slashing barber ran amuck on Broadway for 557 performances and became a film star some 30 years later.

In 1981, Sondheim attempted a remake of the 1934 Moss Hart, George S. Kaufman show called *Merrily We Roll Along*. The play was unsuccessful the first time around, despite critical acclaim. This did not stop Sondheim from bringing it back in 1981 as a musical. After some 52 previews the show finally opened, but lasted only 16 performances. Nonetheless, the musical score spawned a soundtrack that took on a life of its own, with covers of the songs recorded by both Frank Sinatra and Carly Simon. As a result of the score, the musical was reincarnated on numerous occasions in various cities around the country as well as Off Broadway. It would not be a surprise if *Merrily* somehow managed to roll its way back to Broadway yet again.

Despite the box office woes of *Merrily We Roll Along*, Sondheim would rebound in 1984 with lyricist James Lapine and the hit *Sunday in the Park with George*, which ran for over 600 performances. With two scenes some one hundred years apart, the avant-garde show, based in part on a painting of artist Georges Seurat, explores the drive of an artist, and later that of his great grandson. Mandy Patinkin, the Chicago-born son of Russian and Polish-Jewish parents, starred in the show. Patinkin's upbringing included attending religious school and, like many Jewish families, he was introduced to music as a youngster. Then, as a teenager, he would sing in the choir at his synagogue.

Prior to his success in *Sunday in the Park with George*, Patinkin had won a Tony Award for his performance in *Evita* in 1979. He would later go on to star in *The Secret Garden*, a Tony Award–winning show. It was in 1998, however, that he would return to his Jewish roots with a project called *Mamaloshen*. The show was actually a concert by Patinkin, which consisted of classic and contemporary songs sung in Yiddish and was presented Off Broadway and on tour to critical acclaim.

Meanwhile, Sondheim would team with James Lapine again on *Into the Woods*. Bringing the "darker" side of fairy tales to the stage in 1987, as a testament to the messages such tales are really giving our children, the show was a success and ran for 764 performances. The team of Sondheim and Lapine would also join forces on *Passion* in 1994, which, despite a limited run, won the Tony Award for Best Musical.

Sondheim's impact on Broadway was celebrated in the 2001 musical, *Side by Side by Sondheim*. A musical revue, the show chronicled his many years as a composer, featuring his various styles and tunes from many of his shows.

Along with Stephen Sondheim, there was his director James Lapine, also Jewish. Born and raised in Mansfield, Ohio, Lapine and his family moved to Stamford, Connecticut, during his teen years. His interest in school and throughout college was in photography and design. It wasn't until he was working as a designer for the Yale School of Drama, and taught design courses for the university, that he was cajoled by his students into directing a version of Gertrude Stein's play *Photograph*. The show was first produced in New Haven and later Off Broadway. For his efforts, Lapine won an Obie Award. Lapine took to his sudden new career quickly and dipped into his own Jewish background to direct the comedy *Table Settings*, which focuses on an offbeat Jewish family.

Meeting composer William Finn, Lapine also took on the role of librettist on the shows *March of the Falsettos* and *In Trousers* in the early 1980s, the latter of which opened with the song "Four Jews in a Room Bitching." A reworked version of *March of the Falsettos*, simply called *Falsettos*, would make it to Broadway in the early 1990s and win Tony Awards for Best Book and Best Score.

But it was in the early 1980s that Lapine would meet and start working with Stephen Sondheim. He would write the book for *Sunday in the Park with George, Into the Woods* and *Passion*. Together, Sondheim and Lapine developed a chemistry that merged Sondheim's music with the chemistry taking place onstage between the actors.

Like many Broadway directors, Lapine would head to Hollywood in the 1990s to direct feature films. After three highly acclaimed films with modest box office returns, Lapine returned to Broadway. This time he collaborated with Brooklyn-born writer/actress Claudia Shear to create a show about the legendary Mae West entitled *Dirty Blonde*, which opened on Broadway in 2000 and ran for over 350 performances. After teaming with Michael Legrand on a post–World War II musical fantasy flop called *Amour*, Lapine was back on track serving as director on the entertaining box office hit *The 25th Annual Putnam County Spelling Bee* in 2005, which ran for nearly three years.

Like Coleman and Sondheim, another theater veteran to thrive in the late 1980s and through the '90s was Alfred Uhry, who enjoyed a brief taste of Broadway as a lyricist in 1968 with the help of Frank Loesser and a show called *Here's Where I Belong*, which opened and closed the same night. It was not until the mid–1970s that Uhry would truly enjoy his first Broadway success working along with composer Robert Waldman on *The Robber Bridegroom*. The Robin Hood–esque musical saw over 550 performances at Broadway's Helen Hayes Theater and earned Uhry a Tony Award nomination.

Then, in the late 1980s, now in his 50s, the Atlanta-born Jewish lyricist turned his attention to playwriting and quickly emerged as a significant writer for both stage and screen.

Uhry wrote about Southern-based Jews in three plays that became known as the Atlanta Trilogy. The first play, set in Georgia, was about the relationship between an elderly Jewish woman and her African American chauffeur. The Off Broadway Pulitzer Prize–winning drama was called *Driving Miss Daisy*. The play delved gently into the subject of racism and prejudice through a series of events in their sentimental journey together, illustrating the bond these two very different, yet compassionate seniors shared in the eyes of a society wrought with prejudice. The film adaptation later won the Academy Awards for Best Picture and Best Writing of an Adapted Screenplay.

Having now achieved prominence as a writer, Uhry took on anti–Semitism even within the Jewish community itself with his play entitled *The Last Night of Ballyhoo*, a 1996 comedic-drama set at the onset of World War II. The play, about a Southern Jewish family that celebrates Christmas, knows little to nothing about Passover and is even naive to the prejudice that exists within their own Jewish community, received a Tony Award for Best Play. It also generated a lot of discussion about Jewish culture and how it was often misinterpreted even by many Jewish people in a time of growing anti–Semitism.

The third play in Uhry's trilogy brought him back to his musical background as he also served as librettist on *Parade*. Despite being a musical, *Parade* explored the 1913 lynching by the Ku Klux Klan of a Jewish factory manager accused of murder. Once again Uhry explored anti–Semitism and in this case, the founding of the Anti-Defamation League as a response to this unjust crime. While the musical was not successful on Broadway, it won the Tony Awards for best book and best score.

At a time in the 1990s when anti–Semitism and prejudice toward American Jews had become far less outwardly prevalent, Uhry brought very real reminders of such intolerance to the public through his critically acclaimed works.

And Me

It was also in the 1980s that I was fortunate to come into my own as a Broadway producer. Yes, another Jewish boy from Long Island grew up with a love of theater. It all emanated from that first experience, seeing *Little Me* in 1961. Some 20 years later, I had become co-owner of the Palace Theater along with Jimmy Nederlander, and in 1981 I had the pleasure of starting the new decade by working with Lauren Bacall, as the first of three major stars to take the lead role in *Woman of the Year* (the others were Raquel Welch and Debbie Reynolds). The show ran for two years, and each of the stars was marvelous in the lead role.

It was on my next hit show, *La Cage aux Folles* in 1983, that I realized I had actually become a part of something very significant—Broadway. Producer Allan Carr was originally trying to create an American version of the French play and film, *La Cage aux Folles*, called *The Queen of Basin Street*. The original effort did not pan out, but because the show had such potential, Carr forged ahead bringing in Jerry Herman to write both the music and lyrics. I joined the team when they started seeking a theater and became involved as a producer. Soon Harvey Fierstein was brought in to write the book, and Arthur Laurents came onboard to direct. This was truly a very Jewish team. It was also largely a gay team, who looked at me and shook their heads as I was the token heterosexual in the group. Nonetheless, I too appreciate that we were teaming up on something more than just a great comical musical with a fabulous score. We had a cause to rally around as we worked to bring the show to Broadway. It was a call for tolerance and for acceptance of gays in society at a time when such acceptance was still shaky at best.

We opened in Boston in July to great reviews. Of course that made us a little worried because now the New York critics would have higher expectations. The show finally opened in New York in August of 1983. *New York Times* critic Frank Rich called it the "most old-fashioned major musical Broadway has seen since *Annie*, and it's likely to be just as popular with children of all ages."[2] My father, who was always one of my staunchest supporters called that (the "old-fashioned musical" reference) the kiss of death. In fact, after returning to my apartment with some friends, following the lavish opening night party at the Pan Am building, complete with a 28-piece orchestra, my father convinced me that the show was doomed. So, the celebration ended quickly, and I spent the evening alone nursing two bottles of champagne. The next morning, despite a hangover, I remember going to the meeting with the show's creative team and all of the producers. Everyone was all smiles. "We have a big hit on our hands, the money's rolling in," was the theme of this joyful meeting. While my dad thought that the "old-fashioned musical" would be the kiss of death, apparently Broadway needed just that, a good old-fashioned musical, only this one was about accepting gays. Go figure. *La Cage* ran for 1,176 performances.

Despite the success of *La Cage*, we were still the underdogs when it came to the Tony Awards and not expected to top *Sunday in the Park with George*. Much to our surprise, we won for Best Musical, and Arthur, Jerry and Harvey walked off with their own Tonys.

On a side note, shortly thereafter, co-producer Marty Richards was having a fifth anniversary party in the Hamptons, and I was invited. In fact, the whole *La Cage* cast was invited. The setting was a beautiful house on the beach with topiaries, a marvelous ocean view and the Peter Duchin Orchestra playing. After making the rounds, saying hello to the cast and crew of the show, I found that I was seated at a table with Betty Comden and Adolph Green, Phyllis Newman, Bob Fosse, and acclaimed director Josh Logan and his wife, Netta. I recall looking around in awe of these people whose work I had admired for years.

This was a table of Broadway legends—and me. I've never forgotten that evening and how much it meant to me as a still fairly young producer.

And Then Came The Will Rogers Follies

My other significant show during the '80s and '90s was *The Will Rogers Follies*. It was significant to me, not only because it was a hit, but because it gave me the opportunity to actually work with Betty Comden, Adolph Green and Cy Coleman.

Oddly enough, I was almost not involved in *The Will Rogers Follies* at all. As was the case with Alan Menken and our Nederlander audition, the creative team behind the show invited me to a presentation of the show. Sometimes it can be very charming when the writers and composers present their own work, but it doesn't always accomplish the goal of getting a producer on board. I was honored to be sitting in and watching as Betty Comden and Adolph Green played the songs, with Peter Stone (also Jewish) who was writing the book also on hand. Tommy Tune even stopped by for a brief cameo. The problem was, when they were finished, I had to admit that I did not really think they had a full-fledged show on their hands.

This seasoned creative team, however, did not give up that easily. I was then invited to see another presentation at the landmark New York restaurant Tavern on the Green. This time, Keith Carradine was on hand, and he made all the difference in the world. He was funny, insightful and totally brought the show to life. I remember saying that I could certainly watch this guy for two-and-a-half hours. And in the end, not only did I enjoy producing the show with Keith Carradine in the starring role, but theatergoers enjoyed the musical at the Palace Theater for 981 performances. In addition, *The Will Rogers Follies* would go on to win six Tony Awards.

I enjoyed the opportunity to work with Betty Comden and Adolph Green. They were the consummate professionals, always there for meetings, rehearsals and ready to do whatever was necessary. They were indeed troopers, even at one point when Betty broke her leg. The only way to get to the meeting room at the Palace Theater was by a spiral staircase that went down to the basement. Yet, it never slowed Betty down one bit. Even with crutches she went to every meeting and never complained. It was evident that both Betty Comden and Adolph Green simply loved what they did and nothing was going to stop them.

As for Cy Coleman, he was also great to work with, very comfortable in his own genius. I say this because he was a child prodigy and his music was such a part of him that it was innate. He'd simply get up, perform and enjoy every minute of it. He clearly loved his music and his work. I also recall that when we brought Marla Maples in to join the show, Coleman stepped up to help her. An aspiring actress, Maples was known all throughout the media because of her relationship with Donald Trump, whom she would later marry. However, when she auditioned for a role in the show, some of the producers were concerned that she couldn't handle the part. So, Cy Coleman, along with Tommy Tune, volunteered to take the extra time necessary to work with her. Sure enough, after working with Cy, and Tommy, Marla Maples turned out to be a big hit in the show.

Along with the successful shows such as *La Cage* and *Will Rogers* came a few flops along the way. Nonetheless, my experiences during this era as a burgeoning producer were highlighted by working on some marvelous shows with some legendary talents.

The '80s and '90s were indeed a changing time for Broadway. From the new breed of young playwrights focusing their attention on significant social causes, to the mouse that roared, bringing Disney to 42nd Street, the Jewish influence continued with a new generation of names and faces interspersed with some familiar favorites, such as Sondheim and Coleman. And while writers like Alfred Uhry dutifully reminded us of the anti–Semitism that had existed in the past, and was still prevalent to some extent in other parts of the country, I was aware of my good fortune. I was lucky to be working and living in New York City at a time when I was not a victim of the prejudice or persecution that befell so many Jewish people who had come before me. While I was grateful, like so many Jews in the theater industry, I was aware that our Broadway success did not mean we could ever take our good fortune for granted.

8

The New Millennium
Sees Broadway Breakthroughs:
Veterans and Newcomers

The 20th century brought theater from a much-needed form of entertainment and self-expression for the new immigrants to a forum for social and political expression as well as marvelous entertainment. The Jewish influence impacted theater in all facets both on and off stage, broadening the way in which the Jewish people and their culture were presented and perceived by a secular audience. The Jewish contributors to Broadway during the 20th century faced their own challenges, whether it was the Great Depression, anti–Semitism, the war efforts or McCarthyism. Through it all, they never buckled under or stood idly by without being heard. Instead the Jewish people continued to have a voice on stage, and be part of the message, much as Tovah Feldshuh noted earlier. No matter what was taking place socially or politically, the Jewish people let their indomitable spirit continue to shine on the stages of Broadway. By the end of the century, not only had the Jewish people made a significant contribution to Broadway, but their contributions also impacted the way in which theater continues to be presented today.

At the turn of the new century, there was great concern over Y2K. Broadway, however, was always prepared with its own source of backup energy, which came not from technology, but from a wealth of creative talent.

As the new century began, it was clear that the social activism of the 1990s had spilled over into the new era, along with the passion for presenting top-notch entertainment. Of course, as the cost of staging a show, particularly a musical, continued to increase, taking a low-risk route with a proven commodity was still the best bet. With that in mind, revivals continued to be one means of drawing an audience for a musical. Popular movies, such as *Thoroughly Modern Millie*, *The Full Monty* and those with significant cable television exposure—such as *Legally Blonde*, *Shrek*, *The Producers* and the Disney films proved to be another manner in which to find material with a built-in fan base. The music and/or stories of popular entertainers such as Billy Joel, the Four Seasons and Frank Sinatra also provided shows with an established fan base. Even television shows, such as *The Addams Family*, could be fertile sources for musicals with fans at the ready.

While ticket prices limited families from making frequent the ritual of seeing a weekly or monthly Broadway show, as was the case in the 1950s, '60s and '70s (especially for Jewish families), Broadway theater remained very appealing for that special night out. It might cost a family $300, but for a special occasion it became fashionable to see the characters in *The Lion King* or *Mary Poppins* up close performing live onstage.

The number of new shows in a given year continued to be much lower than in the past. Totals were down from over 100 in the early years of the 20th century to around 70 per year in the 1960s to roughly 45 per year by 2005, nearly half of which were revivals. Nonetheless, quality prevailed over quantity, and the first decade saw a number of highly acclaimed productions, and box office hits; I was very happy to be a part of a few of them.

9/11 and Broadway

Before talking about the shows and stars of the decade, it would be remiss not to mention the effects that 9/11/2001 had on Broadway in the early part of the new century. To see Nathan Lane and cast members of *The Producers* come out during the final curtain call and stop the orchestra to ask people to please give money for the ongoing rescue efforts, some ten days after the horrible tragedy, was a testament to how all New Yorkers were pitching in, along with the rest of the country, to help in the aftermath.

In the weeks and months following 9/11, tourism came to a halt, and even many New Yorkers were fearful of coming into Manhattan. People in New York City, Washington, D.C., and all over the country were in shock and disbelief that such a terrorist attack could occur here in the United States.

If it weren't for the both the city and state government pushing to get Broadway up and running as soon as possible, many shows would have closed. The city purchased 50,000 theater tickets, while the state put $1 million behind a promotional campaign for Broadway. The idea was to show that New York City would not shut down and give in to terrorism. The lights on Broadway were, and still are, a symbol of New York's vitality and resolve. Sadly, many of the downtown shows and Off Broadway productions did not get any help from the city or state, and some were forced to close despite very good reviews.

While the theater was up and running within a short time after 9/11, it took time to fill all of the seats again. The usually bustling holiday season was much quieter than in the past, with fewer tourists and a much-subdued holiday spirit. It took time, but the audiences did return. A lot of credit has to be given to the cast members and to the crews who went back to work on Broadway within a few days of the tragedy.

Breakthroughs: The Veterans

MEL BROOKS

Few people have the distinction of winning an Oscar, Grammy, Emmy and Tony Award. Mel Kaminsky, better known as Mel Brooks, is one of them. While Brooks' long list of accomplishments spanned four decades before he landed firmly on Broadway, when he finally "made it," he did so with gusto, presenting one of the biggest musicals in the history of The Great White Way.

Brooks was born in Brooklyn, New York, in 1926, the son of German and Russian Jews. Small and often picked on as a child, Brooks turned to comedy as a means of coping. At 18, he enlisted in the army and went on to see action in Germany during World War II. By the time he returned to Fort Dix in New Jersey, he had been promoted to corporal.

It was after the war that Mel Brooks decided to try his hand at stand-up comedy. Like Woody Allen and Sid Caesar, he would hone his skills at the Catskills resorts. Also, like Allen, he would land a job as one of the staff writers on Caesar's TV series, *Your Show of Shows*.

During the 1960s, Brooks would make his mark in several mediums, teaming with funnyman, and close friend Carl Reiner on the comedy routine *The 2000 Year Old Man*, which emerged from popular sketches to several hit comedy albums. He would also make his mark in television as co-creator (with Buck Henry) of the James Bond spoof sitcom *Get Smart*.

It was also during the 1960s that Brooks would venture into the movie business, first with a small animated film entitled *The Critic* and then with *The Producers*, which was initially rejected by one major studio after another. The storyline about two producers discovering that they could make more money on Broadway with an absolute flop was a marvelously original and unique idea. However, their creation of a mega-flop musical called *Springtime for Hitler* scared the hell out of studio heads, who wouldn't touch the project. Eventually, an independent film company finally made *The Producers* and despite poor reviews and minimal box office numbers won an Oscar for Best Original Screenplay.

Brooks would eventually go mainstream with several classic comedy film satires, poking fun at one film genre after another to the delight of audiences and studio execs. *Blazing Saddles, High Anxiety, Young Frankenstein* and *Silent Movie* were among the classics that secured Brooks' place as a comic genius. Unknown to many, Brooks also did his share of serious films as well, such as *The Elephant Man,* for which he did little promotion. The thinking was that if Brooks lent his name to the film, audiences would have presumed it to be a comedy, rather than the serious dramatic work that it was.

The one area Brooks had not conquered, however, was theater, and Broadway in particular. Brooks had written sketches for *New Faces of 1952* and served as co-writer for the 1957 musical *Shinbone Alley,* which had three lead cats as characters, singing and dancing for only 49 performances long before the megahit musical *Cats.* Although *Shinbone Alley* was later made into an animated film, it did not land Brooks a Broadway hit. *All American,* starring Ray Bolger in 1962, with music by Charles Strouse, faired only slightly better than *Shinbone Alley,* with 80 performances.

Nonetheless, Brooks would finally have his day on Broadway, some 39 years later, with *The Producers.* It was the perfect choice. The quirky comedy had never quite been the mainstream hit that Brooks' later films would become. However, those who knew the film loved it and told their friends about the ingenious plot line. By 2001, when the Broadway show opened, it had a cachet about it as a "cult" favorite. It didn't hurt that Nathan Lane agreed to play one of the lead roles as fictional Broadway impresario Max Bialystock.

The absurdity of the show within the show, the off-beat characters and Matthew Broderick teaming with Nathan Lane made *The Producers* the talk of Broadway, first setting a box office record by amassing over $3 million in ticket sales in one day and then, 2,500 performances later, walking away with a record 12 Tony Awards including Best Musical. Brooks even wrote the song lyrics and contributed to the music. In addition to the Broadway run, the show ran successfully in Great Britain and other parts of the globe, translated into Spanish, Japanese, Danish, Italian, Russian and Hebrew, among other languages. There was a 2005 film, but it was not as well received as the original, which grew in popularity over the many years since its original release. *The Producers* was spoofed by Larry David on his HBO television series *Curb Your Enthusiasm,* in an episode in which David was given a role in the show, essentially to cause the show to fail so that Brooks and his wife, Anne Bancroft, could get out of their endless commitment to it. The plan backfires, and just like *Springtime for Hitler,* Larry David in *The Producers* becomes an unlikely hit.

Brooks would later follow *The Producers* by bringing the 1974 film *Young Frankenstein* to Broadway in 2007. A modest hit, the show ran for nearly 500

PLAYBILL®

ST. JAMES THEATRE

The marvelous film of 1967 *The Producers* came to life at the St. James Theatre in April of 2001 and went on to steal the name of another hit musical when it became the "talk of the town." The buzz about this laugh fest extended far and wide, and twelve Tony Awards later, Mel Brooks knew that he had finally conquered Broadway. The stars were Nathan Lane, left, and Matthew Broderick (courtesy Playbill Inc.).

performances. Whether more of Brooks' films are on the way to Broadway remains to be seen. However, the standard he set for a musical comedy with *The Producers* will be very hard to surpass.

MARSHALL BRICKMAN

Not unlike Mel Brooks, Marshall Brickman proved that it is never too late to have a hit Broadway musical. Jewish on his father's side, and perhaps through his long collaborative career with Woody Allen, Brickman made his way to Broadway in 2005 with the box-office smash *Jersey Boys*.

Brickman was born in Brazil in 1941. Following college, in the early 1960s, his enthusiasm for music led to him form a folk group with Eric Weissberg, who later went on to fame as one of the string-picking participants in "Dueling Banjos," the popular song from the film *Deliverance*. Brickman would move on to play in a band called the New Journeymen with John and Michelle Phillips, later of Mamas and Papas fame.

While Brickman loved folk music, he also had a knack for writing comedy and found his way into television writing for *Candid Camera*, *The Tonight Show* and *The Dick Cavett Show* from the mid– to late '60s. Shortly thereafter he would team up with Woody Allen on Allen's first TV special and then as a co-screenwriter on *Sleeper, Annie Hall, Manhattan*, and years later, on *Manhattan Murder Mystery*.

However, Brickman had not yet ventured into writing for the theater until *Jersey Boys*. While more of a folk music enthusiast than a Four Seasons fan, Brickman, in his early 60s, decided to team with former actor and advertising writer Rick Elise on the book for *Jersey Boys*. The show hit Broadway in 2005, winning the Tony Award for Best Musical. It has been running ever since. While Brickman acknowledged in several interviews that in the process of writing the book for the musical he was learning a lot from those with more theatrical background than himself, he was also pleased with his ability to work his comedy into the dialogue as he wrote. "A laugh in the theater is not a superficial thing," explained Brickman in an interview about co-writing *Jersey Boys*. "If you can get 1,500 people to all laugh at the same time about the same thing, then you've extracted some kind of basic truth about whatever it is that the laugh is,"[1] adds Brickman.

Enjoying their newfound Broadway success, Brickman and Elise teamed up again on the 2010 musical *The Addams Family*. While Brickman is better known for his work with Woody Allen and his appearance in *Annie Hall*, he has, like Mel Brooks, added Broadway success to an already highly impressive resume.

MARC SHAIMAN

Another of the seasoned Broadway breakthroughs of the 2000s came from Marc Shaiman. While certainly younger than Brooks or Brickman, Shaiman had also amassed a significant list of major credits when he strolled onstage to collect his two Tony Awards for *Hairspray* in 2003.

Unlike many of the Jewish composers of the early 20th century who left college to pursue music, Shaiman actually left both high school and his life in New Jersey to move to New York City at the age of 16. Already an accomplished piano player, with a fixation on Bette Midler, Shaiman wrote and performed in many shows on the Lower East Side before finally meeting Midler and, in time, becoming her musical director. He would also go on to work with Midler as a co-producer on a number of her records. In fact, it was thanks to the Divine Miss M that Shaiman would get his first taste of Broadway working on her show *Divine Madness*. He would also get to work on Peter Allen's show *Up in One*. Both shows, however, would have short runs on Broadway.

It was in film that Shaiman would make a name for himself, writing music and/or film scores for Midler's films *Big Business* and *Beaches*, as well as for *Broadcast News*, *When Harry Met Sally…*, *City Slickers*, *George of the Jungle* and *The Wedding Planner* to name a few.

But it wasn't until 2002 that Shaiman, who always had a Broadway musical flair, would enjoy his first major box-office success, *Hairspray*, which topped 2,600 performances and became a favorite on film as well, … with a less notable sequel. In 2005, Shaiman worked on the musical version of Neil Simon's *The Odd Couple*. Despite a cast that featured Nathan Lane and Matthew Broderick, the show ran for only seven months. He would then not only do the music and lyrics for *Martin Short: Fame Becomes Me*, but he would also play piano and perform as one of the Comedy All-Stars in Short's 2006 Broadway show. Shaiman has now firmly established himself as a sought-after Broadway composer and lyricist.

BILLY JOEL

While Joel personally did not find himself on the Broadway stage, he joined the litany of famous composers and lyricists whose music brought home a major hit show. Often thought to be Italian, Joel was born to Jewish parents on Long Island where he grew up and almost finished high school, opting for a musical career instead. He would ultimately get his high school degree 25 years after leaving school.

Joel's dad was a classical pianist, so he learned to play at an early age. But he credits seeing the Beatles on *The Ed Sullivan Show* in 1964 as the impetus for wanting to be a rock star. Forming a band in his teens and playing session for several years, Joel would finally land a recording deal and record his first solo album, *Cold Spring Harbor*, which was mixed poorly and, as a result, proved to be a disappointment. Joel would, however, break through shortly thereafter with the song and album *Piano Man* generating tremendous attention, first in New York and later, nationwide. In the late '70s, Joel would reach superstar status with the album *The Stranger* and hits such as "Just the Way You Are" and "Movin' Out." He would continue with string of major pop hits and platinum-selling albums while touring the world. Today, although he has long since stopped recording, he continues playing arenas and even stadiums.

The idea for a Broadway musical featuring dance numbers to Joel's popular songs emerged from dancer/choreographer Twyla Tharp who, like Joel, had launched her career in the mid-'60s, forming her own dance troupe. It was in 2000, having just put together an entirely new troupe, that she decided to develop dances to Joel's popular songs. In October of 2002, the musical *Movin' Out* opened on Broadway, featuring Joel's music and Tharp's choreography. The show would run for 1,303 performances over three years. As a result, both Tharp and Joel would walk away with Tony Awards for doing what they do best, creating music and dance.

CAROLE KING

Another Jewish latecomer to Broadway made it big by virtue of being one of the most prolific songwriters of the 1960s and '70s. Born Carole Klein, music was her passion throughout her childhood and teenage years. It was during her teens that she met her soon-to-be-husband Gerry Goffin while attending Queens College. Klein, soon to become known as Carole King, had spent years playing piano, writing songs, and recording demos. She had a knack for catchy tunes that resulted in an amazing string of hits by other artists, starting with the Shirelles' 1960 hit "Will You Love Me Tomorrow" and proceeding through pop classics, such as "Up on the Roof" by the Drifters, "One Fine Day" by the Chiffons, "(You Make Me Feel Like) a Natural Woman" by Aretha Franklin, "You've Got a Friend" by James Taylor, and many others. Even King's babysitter (known on her record as Little Eva) had a hit song that started a dance craze, "The Loco-Motion."

At the start of the 1970s, King would record a couple albums of her own, starting with the appropriately titled *Writer*, which saw minimal success in 1970, and followed by *Tapestry* in 1971, which became a classic multimillion-selling album featuring her own renditions of several of her classic songs, coupled with some brand-new tunes, such as "It's Too Late" and "I Feel the

Earth Move," which became two of her signature hits. This also led to several major hit albums and popular songs for King, as a performer, throughout the rest of the decade.

As for Broadway, King's music has been featured in a few shows, including the musical revue *Uptown … It's Hot* and the recent revival of *The Real Thing*. King also had her first and only performing role, when she stepped in for a year to play Mrs. Johnstone, in the mid–'90s musical *Blood Brothers*, which ran for 840 performances.

But it wasn't until the sixth decade of her long career that a massive baby boomer audience would find themselves sitting in the Stephen Sondheim Theatre singing along to hit after hit in the biographical production *Beautiful: The Carole King Musical*, which opened in January 2014 to great reviews and packed houses. Featuring Jessie Muller in the lead role, for which she won the 2014 Tony for Best Performance in a Leading Role, *Beautiful* is still running today, encompassing the music and the story of Carole King, who, now in her '70s, is enjoying the new wave of attention and appreciation.

DAVID, ALEXANDER, AND SHAPIRO

No, it's not a law firm. David, Alexander, and Shapiro are three of the principals who brought *Fish in the Dark* to Broadway in 2015. Two of the main cogs in the success of the television show *Seinfeld*, co-creator and writer Larry David and Jason Alexander (who is forever enshrined in sitcom folklore for his role as George Costanza) teamed up with a talented young director, Anna D. Shapiro, for this much talked-about stage comedy.

David, who hails from Sheepshead Bay in Brooklyn, started out as one of many Jewish stand-up comics trying to get stage time at the New York comedy clubs. He later wrote for, and performed in, the early 1980s ABC sketch comedy series *Fridays*. Then in 1988, he teamed with fellow stand-up comic and good friend Jerry Seinfeld to pitch a sitcom to NBC, and the rest, as they say, is television history.

Nearly twenty years after leaving Seinfeld, Larry David would make his Broadway debut in the play *Fish in the Dark*, for which he also wrote the book. The show about bad behavior following a death in the family incorporated David's cynical and overly critical *Curb Your Enthusiasm* persona. While *Fish* did not have a long run, it set box-office records for advance ticket sales for a spring opening, taking in $13.5 million. David played the lead role for just over half of the 173 performances before turning the reigns over to none other than Jason Alexander, who essentially played David on *Seinfeld*.

For Alexander, Broadway was already familiar territory. Born in Newark,

New Jersey, to Jewish parents, Alexander wanted to pursue more serious acting roles but was guided to comedy after leaving Boston University. Prior to his *Seinfeld* experience, he would sing and dance his way into Broadway musicals, including a brief revival of *Merrily We Roll Along* in 1981, *The Rink* in 1984, and as Stanley in Neil Simon's hit comedy *Broadway Bound* in 1986. He would also appear in *Jerome Robbins' Broadway* and the comedy-thriller *The Accomplice*. Since the finale of *Seinfeld*, he has appeared on a number of television shows, including Larry David's *Curb Your Enthusiasm* and in several movies. He has also directed several theatrical productions in his home away from home, Los Angeles. While many *Seinfeld* fans are still surprised to hear Alexander's vocal abilities, Broadway theatergoers will not be surprised to see him return to the stage in the not-too-distant future.

As for Anna D. Shapiro, the young director and graduate of the Yale School of Drama, she knew she had a major challenge when taking on *Fish*. In an interview with *Jewish Week* magazine, Shapiro said of Larry David, "I adore the guy; he's been so seminal in the formation of my own sense of humor. I didn't want him to think that I wasn't funny."

Shapiro came to New York from the Steppenwolf Theater Company in Chicago, where she has since returned, having been named artistic director. She made her Broadway directorial debut with the original play *August: Osage County* in 2007, which ran for 648 performances and from which she walked away with a Tony Award for direction and a husband, marrying the lead Ian Barford. More recently, she directed James Franco in John Steinbeck's *Of Mice and Men*. *Fish*, however, brought Shapiro closer to her Jewish roots, as the family that she and David brought to the stage hit closer to home

It's also worth noting that New York native David Yazbek, whose mother was Jewish and father Lebanese, wrote the music for *Fish in the Dark*. A musician, composer, orchestrator, arranger, and lyricist, Yazbek first hit Broadway at the age of 39 writing the music and lyrics for the adaptation of the hit comedy *The Full Monty*, which ran for over 700 performances. Yazbek went on to write music and lyrics for *Dirty Rotten Scoundrels* and a Lincoln Center Theater production of *Women on the Edge of a Nervous Breakdown*, also adding vocal arrangements and additional orchestrations before moving on to *Fish*.

And the Newcomers

Adam Guettel

Along with the Adlers and the Hammersteins, another remarkable Broadway family would be the Rodgers family. The daughter of composer Richard

Rodgers, Mary Rodgers composed the music for several Broadway shows including the successful 1959 musical *Once Upon a Mattress*. It was, therefore, not a surprise when her son Adam Guettel would emerge as a young soprano by the age of ten, singing at the New York City Opera and at the Metropolitan Opera House. But by the age of 13, Guettel's voice was changing and his opera career appeared to be behind him. The young child protégé was not at all unhappy to be changing careers, wanting to follow his musical dreams.

After graduating from Yale University in 1987, Guettel began writing music, first as a young rock and roller and later as a Rodgers. He clearly had his own creative instincts, but his lineage was present in his composition. "I grew up in great privilege; I was given a great heritage,"[2] explained Guettel in an interview for *The Jewish Exponent*, adding that he writes out of fundamental values that connect with Jewishness and the stage.

Unfortunately his composer grandfather died when he was 14. "If I had had the chance, there are thousands of questions I had wanted to ask him. I would have loved to have known his thoughts,"[3] said Guettel, who first drew attention and favorable reviews for his music and lyrics for *Floyd Collins*, a 1996 musical about a man trapped in a Kentucky cave. Several musicals later, in 2003, his work based on an Elizabeth Spencer novella, *The Light in the Piazza*, would be staged first in Seattle and then in Chicago, before opening on Broadway for a run of 504 performances. The score, complete with classical music and opera, won Tony Awards for Best Original Score and Best Orchestration.

While differences between the creative team members ended Guettel's next project, a musical version of the popular film *The Princess Bride*, he continues to work on musical adaptations of other written works while also teaching musical theater performance and songwriting at many esteemed universities, including Harvard, Yale, and Princeton.

Zach Braff

Following in the footsteps of Jennifer Jason Leigh, Natalie Portman, and others, a pre-teen Zach Braff honed his acting skills in at the Stagedoor Manor theatrical camp in upstate New York. He then went on for a degree in film at Northeastern University. The Jersey-born Braff's father came from Jewish roots, while his mother converted to Judaism. Braff came to notoriety in the hit sitcom *Scrubs* and followed with a film career that included *Garden State*, *Oz the Great and Powerful*, *Wish I Was Here*, and Woody Allen's *Manhattan Murder Mystery*. More recently, he made his Broadway debut in Woody Allen's *Bullets Over Broadway* in 2014. While Braff is very likely to return to the Broadway stage in the not-too-distance future, his latest venture has been directing the remake of the 1979 comedy film *Going in Style* with a cast that features Morgan Freeman, Michael Caine, Alan Arkin, Matt Dillon, Christopher Lloyd, and Ann-Margaret.

IDINA MENZEL (AND *WICKED*)

Along with *The Producers*, one of the most highly acclaimed shows of the past decade featuring many Jewish contributors, has been *Wicked*, which as of the updated version of this book has topped 5,000 performances on Broadway. The idea for the show *Wicked* came from Stephen Schwartz, who in 1998 procured the rights to Gregory Maguire's 1995 novel *Wicked: The Life and Times of the Wicked Witch of the West*. The story focused on the witches from *The Wizard of Oz*. Schwartz (discussed in greater detail in Chapter 6), had enjoyed great Broadway success with *Godspell* and *Pippin* back in the 1970s before moving on to write the music for animated Disney films of the 1990s. For *Wicked*, however, he would team up with Emmy Award–winning television writer Winnie Holtzman to write the book. Holtzman was well versed in musical theatre writing, having studied at New York University with the likes of Stephen Sondheim, Hal Prince, Comden and Green and Leonard Bernstein. Nonetheless, *Wicked* marked her debut on Broadway.

Numerous performers, including Joel Grey, have come and gone during the ongoing success of the show; however, one of the most notable was Idina Menzel. Born Idina Mentzel, the Jewish actress/singer from Syosset changed her last name because it was so often mispronounced. Menzel grew up singing the songs from *Annie* and dazzling her fellow summer campers with her rendition of *The Way We Were*. After playing Dorothy in *The Wizard of Oz* in high school, the young performer would hone her singing talent fronting for wedding bands.

Then in the mid–1990s, an audition for a new Broadway show called *Rent* would change her life forever. She landed the role and the show landed on Broadway in 1996. After a short stint in *The Wild Party* at the Manhattan Theatre Club and playing Fanny Brice in a *Funny Girl* concert at the New Amsterdam Theater in 2002, she would go on to be part of the original cast *Wicked* in 2003, where she would play Elphaba, a.k.a. the Wicked Witch of the West, for a year and a half. For her bewitching performance, she won the Tony Award for Best Performance by a Lead Actress in a Musical. She would later return to the role in London in late 2006.

Her concert performances and appearances in the hit television series *Glee* continued to spotlight Menzel's vocal talents. But what better way to climb to new career heights than to provide the voice of the queen in a hugely successful animated Disney film? The film was *Frozen*, and Menzel had the privilege of singing "Let It Go" not only in the film, but at the 2014 Academy Awards. The song won the Oscar for Best Song in a Motion Picture while becoming a hugely popular hit. It was also in 2014 that Menzel returned to Broadway as the lead in the musical *If/Then*, a show that offers visions of what a woman's life might have been like depending on the paths she chose. The musical ran for a year on Broadway.

JEFF MARX AND ROBERT LOPEZ

Most composers or lyricists do not grow up with the dream of bringing an adult puppet show to Broadway. Jeff Marx, nonetheless, had his breakthrough on Broadway in that very manner, collaborating with his partner Robert Lopez on the musical *Avenue Q*. Marx, who grew up in Hollywood, Florida, was destined to be a lawyer, having passed the bar. However, it was upon meeting Lopez that they decided to try their hand at writing. Together they worked on a Muppet movie script, for which they won a $150,000 award. The movie was never produced, but Marx and Lopez decided that since there was a universal love for puppets, they would create their own with a new story, one that appealed to adults. Thus, a five-year project began, which culminated in *Avenue Q*, the story of a wide-eyed college grad who comes to New York City with big dreams and little money. He ends up on the Lower East Side with a host of unique and entertaining characters, which included former television personality Gary Coleman.

In an interview for the student newspaper of the University of Kansas, Marx explained that he and Lopez spent a long time creating an adult version of Sesame Street. They wanted to create a show about their friends and themselves. "It's not just funny because they say 'fuck' all the time like we do, it's entertaining because they are dealing with real issues like being closeted, still getting money from their parents and obsessions with porn,"[4] explained Marx in the interview.

The producer of *Rent*, Jeff Seller was quite impressed with *Avenue Q* and helped bring it to Off Broadway in early 2003. After great reviews and constant sellouts, the show then moved to Broadway that summer where it played for over 2,500 performances in a six-year run. Marx and Lopez won Tony Awards for Best Musical and Best Original Score. Lopez would go on to write the book, lyrics, and music for the smash satire *The Book of Mormon*, which took Broadway by storm in 2011, while Marx has written and co-written songs for television.

MICHAEL MAYER

Michael Mayer was not entirely new to Broadway when he became director on *Thoroughly Modern Millie*, which I had the pleasure of producing in 2002. His Broadway credits actually dated back to the late 1990s with a musical called *Triumph of Love* in 1997 and a revival of *You're a Good Man, Charlie Brown* in 1999.

Born in Maryland, Mayer came to New York City after high school where he studied acting and graduated from New York University with an M.F.A. in theater. Like many directors, Mayer began as an actor but developed an interest in directing as he became more involved in theater. In 1999, Mayer joined forces with Dick Scanlon, Jeanine Tesori, Richard Morris and myself to bring the 1967 film *Thoroughly Modern Millie* to the stage for the first time. From the tryouts in La Jolla, California, to opening night at the Marquis Theater on Broadway in 2002, Mayer worked diligently helping to bring a show that was a little too long for a musical (at three hours) down to a more manageable length (two and a half). He also worked with three Millies in the process. Kristin Chenowith was the first Millie, but she had television and film projects that precluded her continuing in the show. Erin Dilly was the next Millie. But Dilly as Millie did not make it to Broadway. When she took ill, her replacement, Sutton Foster, took over the role. I recall, upon seeing Foster perform, Mayer exclaimed, "There's Our Millie!" And sure enough, Foster, who was thrust into the role and landed ever so quickly on Broadway, ended up walking away with the Tony Award for Best Actress in a Musical. *Millie*, meanwhile, was awarded Best Musical.

As for Mayer, while *Millie* ran for over 900 performances, he would move on to *Spring Awakening*, the coming-of-age musical for which he would win a Tony Award for Best Director. Most recently, Mayer joined forces with Billy Joe Armstrong, lead singer of the rock band Green Day, to bring the band's megaselling album *American Idiot* to Broadway. The show, which gained momentum in Berkeley, California, moved to the St. James Theater on Broadway in March of 2010, marking three original musicals, and five Broadway shows total, in a span of just eight years for Mayer. More recently, Mayer directed the revival of a musical dealing with a rock star's gender identity issues, titled *Hedwig and the Angry Inch*, which ran Off Broadway for two years in the late 1990s. The Broadway rendition debuted in 2014 and ran for over 500 performances.

MATT STONE

Another newcomer to Broadway has made the transition from animated television success. Stone, along with Trey Parker, were the creators, writers, and driving force behind the satirical, animated, edgy television comedy *South Park* and the movie *South Park: Bigger Longer & Uncut*. They would later move from animation to film's raunchiest marionette movie of all time, *Team America: World Police*. The 2004 film was given an NC-17 rating before eventually being reduced to an R rating just prior to release.

While the Texas-born-and-raised Stone is half–Jewish, his theatrical success has been 100 percent Mormon, since he is the cowriter of one of Broadway's biggest hits of the twenty-first century, *The Book of Mormon*. Teaming with Parker and *Avenue Q* co-lyricist and co-composer Robert Lopez, Stone was a driving force on *Mormon*, serving as cowriter, co-lyricist, and co-composer. *New York Times*' critic Ben Brantley wrote of *Mormon* that "it is as blasphemous, scurrilous, and more foul-mouthed than David Mamet on a blue streak. But trust me when I tell you that its heart is as pure as that of a Rodgers and Hammerstein show."

Meanwhile, five years after capturing an amazing eleven Tony Awards in 2011, the show is the still filling seats nightly. Stone, who epitomizes a new breed of daring satirists taking aim at politics, religion, and several less controversial topics, will likely be back on Broadway soon, unless television and/or film opportunities preclude his imminent return.

Adam Jacobs

Starring as Aladdin in the Disney musical of the same name, young Jewish-Filipino actor Adam Jacobs is one of the most highly acclaimed young performers in the business. The California native began his road to the magic carpet by studying piano as a youngster at the San Francisco Conservatory of Music. Jacobs soon discovered his passion for acting and attended the American Conservatory Theater (ACT), also in San Francisco, and the California Institute of the Arts (CSSSA), in Valencia, before heading east to New York University's Tisch School of the Arts.

From this extensive theatrical training, Jacobs would move into regional theater and perform on cruise ships and on land in a touring company of *Les Misérables*. This would lead to his role in the Broadway musical version and ignite his career, which would lead to two stints in *The Lion King*.

Then in 2014, Adam came to Broadway as the first non-animated Aladdin, and audiences and critics were pleased. The *Hollywood Reporter* wrote, "Jacobs packs plenty of charm into the role and is an ideal incarnation of the handsome Disney cartoon hero." And while Jacobs brings Aladdin to life, it should be noted that his little sister, Arielle, not to be outdone, made her Broadway debut in the musical *Into the Heights* before taking over as Nessarose in *Wicked* in

2015. In keeping with the family ties to Broadway, Adam's wife, Kelly Jacobs, stepped into the ensemble of Disney's *Mary Poppins* in 2012 and enjoyed a year with the show before it closed. Now the question is how much more talent will emerge from the Jacobs family?

LISA KRON

One of the other newcomers to Broadway is Lisa Kron, who stepped up to accept a pair of Tony Awards in 2015 for lyricist and libretto for *Fun Home*, the musical based on the graphic novel by Alison Bechdel. She also collaborated with Broadway veteran Jeanine Tesori on the play *Ver**zon*. Kron, who had one previous short stint on Broadway with a 2006 show she wrote and performed in, *Well*, has been writing and starring in her own shows since she left Michigan for New York City more than twenty years ago. Some of her works have landed in a variety of locations, from Lincoln Center to London.

Kron's father is a Holocaust survivor whose parents died in the death camps, while her mom converted to Judaism once she was married. Kron commented in her play *Well* that she, along with her brother and father, feel like outsiders in their own family, which exists only of her mother's non–Jewish relatives.

From her many years of writing and performing in plays primarily about life, lesbians, and family, it is likely that now being on a grander stage, Kron will have opportunities to continue bringing both humor and pathos to Broadway in the years ahead.

JUDY KUHN

Starring in Kron and Tesori's *Fun Home* is Judy Kuhn, a native New Yorker who grew up in Maryland, went to Oberlin College in Ohio, and moved to Boston before returning to the Big Apple.

Judy would debut on Broadway in *The Mystery of Edward Drood* before landing the role of Cossette in the original 1987 cast of *Les Misérables*. Ten years later, she would appear in the tenth anniversary celebration of the classic show before returning in 2007 in the *Les Miz* revival.

A talented singer, Kuhn has also used her incredible voice to the delight of Disney fans as the singing voice of Pocahontas in the 1995 animated film, as well as in the sequel *Pocahontas II: Journey to a New World*, then later as Princess Ting-Ting in the *Mulan II* video.

Having released two solo albums of classics in recent years, she generated some terrific reviews. The *New York Times* described her as a singer with

Opening on April 19, 2015, *Fun Home* brought three decades of a woman's exploration of her relationship with her father to the stage in a show that begs the universal question: Who are these strange people who created me? Apparently, the answers made an impact, as *Fun Home* drew tremendous critical acclaim and garnered five Tony Awards (courtesy Playbill Inc.).

"passionate restraint ... conveying as much insight and empathy as more overtly dramatic singers without straining for a show-stopping theatricality; her delivery is refined but not prim, her intonation impeccable."

ROBERT FREEDMAN

While the Tony Award–winning Robert L. Freedman (Best Book of a Musical) may be a newcomer to Broadway with the musical smash hit *A Gentleman's Guide to Love and Murder,* he is not new to critically acclaimed screen plays. Freedman enjoyed years of television writing success, starting with TV movies of the week for NBC and CBS in the early 1980s and continuing into the '90s when he scored big with a television presentation of *Cinderella* featuring Brandy and Whitney Houston.

The bicoastal writer, who hails originally from Los Angeles, received his undergraduate degree from UCLA. Venturing east, he then earned master's degrees in dramatic writing and musical theatre from the Tisch School of the Arts at New York University. From early shows at UCLA and the Collective Actor's Theater in New York, Freedman would tackle the *Beast of Broadway,* a one-man show he co-wrote about the life of David Merrick.

Not long after, Freedman moved on to *Gentleman's Guide,* which opened in Hartford, Connecticut, and moved to San Diego prior to reaching Broadway in late 2013. But it wasn't until the 2014 Tony Awards that the show took off and Freedman and co-lyricist/composer Steven Lutvak knew they had a major hit on their hands, which ran for 905 performances before heading out on tour.

Steven Lutvak has been called "an upper-middlebrow Billy Joel crossed with a lower-highbrow Tom Lehrer, with a pinch of Debussy," by *New York Times* writer Stephen Holden. Prior to *Gentleman,* Steven wrote the title track to the documentary *Mad Hot Ballroom.* He also has two solo albums, *The Time It Takes* and *Ahead of My Heart.*

Ladies Taking Charge

ANITA WAXMAN

No, Broadway producers need not be members of the good old boys' club. Anita Waxman, along with partner Elizabeth Williams, certainly proved that point during the first decade of the new century.

Waxman, who hails from California, turned to theater after a lucrative corporate career in which she was the founder and chairman of Howe-Lewis International Incorporated, a very successful management consulting and executive search service firm. Waxman, who first reached Broadway in 1986 as producer of an original comedy called *Wild Honey*, met the Southern-born Williams in 1998. Williams had already been involved in a few Broadway productions herself, including *Into the Woods* and *The Secret Garden*.

The pair ended the 1990s with a revival of the historic musical *1776* and a revival of the tragedy *Electra* before making their mark by bringing four shows to Broadway in 2000, *The Real Thing*, *The Music Man*, *A Moon for the Misbegotten*, and *The Wild Party*. The shows combined for two-dozen Tony Award nominations. They added two more productions in 2001 including the hit *Noises Off*, followed by five more over the next couple of years, topping even the prolific David Merrick who launched shows at a frenetic pace in the 1960s. In 2004 they were behind the original musical *Bombay Dreams* about a boy from India who dreams of escaping the slums for movie stardom in Bollywood. The musical ran for 284 performances.

In recent years, Waxman and Williams have gone their separate ways, but Waxman has continued to produce shows featuring a wide range of well-known leading men, from Jesus Christ (*Jesus Christ Superstar*) to Charlie Chaplin (in the brief run of *Chaplin*) to *Rocky* (in the multi-million-dollar extravaganza) to *Doctor Zhivago*, which unfortunately did not last long on Broadway.

Waxman, who grew up in California before becoming a major force in New York Theater, never forgot her Jewish roots. After enduring nearly a year of the emotionally challenging adoption process in Russia, she was finally able to bring her son home from a Russian orphanage in the 1990s. With memories of the orphanage etched in her mind, she helped fund and open the Passin-Waxman Center, a privately funded Jewish children's home in the center of Moscow, the first Jewish orphanage in the Russian capital since Stalin's purge. Ironically, her son's name when they met was Yuri Antipov, which combines the names of two of *Zhivago*'s protagonists, Pasha Antipov and Yuri Zhivago.

Carole Shorenstein Hays

Another prominent producer in recent years is Carole Shorenstein Hays, born and raised in San Francisco. Seeing musicals with her parents in the 1950s got Hays hooked on theater. She would later follow her dreams to New York City where she attended New York University.

Carole's dad, a successful real estate mogul, was friends with George Steinbrenner and Jimmy Nederlander, who mentored Carole from a young age. "When it comes to theatre," she says, "I learned everything from Jimmy Nederlander. He is masterful. There's no better theater person."[5]

Her first taste of Broadway was in 1979 when she worked with me on Jerry Herman's *The Grand Tour*. A few shows later she was on her own producing *Fences* in 1987. After producing a string of Broadway shows including *Take Me Out*; *The Tale of the Allergist's Wife*; *Caroline, or Change*; and *Doubt*; and amassing five Tony awards, Hays went full circle bringing *Fences* back to Broadway in 2010. The following year, Hays would be part of the production of *War Horse*, which ran for over 700 performances at Lincoln Center's Vivian Beaumont Theater. I also had the honor of being part of the successful run of this marvelous show. Knowing and working with Hays over the years, I can attest to the fact that she is, not unlike myself, always thinking about the next potential hit show.

DARYL ROTH

Another of the most celebrated women behind the scenes on Broadway is Daryl Roth, who was named by *Crain's* magazine as one of the "100 Most Influential Women in Business."

Roth grew up in a Jewish home in Wayne, New Jersey. Being within an hour of the city, her parents took her and her sister to see Broadway shows often during the 1950s. Despite her love of Broadway, she followed a different career path, establishing herself as an interior decorator before venturing into the theater as a producer in her 40s with the 1989 Richard Maltby, Jr., David Shire show *Closer Than Ever*, an award-winning Off Broadway musical revue. Just two years later, she would get a taste of Broadway with *Nick and Nora*, which, unfortunately lasted less than two weeks. Since her inauspicious Broadway debut, Roth has emerged as a prolific producer with a long and impressive list of shows, including *Proof, The Tale of the Allergist's Wife, Curtains, August: Osage County, Caroline, or Change, Fela!*, the 2009 revival of *A Little Night Music, Driving Miss Daisy*, the return of *Annie* in 2012, and Cyndi Lauper's *Kinky Boots*. During this run of success, she also brought Larry Kramer's *The Normal Heart* to Broadway, the groundbreaking show illuminating the early years of the AIDS epidemic. She told *Playbill* magazine that show was "full of everything we love about theatre, everything good theatre strives to be."

While producing a string of Broadway hits over the past 25 years and bringing six Pulitzer Prize–winners to the stage, Roth also found the time to revive a landmark building on 15th Street in Manhattan, in the heart of Union Square, where she established the Daryl Roth Theater in a former Union Square Savings Bank. Today, the Off-Broadway location is home to three venues, including DR2 and the D Lounge.

Like Mother, Like Son

JORDAN ROTH

Daryl Roth has apparently passed her Broadway lineage on to her son, who has combined his theater degree from Princeton and his MBA from Columbia Business School to lead Jujamcyn Theaters to tremendous success. In a town where the Shuberts and Nederlanders have presided over the Broadway theater community for years, Roth, principal owner of Jujamcyn Theaters, has also played a major role, owning five venues and bringing a long list of hits to Broadway over the past decade. Initially a producer, who brought the cult favorite *Rocky Horror Show* to the Circle in the Square in 2000, with a host of popular performers moving in and out of the leading roles, he would later move into Jujamcyn in 2005 as a producer. A year later, he became a vice president, and by 2009, he was president and co-owner with Rocco Landesman. When Landesman decided to sell his shares of the business, he sold them to Roth, who became a rare theater impresario before the age of forty.

Roth kept an eye out for innovative productions that would expand the theater audience. With his mom as one of the producers, he served as creative director on the musical comedy *Curtains*, starring David Hyde Pierce in 2007. The show ran for over a year, and the Jordan Roth era had begun. Among the shows that would follow would be the original musical *A Catered Affair*, a successful revival of *Gypsy* starring Patti LuPone, *Fela!*, Green Day's *American Idiot*, two revivals of *Hair*, and revivals of other favorites, including *A Little Night Music* and *How to Succeed in Business Without Really Trying*, plus an original comedy/drama called *Claybourne Park*. Stepping it up a notch, Roth's involvement in contemporary Broadway would also include award-winning shows, such as *The Book of Mormon*, *Jersey Boys*, *Kinky Boots*, and *A Gentleman's Guide to Love and Murder*.

While sprinkling in some "more traditional revivals," such as the recent return of Arthur Miller's *The Crucible*, Roth has shown a penchant for bringing in fresh ideas, which perhaps dates back to his pre–Broadway days when he staged an audience participation production of *The Donkey Show* in which Shakespeare and disco united in a production described as a "magic fantasia." The distinctive *Donkey Show*, which took place in a New York City disco, ran for six years.

Among Others

The new century marked a marvelous opportunity for young Jewish playwrights, lyricists and composers to make their way to Broadway. Lisa Lambert, an actress and writer from Washington, D.C., made her mark on Broadway and won Tony Awards for Best Composer and Best Lyricist for her work on *The Drowsy Chaperone* in 2006. *Chaperone* spoofed musicals of the 1920s, '30s and '40s with a show-within-a-show dream sequence featuring the infamous Man in the Chair, who serves as the narrator of this original musical comedy that first gained momentum in Toronto over several years.

Another Tony Award–winning Jewish-born newcomer to Broadway in recent years, Rachel Sheinkin, won the prestigious honor for writing the book to the quirky comedy *The 25th Annual Putnam County Spelling Bee*. Sheinkin's road to Broadway began after graduating with a master of fine arts from Yale University and continued with her fellowship at the Manhattan Theatre Club. *Spelling Bee* originated from an improvisational work of actress Rebecca Friedman in an improv workshop. Little by little, the show grew and Sheinkin was brought in to help transform improv into an actual script with the help of James Lapine and William Finn. From Massachusetts workshops to Off Broadway success and on to a lengthy Broadway run, the musical highlighted the writing of Sheinkin while still including opportunities for improvisational material.

The Addams Family: Funny, They Didn't Look Jewish

Unlike *The Producers* or *Wicked*, the reviews for *The Addams Family* were not good. But unlike days of old where such negative press would have instantly sunk a new show, the modern era of social media and viral promotion, plus the TV culture of a classic sitcom, coupled with a few major stars, including Nathan Lane, and a few Jews who believed in the project (Marshall Brickman, Jimmy Nederlander and Jerry Zaks) made *The Addams Family* a box office hit grossing over $6.5 million in the first six weeks. The show did slow down, after that frenetic start, but continued for a run of 722 performances.

One of the reasons for such success, and certainly not a target of the critic's wrath, was Bebe Neuwirth. When Beatrice "Bebe" Neuwirth stepped into the role of Morticia Addams, she bridged the two mediums for which she is best known, television and Broadway.

The daughter of a mathematician and an artist, the Jewish-born actress hails from Newark, New Jersey, where she took up dancing at the age of five and went on to train in both dance and music at the famed The Juilliard School. She made it to Broadway in the 1980s in *A Chorus Line* followed by the revivals of *Little Me* and *Sweet Charity*, winning Neuwirth her first of two Tony Awards. Despite her highly acclaimed Broadway skills, she became forever known as

Bebe Neuwirth has won over fans and critics for her range of roles, from Lilith in *Cheers* and Lola in *Damn Yankees* to Velma Kelly in *Chicago* and Morticia Addams in the *Addams Family* (photograph by Rob Rich).

Lilith Crane from her role on the top-rated television series *Cheers*, which spilled over to occasional appearances on the spin-off *Frasier*. She also won two Emmys for her character and even brought some of her Jewish identity to the role. Lilith turned out to be Jewish somewhere during the long run of *Cheers*, to the surprise of even Bebe Neuwirth. The name Lilith also turned out to have a historical reference in Jewish folklore as the demonic first wife of Adam.

Returning to Broadway in the mid–1990s, Neuwirth won a Tony Award for her role in the revival of *Damn Yankees*. But it was in the musical revival of *Chicago* that she was finally able to establish her Broadway identity and move away from being forever known as "Lilith." Neuwirth would appear in the revival first in 1996 and then return in 2006, after mounting her own Off Broadway production called *Here Lies Jenny* in 2005, inspired by the music of Kurt Weill. And yet, after proving herself a multi-talented stage performer during three decades on Broadway, the versatile Neuwirth opted to return to television in a dramatic role in the CBS series *Madam Secretary*.

It should also be noted that Neuwirth appeared in Barry Levinson's film *Liberty Heights*, playing the Jewish mother in a semi-autobiographical story about a family growing up in Baltimore in the 1950s.

The Return of Fiddler

In November of 2015, *Fiddler on the Roof* returned once again to the Broadway stage, opening at the Broadway Theatre and starring Danny Burstein and Jessica Hecht. The son of a Costa Rican Catholic mom and a Jewish dad from Brooklyn, Burstein was born in Mount Kisco, New York, although his family was living in the Bronx at the time. Raised by his mom and stepdad, Burstein had a passion for theater from an early age. By 14, he had developed his skills and auditioned along with more than 4,000 other students to get into the prestigious High School of Performing Arts. "By some stroke of luck, I was one of the 128 that made it in, which started me on my path to being an actor," said Burstein in an interview. After graduating from Queens College, the young actor would head out west to get a master's degree in acting. Then, upon returning to New York in 1990, Burstein would spend a semester teaching at Queens College before making the tough decision that many actors had faced before him, to leave the safe job and take the plunge into an acting career.

More than 25 years later, Burstein clearly knows he made the right choice. He would make his Broadway debut in a revival of the play *A Little House on the Side*. Although it was a small role and the show closed in a couple of months,

You can't keep a great musical down. *Fiddler on the Roof* returned to Broadway for the fifth time in late 2015, bringing fans back to once again share the joy and emotion of the timeless show. From left, Melanie Moore, Alexandra Silber and Samantha Massell (photograph by Joan Marcus).

it was the inauspicious start of a Broadway career that would eventually lead to a starring role in the musical comedy the *Drowsy Chaperone*, which ran for 674 performances. He would later land the lead in the musical drama *Follies*, with Elaine Paige and Bernadette Peters, and then appear in a revival of Odets' *Golden Boy* in 2012. Then, after a short stint in the 2014 revival of *Cabaret*, he would land the prestigious role of Tevye in the latest revival of *Fiddler*.

Meanwhile, Danny's wife, Rebecca Luker, has also enjoyed a long and successful Broadway career, starting with *Phantom of the Opera* as Princess Daaé prior to appearing in revivals of *The Sound of Music*, *The Music Man*, and *Nine* before moving to Disney's *Mary Poppins* and Rodgers and Hammerstein's *Cinderella*.

Alongside of Burstein as Tevye in *Fiddler* is actress Jessica Hecht as Golde. While not quite a New York Jew (Hecht was born in New Jersey and later moved with her family to Connecticut), she was never far from the Big Apple, where she graduated from the New York University Tisch School of the Arts in 1987.

Hecht's foray into show business began when she took a job as a nanny to *Cheers* star George Wendt's children after making her move to Los Angeles. However, within a year, she landed two appearances on *Seinfeld* in the always-

Danny Burstein as Tevye in the latest revival (photograph by Joan Marcus).

challenging role of trying to date George Costanza. This would open the door to numerous television and film roles, including a recurring regular stint on *Friends* as Susan, the lesbian lover and later wife of Ross's ex-wife, Carol.

After a long list of film credits, including the highly acclaimed hit *Sideways,* Hecht would find her way to Broadway in the 1997 comedy *The Last Night of*

Ballyhoo. From the tragedy of *Julius Caesar* to the comedy of *Brighton Beach Memoirs* to the dramatic *View from a Bridge,* Hecht demonstrated her versatility as a stage performer. However, the role of Golde has also proved to be important to her from a spiritual sense as well as for her career.

Furman, Furman, Seller and the Rise of Hamilton

While Alexander Hamilton was not Jewish, several of the key people behind the runaway box-office smash hit musical *Hamilton* are. They have pooled their resources to create a unique production fusing modern music with American history that has gobbled up awards and packed houses with the hottest tickets New Yorkers have seen in years.

Roy Furman, vice chairman of Jefferies Group, LLC, and chairman of Jefferies Capital Partners, a group of private equity funds, has been a fan of the arts for years, serving as vice chairman of Lincoln Center for the Performing Arts and chairman emeritus of the Film Society of Lincoln Center. He has put his name and finances behind a wide range of Broadway productions, but none that have rivaled the success of *Hamilton.* Furman's involvement in theater dates back to his days as chairman and CEO of Livent and the original musical drama of the show *Parade* in December 1998. He has since been among the producers of a number of hits, including *Spamalot, The Color Purple, Legally Blonde, The Book of Mormon, War Horse,* Rodgers and Hammerstein's *Cinderella, Rocky, Bullets Over Broadway, The Drowsy Chaperone, An American in Paris, The Humans,* and now *Hamilton.*

Taking a cue from dad, Jill Furman, a Brown University graduate, went from acting to serving as an associate producer to joining the ranks of full-fledged producer on *The Drowsy Chaperone* in 2006. Then, shortly after the opening of her next production, with her dad, *In the Heights,* she married Richard Willis, who was born in Stratford-upon-Avon and was, naturally, appearing in Shakespearean roles by the age of six.

As for Jeffrey Seller, the lead producer on *Hamilton,* he worked closely, over the five-year gestation period of the show with Lin-Manuel Miranda, who not only stars in the production, but also wrote the music and lyrics. The pair had worked together previously on *In the Heights.*

Seller worked his way up the ladder as a publicist and booking agent before making his way into producing, where he struck gold with an award-winning trio of shows, along with his partner Kevin McCollum. Spread out over twelve years, they enjoyed the success of *Rent,* which opened in 1996; *Avenue Q,* which bowed in 2003; and *In the Heights,* which debuted in 2008. After the disappointing musical *The Last Ship*, it was on to the triumphant *Hamilton*, which opened in August 2015. It was also during the run of *Hamilton* that Seller and McCollum took a page out of the Joseph Papp theater playbook when they decided to make tickets more accessible for the mainstream audience. Knowing that the musical would have strong appeal to the twenty-something demographics, they wanted affordable tickets to be available. As a result, they created Rush Tickets, using a lottery to sell $20 tickets to see the show.

Bring On the Jews

From the Yiddish theater that started the 20th century to *The Producers* that ushered in the 21st century, the Jewish people have never stopped contributing to Broadway in a major way. Since the Tony Awards were first given out in 1947, 69 percent of composers, 70 percent of lyricists and 56 percent of librettists have been Jewish.[6] Add to this total the numerous awards for directing, acting, choreography and playwriting as well as the many Jewish producers stepping up to accept awards for Best Musical or Best Play, and you have an unprecedented contribution to Broadway.

But perhaps it was the song in the comedic musical hit *Spamalot* that best summed up the Jewish influence on Broadway:

You Won't Succeed On Broadway
by Eric Idle and John Du Prez

ROBIN: In any great adventure,
  if you don't want to lose,
  victory depends upon
  the people that you choose.
  So, listen, Arthur darling,
  closely to this news:
  We won't succeed on Broadway
  if we don't have any Jews.
  You may have the finest sets,
  fill the stage with Penthouse Pets,
  You may have the loveliest costumes and best shoes.
  You may dance and you may sing,
  But I am sorry, Arthur King,
  you'll hear no cheers, just lots and lots of boos.

MINSTRELS: *Boo!*
ROBIN: You may have butch men by the score,
  whom the audience adore,
  you may even have some animals from zoos.

Though you've Poles and Krauts instead,
you may have unleavened bread,
but I tell you, you are dead
if you don't have any Jews.
They won't care if it's witty, or ev'rything looks pretty.
They'll simply say it's shitty, and refuse.
Nobody will go, sir,
if it's not kosher, then no show, sir.
Even goyim won't be dim enough to choose.
Put on shows that make men stare,
with lots of girls in underwear.
You may even have the finest of reviews.

MINSTREL: *You're doing great!*

ROBIN: But the audience won't care, sir,
as long as you don't dare, sir,
to open up on Broadway,

ARTHUR & PATSY: *If you don't have any Jews.*

ROBIN: You may have dramatic lighting,
or lots of horrid fighting.
You may even have some white men sing the blues.
Your knights might be nice boys,
but sadly, we're all goys,
and that noise that you call singing you must lose.
So, despite your pretty lights
and naughty girls in nasty tights,
and the most impressive scenery you use,
you may have dancing *mano e mano,*
you may bring on a piano,
but they will not give a damn-o
if you don't have any Jews.

ALL: *Hey!*

ROBIN: Oh, oy!
You may fill your play with gays,
have Nigerian girls in stays.

WOMEN: You may even have some shiksas making stews.

ROBIN & MEN: You haven't got a clue,
if you don't have a Jew,
all of your investments you are going to lose.

ROBIN: There's a very small percentile
who enjoys a dancing gentile.
I'm sad to be the one with this bad news.

ALL: But never mind your swordplay.
You just won't succeed on Broadway.
You just don't succeed on Broadway
if you don't have any Jews.

ROBIN: *Papa, can you hear me?*
  To get along on Broadway,
  to sing your song on Broadway,
  to hit the top on Broadway and not lose.
  I tell you, Arthur King, there is one essential thing.
  There simply must be, simply must be Jews.
  There simply must be, Arthur, trust me,
  simply must be Jews.

Ironically, other than Mike Nichols, there were not many Jews associated with the hit musical *Spamalot* (other than some of the producers), which debuted on Broadway in 2005 and ran for over 1,500 performances. Nonetheless, the song was widely received in the good humor in which it was intended and was certainly inspired by the Jewish contribution to Broadway.

Setting the Stage for the Future

As we wind our way through the second decade of the new century, I'm happy to see that Jewish themes continue to provide fodder for clever playwrights, and many such shows have been thriving Off Broadway.

Jewish comedy is featured in Steve Solomon's *My Mother's Italian, My Father's Jewish and I'm in Therapy.* Also writing from his personal experiences, Solomon, in true Sid Caesar–style, packed some 30 characters into his 90-minute show that went from Off Broadway to a run on Broadway in 2006. Having honed his skills on the comedy club circuit, Solomon brought back some of the Catskills-style humor in the culture-crossing comedy that tackled kosher cooking by non–Jews and other such interfaith themes.

Then there are the plays of Daniel Goldfarb, the Jewish playwright and graduate of both The Juilliard School and New York University. "It's difficult to think of a playwright of Mr. Goldfarb's generation who has written about Jewish themes for mainstream theater audiences more consistently than he has,"[7] noted Jason Zinoman in the *New York Times*. Goldfarb ushered in the new decade with his first play, *Adam Baum and the Jew Movie* about a non–Jew trying to write a movie about anti–Semitism in the Golden Age of Hollywood. Goldfarb also wrote the Off Broadway show *Modern Orthodox* about a secular Jewish couple that takes in an Orthodox Jewish man. The show focuses on the impact of modern secular Jews on the life of the Orthodox Jew.

A more recent show by Goldfarb, *The Retributionists*, took a similar storyline to the film *Inglourious Basterds* (which came out roughly at the same time). *The Retributionists* explored the little-known underground Jewish revolutionaries who sought revenge upon the Germans after the war, pledging to kill one German for every Jew who was killed.

While Goldfarb does not want to become known solely as a Jewish playwright, his works have expanded the ever-growing library of Jewish theater works that have emerged in recent years. Nonetheless, he did go mainstream, hitting Broadway by writing the book for *Martin Short: Fame Becomes Me*, as well as his latest Off Broadway show, *Piece of My Heart: The Bert Berns Story* about the little-known songwriter who wrote over 50 charting singles in seven years (including "Hang on Sloopy," "Cry, Baby," and "Twist and Shout") before a fatal heart attack took his life at the age of 38.

Other shows like *Jewtopia*—a very successful Off Broadway comedy about two young men, one Jewish and one Gentile, who are teaching one another how to win over women of the opposite religion enjoyed long runs Off Broadway with secular audiences.

New plays from Jewish playwrights continue to guide us further into the second decade of the century by tapping into the latest social, political, and cultural issues, much in the same manner as so many previous Jewish playwrights who have been the voice of social conscience for more than a century. There is some concern today, however, as many young people, not only Jews, are losing touch with their culture and history. And while attending a revival of *Fiddler on the Roof* should now serve as requisite for each new generation of Jews, it's not enough. There is a growing disconnect. The vast majority of the roughly five million American-Jewish adults has now far surpassed assimilation and has succeeded in many industries, so much so that young Jews have little connection with the immigrant experiences of the millions who struggled before them to build a new life on the Lower East Side of Manhattan or on the streets of Brooklyn. Part of the problem is said to stem from the high intermarriage rate, which, according to a *New York Times* poll, indicates that nearly 58 percent of Jews are marrying outside of their faith, a significant increase from 1970, where the percentage of out-of-faith marriages was only 17 percent. It was also noted in the same poll that some 65 percent of Jews did not even belong to a synagogue. Most, however, do show support for Israel. It's also worth mentioning that "secularism" has become increasingly common among the overall American population.

So, what's next? It's now up to the 60-plus percent of practicing Jews to continue instilling an appreciation of the arts in their children in hopes that, along with self-expression, some of their Jewish culture makes its way into their music, their writing, and their performances. While theater life can still be a bit daunting, there remain many opportunities for Jewish talent in mainstream theater to infuse some of their Jewishness.

Epilogue

Our country is still young and our cultural contribution to the world is just beginning. The Jewish participation in the last century reflected the opportunity, growth, social responsibility and diversity that only a new democratic republic could offer. As such, Jewish involvement in the fabric of American theater is so interwoven that you cannot tear them apart. One question I set out to answer in this book is why the Jewish community was so active in the American theater? Could it be, as Ellen Adler suggested to me, in our interview, that the culture, music and literature were such an intrinsic part of Jewish life that they spilled over into this new American way of life? Or perhaps it is as Tovah Feldshuh said to me, that America offered a society and financial environment based on meritocracy. If you had the talent, you reaped the rewards and there were opportunities in America that were not available to Jews in other parts of the globe.

Historically, Charles Strouse felt the world of music and theater had been exclusively the domain of the wealthy, elite or royalty. The Italian, German, Austrian and French people had their opera, but there were no Jewish composers at the court of Franz Josef or Napoleon Bonaparte. When a new form of "mass" entertainment was created, like the American musical (a totally American creation along with jazz music), the Jews participated. Unlike other professions, many of which excluded Jews, this was an opportunity for the Jewish people to excel, and they did, becoming experts.

Similarly, the African American community, once liberated, has also become a force in American theater. In addition, our English cousins and the Irish have been major contributors to 20th century American theater. Likewise, going forward, as the makeup of our country changes, it should be reflected in our culture. All this notwithstanding, the Jewish contribution to American theater continues to reshape and re-define us as a people and as Americans.

As for me personally, I am now, along with my wife, Bonnie, working hard to bring classic Broadway works from the always-diverse theater population to a much broader audience, thanks to the latest in new high-definition technology. BroadwayHD has made some of the shows listed in this book, along with many others, widely available, thanks to online streaming. Now you can enjoy the Broadway experience in the comfort of your own home. Visit BroadwayHD.com for a listing of the many full theater productions we have available.

Chapter Notes

Chapter 1

1. Edna Nahshon, "The Golden Epoch of Yiddish Theatre in America: A Brief Historical Overview," http://www.jewish-theatre.com/visitor/article_display.aspx?articleID=1411.
2. Nahma Sandrow, *Vagabond Stars: A World History of Yiddish Theater* (Syracuse, NY: Syracuse University Press, 1995).
3. *Ibid.*
4. *Ibid.*
5. *Ibid.*
6. Adler Family, www.eilatgordinlevitan.com/kurenets/k_pages/adler.html.
7. Nahma Sandrow, personal interview, October 2009, New York City.
8. *Ibid.*
9. Ellen Adler, personal interview, October 2009, New York City.
10. *Ibid.*
11. Sandrow, *Vagabond Stars.*
12. Anastasia Tsioulcas, "Michael Tilson Thomas Invites You to Meet His Grandparents—the Amazing Thomashefskys" http://www.jewish-theatre.com/visitor/article_display.aspx?articleID=1434.

Chapter 2

1. Wayne Keyser, "Vaudeville & Burlesque History & Lingo," http://www.goodmagic.com/carny/vaud.htm.
2. John Kenrick, "A History of The Musical. Vaudeville—Part II," http://www.musicals101.com/vaude2.htm.

Chapter 3

1. Jerry Klinger, "America Was different. America Is different." http://www.jewishmag.com/86mag/usa10/usa10.htm.

2. Michael Palomino, "Jews in the 'USA' 06: 1929–1939," http://www.geschichteinchronologie.ch/USA/EncJud_juden-in-USA06_1929-1939.html.
3. "The Dearborn Independent," http://freemasonry.bcy.ca/anti-masonry/dearborn.html.
4. Klinger, "America Was different."
5. Ellen Adler, personal interview, October 2009, New York City.
6. Nate Bloom, "Irving Berlin, Ellin MacKay and White Christmas," http://www.interfaithfamily.com/arts_and_entertainment/popular_culture/Irving_Berlin_Ellin_McKay_and_White_Christmas.shtml.
7. Richard Reublin, "Irving Berlin, the Dean of American Songwriters," http://parlorsongs.com/bios/berlin/iberlin.php.

Chapter 4

1. Ellen Adler, personal interview, October 2009, New York City.
2. Tom Oppenheim, Speech delivered to the Jewish Historical Society of New York, October 2009, New York City.
3. "About Us," http:www.stellaadler.com/about.html.
4. Oppenheim, Speech.
5. Janine Parker, "Jerome Robbins (1918–1998)," http://www.bostonphoenix.com/archive/dance/98/08/06/JEROME_ROBBINS.html.
6. Ellen Schrecker, *The Age of McCarthyism: A Brief History with Documents* (New York, St. Martin's, 1994).

Chapter 5

1. Lillian Hellman, http://www.quotationspage.com/quotes/Lillian_Hellman.

2. Zero Mostel biography, http://www.imdb.com/name/nm0609216/bio.

3. Bill Blankenship, "Inherit the Controversy," http://cjonline.com/stories/030201/wee_inherit.shtml.

4. Stewart F. Lane, *Let's Put On a Show* (New York: Working Arts Library, 2007).

Chapter 6

1. Ellen Adler, personal interview, October 2009, New York City.

2. Charles Strouse, personal interview, April 2010, New York City.

3. *Ibid.*

4. *Ibid.*

5. Tovah Feldshuh, personal interview, May 2010, New York City.

6. *Ibid.*

7. *Ibid.*

8. *Ibid.*

9. *Ibid.*

10. *Ibid.*

11. Howard Kissel and Jay Maeder, "Joe Papp the Torrent," www.nydailynews.com/archives/news/1999/07/25/1999-07-25_joe_papp_the_torrent.html.

Chapter 7

1. R.J. Donovan, "Family Matters," http://www.onstageboston.com/Articles/2005/11/November/revrosen.html.

2. Frank Rich, "Stage: The Musical 'Cage aux Folles,'" http://www.nytimes.com/1983/08/22/arts/stage-the-musical-cage-aux-Folles.html.

Chapter 8

1. Dennis Brown, "Jersey Boys Writer Marshall Brickman Is No Career Counselor—but He's a Great Interview," http://www.riverfronttimes.com/2008-04-23/culture/too-good-to-be-true-jersey-boys-writer-marshall-brickman-is-no-career-counselor-mdash-but-he-s-a-great-interview/.

2. Michael Elkin, "'Light' of His Life?: Composer Adam Guettel Settles the Score on an Important and Revealing Question: Who Has Impacted Him the Most?," http://www.jewishexponent.com/article/20015.

3. *Ibid.*

4. Anna Sobering, "Q&A with Jeff Marx, Co-Creator of Broadway musical 'Avenue Q.'" http://www.kansan.com/news/2010/mar/11/q-jeff-marx-co-creator-broadway-musical-avenue-q/.

5. Mervyn Rothstein, "A Life in the Theatre: Carole Shorenstein Hays," http://www.playbill.com/news/article/140734-A-Life-in-the-Theatre-Carole-Shorenstein-Hays.

6. "Jewish Recipients of the Antoinette Perry (Tony) Award for Best Musical Production," http://www.jinfo.org/Tony_Award_Musical.html.

7. Jason Zinoman, "At Ease in His Own Pigeonhole," http://www.nytimes.com/2009/08/16/theater/16Zino.html.

Bibliography

Books

Green, Stanley. *Broadway Musicals, Show by Show*, 3d ed. Milwaukee: Hal Leonard, 1990.

Lane, Stewart F. *Let's Put On a Show*. Portsmouth, NH: Heinemann, 2007.

Sandrow, Nahma. *Vagabond Stars: A World History of Yiddish Theater*. Syracuse: Syracuse University Press, 1995.

S.D., Trav. *No Applause—Just Throw Money: The Book That Made Vaudeville Famous*. New York: Faber and Faber, 2005.

Personal Interviews/Visits

Adler, Ellen. Personal interview, New York City, October 2009.

Feldshuh, Tovah. Personal interview, New York City, May 2010.

Sandrow, Nahma. Personal interview, New York City, October 2009.

S.D., Trav. Personal interview, New York City, October 2009.

Shubert Archives. Personal visit, New York City, February 2010.

Strouse, Charles. Personal interview, New York City, April 2010.

Speeches

Oppenheim, Tom. Speech delivered to the Jewish Historical Society of New York, New York City, October 2009.

Websites

Adler Family, http://www.eilatgordinlevitan.com/kurenets/k_pages/adler.html.

Alan Brody, www.alanbrodyworks.com.

American Theatre Wing, http://americantheatrewing.org.

Answers.com, www.answers.com.

BroadwayWorld.com, www.broadwayworld.com.

Charles Strouse, www.charlesstrouse.com.

Corine's Corner, www.corinescorner.com.

Encyclopedia of World Biographies, www.notablebiographies.com.

Film Reference, www.filmreference.com.

Internet Broadway Database, www.ibdb.com.

Jerry Herman, www.jerryherman.com.

Jewish Theatre, www.jewish-theatre.com.

Jewish Virtual Library, www.jewishvirtuallibrary.org.

Jinfo.org, www.jinfo.org.

Mahalo.com, www.mahalo.com.

Musicals 101, www.musicals101.com.

New Georgia Encyclopedia, www.newgeorgiaencyclopedia.org.

PBS, www.pbs.org.

Public Theater, www.publictheater.org.

Quotationspage.com, www.quotationspage.com.

Songwriters Hall of Fame, www.songwritershalloffame.org.

Stella Adler.com, www.stellaadler.com.

Talkin' Broadway, www.talkinbroadway.com.

Whole New World of Alan Menken, www.alanmenken.info/biography/biography.html.

Online Articles

Berry, Melissa. "A Date with the Thomashefskys at Disney Concert Hall." http://www.buzzine.com/2009/01/a-date-with-the-thomashefskys/.

Blankenship, Bill. "Inherit the Controversy." http://cjonline.com/stories/030201/wee_inherit.shtml.

Bloom, Nate. "Irving Berlin, Ellin MacKay and White Christmas." http://www.interfaithfamily.com/arts_and_entertainment/popular_culture/Irving_Berlin_Ellin_McKay_and_White_Christmas.shtml.

Brown, Dennis. "Jersey Boys writer Marshall Brickman Is No Career Counselor—but He's a Great Interview." http://www.riverfronttimes.com/2008-04-23/culture/too-good-to-be-true-jersey-boys-writer-marshall-brickman-is-no-career-counselor-mdash-but-he-s-a-great-interview/.

"The Dearborn Independent." http://freemasonry.bcy.ca/anti-masonry/dearborn.html.

Donovan, R.J. "Family Matters." http://www.onstageboston.com/Articles/2005/11/November/revrosen.html.

Edelman, Marsha B. "Leonard Bernstein: Jewish America's Favorite (Musical) Son: A Celebrated American Composer, Conductor, Teacher, and Pianist Who Infused His Work with His Jewish Heritage." http://www.myjewishlearning.com/culture/2/Music/American_Jewish_Music/Leonard_Bernstein.shtml.

Elkin, Michael. "'Light' of His Life? Composer Adam Guettel Settles the Score on an Important and Revealing Question: Who Has Impacted Him the Most?" http://www.jewishexponent.com/article/20015.

Kenrick, John. "A History of the Musical. Vaudeville—Part II." http://www.musicals101.com/vaude2.htm.

Keyser, Wayne. "Vaudeville & Burlesque History & Lingo." http://www.goodmagic.com/carny/vaud.htm.

Kissel, Howard, and Jay Maeder. "Joe Papp the Torrent." http://www.nydailynews.com/archives/news/1999/07/25/1999-07-25_joe_papp_the_torrent.html.

Klinger, Jerry. "America Was different. America Is different." http://www.jewishmag.com/86mag/usa10/usa10.htm.

Medoff, Rafael. "The Bergson Group vs. the Holocaust—and Jewish Leaders vs. Bergson." http://www.jewishpress.com/pageroute.do/21747/.

Nahshon, Edna. "The Golden Epoch of Yiddish Theatre in America: A Brief Historical Overview." http://www.jewish-theatre.com/visitor/article_display.aspx?articleID=1411.

O'Donnell, Edward T. "82 Years Ago: Abie's Irish Rose." http://www.edwardtodonnell.com/hibchronabiesirishrose.html.

Palomino, Michael. "Jews in the 'USA' 06: 1929–1939." http://www.geschichteinchronologie.ch/USA/EncJud_juden-in-USA06_1929-1939.html.

Parker, Janine. "Jerome Robbins (1918–1998)." http://www.bostonphoenix.com/archive/dance/98/08/06/JEROME_ROBBINS.html.

Pogrebin, Robin. "How Broadway Bounced Back After 9/11; But Downtown Theater Lacked the Right Ties." http://www.nytimes.com/2002/05/22/theater/how-broadway-bounced-back-after-9-11-but-downtown-theater-lacked-the-right-ties.html.

Reublin, Richard. "Irving Berlin, the Dean of American Songwriters." http://parlorsongs.com/bios/berlin/iberlin.php.

Rich, Frank. "Stage: The Musical 'Cage Aux Folles.'" http://www.nytimes.com/1983/08/22/arts/stage-the-musical-cage-aux-Folles.html.

Rose, Frank, and Erin M. Davies. "Can Disney Tame 42nd Street?" http://money.cnn.com/magazines/fortune/fortune_archive/1996/06/24/213770/index.htm.

Rothstein, Mervyn. "A Life in the Theatre: Carole Shorenstein Hays." http://www.playbill.com/news/article/140734-A-Life-in-the-Theatre-Carole-Shorenstein-Hays.

_____. "Stage Struck. A Funny Thing Happened on Tony Winner Jerry Zak's Way to Med School: He Became a Broadway Director." http://www.cigaraficionado.com/Cigar/CA_Profiles/People_Profile/0,2540,104,00.html.

Schneider, Danielle. "On This Day in NY History: Blacklisted Comic Genius Zero Mostel Is Born." http://www.examiner.com/ny-in-new-york/on-this-day-ny-history-blacklisted-comic-genius-zero-mostel-is-born.

Schrecker, Ellen. "Communism and National Security: The Menace Emerges," from Chapter 3 of *The Age of McCarthyism: A Brief History with Documents*." www.writing.upenn.edu/~afilreis/50s/menace-emerges.html.

Sobering, Anna. "Q&A with Jeff Marx, Co-Creator of Broadway musical 'Avenue Q.'" http://www.kansan.com/news/2010/mar/11/q-jeff-marx-co-creator-broadway-musical-avenue-q/.

Tsiublana, Anastasia "Michael Tilson Thomas Invites You to Meet His Grandparents—the Amazing Thomashefskys." http://www.jewish-theatre.com/visitor/article_display.aspx?articleID=1434.

Warnke, Nina. "Immigrant Popular Culture as Contested Sphere: Yiddish Music Halls, the Yiddish Press, and the Processes of Americanization, 1900–1910." http://jtheater.tripod.com/warnke.htm.

Zinoman, Jason. "At Ease in His Own Pigeonhole." http://www.nytimes.com/2009/08/16/theater/16Zino.html.

Further Reading

JACOB ADLER
Jacob Adler: A Life on the Stage—A Memoir by Jacob Adler and Lulla Rosenfeld.

STELLA ADLER
Stella Adler on the Art and Technique of Acting by Howard Kissel.
The Art of Acting by Stella Adler.

WOODY ALLEN
Woody Allen on Woody Allen: In Conversation with Stig Bjorkman by Woody Allen with Stig Bjorkman.

IRVING BERLIN
As Thousands Cheer: The Life of Irving Berlin by Laurence Bergreen.
Irving Berlin: Songs from the Melting Pot by Charles Hamm.

LEONARD BERNSTEIN
Leonard Bernstein: American Original by Burton Bernstein and Barbara Haws.
Leonard Bernstein: The Political Life of an American Musician by Barry Seldes.

BOUBLIL AND SCHONBERG
The Musical World of Boublil and Schonberg: The Creators of Les Misérables, Miss Saigon, Martin Guerre and The Pirate Queen by Margaret Vermette.

FANNY BRICE
Fanny Brice: The Original Funny Girl by Herbert G. Goldman.
Funny Woman: The Life and Times of Fanny Brice by Barbara W. Grossman.

MEL BROOKS
It's Good to Be the King: The Seriously Funny Life of Mel Brooks by James Robert Parish.

EDDIE CANTOR
Eddie Cantor: A Life in Show Business by Gregory Koseluk.

GEORGE GERSHWIN
Fascinating Rhythm: The Collaboration of George and Ira Gershwin by Deena Ruth Rosenberg.
George Gershwin: An Intimate Portrait by Walter Rimler.
George Gershwin: A New Biography by William G. Hyland.

IRA GERSHWIN
Ira Gershwin: The Art of the Lyricist by Philip Furia.

JACOB GORDIN
Finding the Jewish Shakespeare: The Life and Legacy of Jacob Gordin by Beth Kaplan.

OSCAR HAMMERSTEIN II
Getting To Know Him: A Biography of Oscar Hammerstein II by Hugh Fordin.
The Wordsmiths: Oscar Hammerstein II and Alan Jay Lerner by Stephen Citron.

MOSS HART
Act One: An Autobiography by Moss Hart.
Dazzler: The Life and Times of Moss Hart by Steven Bach.

LILLIAN HELLMAN
Conversations with Lillian Hellman (Literary Conversations Series) by Lillian Hellman.
An Unfinished Woman: A Memoir by Lillian Hellman and Wendy Wasserstein.

AL JOLSON

Al Jolson: A Bio-Bibliography by James Fisher.
Al Jolson, You Ain't Heard Nothin' Yet! by Robert Oberfirst.
Jolson: The Legend Comes to Life by Herbert G. Goldman.

GEORGE S. KAUFMAN

George S. Kaufman: An Intimate Portrait by Howard Teichmann.

JEROME KERN

Jerome Kern by Stephen Banfield.
Jerome Kern: His Life and Music [paperback] by Gerald Bordman.

TONY KUSHNER

The Theater of Tony Kushner: Living Past Hope by James Fisher.
Understanding Tony Kushner by James Fisher.

LERNER AND LOEWE

The Musical Worlds of Lerner and Loewe by Gene Lees.

DAVID MERRICK

David Merrick: The Abominable Showman by Howard Kissel.

ARTHUR MILLER

Arthur Miller by Christopher Bigsby.
Arthur Miller: His Life and His Work by Martin Gottfried.
Conversations with Miller by Mel Gussow.
Miller in an Hour by James Fisher.

ZERO MOSTEL

Zero Dances: A Biography by Arthur Sainer.
Zero Mostel: A Biography by Jared Brown.

CLIFFORD ODETS

Clifford Odets: American Playwright: The Years from 1906 to 1940 by Margaret Brenman-Gibson.

JOSEPH PAPP

Joe Papp: An American Life by Helen Epstein.

JEROME ROBBINS

Jerome Robbins: His Life, His Teacher, His Dance by Deborah Jowitt.
Somewhere: The Life of Jerome Robbins by Amanda Vaill.

RICHARD RODGERS

Richard Rodgers, Musical Stages: An Autobiography.
The Richard Rodgers Reader by Geoffrey Block.

RODGERS AND HAMMERSTEIN

Rodgers & Hammerstein by Ethan Mordden.
The Sound of Music: The Story of Rodgers and Hammerstein by Frederick Nolan, Oscar Hammerstein, and Richard Rodgers.

STEPHEN SCHWARTZ

Defying Gravity: The Creative Career of Stephen Schwartz, from Godspell to Wicked by Carol de Giere.

NEIL SIMON

Play Goes On: A Memoir by Neil Simon.

STEPHEN SONDHEIM

Art Isn't Easy: The Theater of Stephen Sondheim by Joanne Gordon.

LEE STRASBERG

A Dream of Passion by Lee Strasberg.
The Lee Strasberg Notes by Lola Cohen.

BARBRA STREISAND

The Importance of Being Barbra: The Brilliant, Tumultuous Career of Barbra Streisand by Tom Santopietro.

CHARLES STROUSE

Put on a Happy Face: A Broadway Memoir by Charles Strouse.

WENDY WASSERSTEIN

Wendy Wasserstein: A Casebook by Claudia Barnett.

MISCELLANEOUS

Are You Now or Have You Been: The Investigation of Show Business by the Un-American Activities Committee 1947–1958 by Eric Bentley.
Broadway: The American Musical by Michael Kantor and Laurence Maslon.
Broadway and the Blacklist by Lillian Hellman Scoundrel Time.
Broadway Musicals Show by Show by Stanley Green.

Coming Up Roses: The Broadway Musical in the 1950s by Ethan Mordden.

Enchanted Evenings: The Broadway Musical from Show Boat to Sondheim by Geoffrey Block.

Making Americans: Jews and the Broadway Musical by Andrea Most.

The Musical: A Look at the American Musical Theater by Richard Kislan.

Musical Comedy in America: From The Black Crook *to* South Pacific, *from* The King & I *to* Sweeney Todd by Cecil A. Smith and Glenn Litton.

No Applause—Just Throw Money: The Book That Made Vaudeville Famous by Trav S.D.

The Poets of Tin Pan Alley: A History of America's Greatest Lyricists by Phillip Furias.

Stardust Lost: The Triumph, Tragedy, and Meshugas of the Yiddish Theater in America by Stefan Kanfer.

Vagabond Stars: A World History of Yiddish Theater by Nahma Sandrow.

Wit's End: Days and Nights of the Algonquin Round Table by James R. Gaines.

And for those interested in producing their own show:

Let's Put On a Show by Stewart F. Lane.

Index

Numbers in **bold italics** indicate pages with photographs.

225